Date Due

APR 1 2 2001		
APR 3 0 2002		

in U S A

JEAN BÉLIVEAU
My Life in Hockey

JEAN BÉLIVEAU

My Life in Hockey

with Chrys Goyens and Allan Turowetz

M&S

Canadian Cataloguing in Publication Data

Béliveau, Jean, 1931-
  Jean Béliveau : my life in hockey

Includes index.
ISBN 0-7710-1107-5

1. Béliveau, Jean, 1931- . 2. Montreal Canadiens (Hockey team).
3. Hockey players – Canada – Biography. I. Goyens, Chrys.
II. Turowetz, Allan, 1948- .   III. Title.

GV848.5.B4A3   1994   796.962'092   C94-932067-6

The publishers acknowledge the support of the Canada Council and the Ontario Arts Council for their publishing program.

Typesetting by MacTrix DTP

Interior photographs courtesy the private collection of Jean Béliveau. Credits cited with individual photographs. Copyright is retained by the original photographers.

Printed and bound in Canada

McClelland & Stewart Inc.
The Canadian Publishers
481 University Avenue
Toronto, Ontario
M5G 2E9

1 2 3 4 5   98 97 96 95 94

*This is a rare opportunity for one to reflect upon
and rejoice in his family.
This book is dedicated to my wife Élise,
my daughter Hélène, and granddaughters Magalie
and Mylène, with all of my love.
As well, I dedicate this work to my father Arthur
and my mother Laurette, who were inspirations and examples
to me of the benefits of hard work, love, and faith,
and to my stepmother Mida, who made my father so happy
in his later years. Finally, to my brothers and sisters,
living and passed away: Guy, Michel, Mimi,
Madeleine, Hélène, Pierre, and André.*

Contents

Foreword
by Dick Irvin

During the 1979 Stanley Cup finals, I was working with the *Hockey Night in Canada* crew at Madison Square Garden, in New York, where the Rangers were playing the Montreal Canadiens. Just prior to the opening faceoff, I noticed the fans in a section below our broadcast location rising to applaud someone coming up the steps to his seat. I peered over their heads to catch a glimpse of the object of their affection, thinking that, this being New York, I would find a Broadway star or a movie idol. Instead, I saw that it was Jean Béliveau. The former Canadiens great was acknowledging their salute in his typical humble fashion, head cocked slightly to one side, a look of near embarrassment on his face. He waved slightly as he took his seat. Being a Béliveau fan, I was tempted to join in the applause, but we were on the air and Danny Gallivan was into his pre-game commentary.

Those fans in New York were saluting a former hockey star who had been retired from the game for eight years. Obviously, their memories of his greatness as an athlete, and his class and grace as a man, were still very warm, even though he had played against their hometown Rangers for eighteen seasons. It was a moment that said so much about Jean Béliveau, and I was not surprised.

After gaining his first measure of fame as the best player in amateur hockey while playing for junior and senior teams in Quebec City, Jean signed with the Montreal Canadiens in October 1953, and played in the NHL All-Star Game at the Montreal Forum that same night. I was at that game, and I was also in Chicago Stadium May 18, 1971, the evening he played his last game. Looking back at all the games in between, the memories flow.

From the time he scored forty-seven goals in his first half-season in junior hockey, Jean Béliveau was a dominant player on every team he played for, and in almost every game he played. If there is a current star who to some degree mirrors Jean, it is Mario Lemieux. Watching Mario at the top of his game when he led the Pittsburgh Penguins to Stanley Cups in 1991 and 1992, I often thought of Jean during his ten Stanley Cup-winning years with the Montreal Canadiens. Brilliant goals, brilliant assists, leadership, he always was the dominating presence in the game, the player you had to watch because at any moment he might engineer a dramatic, game-winning turn of events.

When Jean Béliveau joined the Montreal Canadiens, he skated into a lineup full of superstars on a team that would win a record five straight Stanley Cup championships beginning in 1956. Ten years later, those older superstars were gone, and Jean was the captain and undisputed leader of yet another dynasty at the Montreal Forum.

Reminisce today with members of the Montreal team that won four Cups in five years in the late 1960s (a team underrated by hockey historians, as Jean discusses in this book), and you hear countless stories about "Big Jean" and how much he meant to them as a teammate, leader, and friend.

Rarely does a supreme athlete retire from his game when a few more lucrative seasons could lie ahead. Jean Béliveau was the exception. When he captained the Montreal Canadiens to an unexpected Stanley Cup in 1971, after a season in which he registered 76 points in 70 games, Jean had already made up his mind to retire. The playoffs that year would be his last hurrah. And what a hurrah it was!

Montreal lost the first game of the first series to the heavily favoured Boston Bruins and were trailing 5–1 in the second period of the second game. Then, Big Jean took over, winning faceoffs and making passes the way he did during his greatest years. He scored two goals, and set up John Ferguson for two more, including the winning goal late in the third period. At the age of thirty-nine, late into his eighteenth and final season, Big Jean had turned back his personal hockey calendar. It was something to behold.

The Canadiens won that game 7–5, went on to eliminate the Bruins in seven games, and eventually won the Stanley Cup in a steamy Chicago Stadium May 18. We all got our final look at Béliveau the player that night. When the game was over, he carried the Stanley Cup off the ice, triumphant in victory, a fitting and unforgettable ending to a marvellous career.

I was fortunate to watch Jean Béliveau play from the start to the finish of his NHL career, and am still fortunate to consider him a friend. Now, via his own words in the pages of his book, you can share his multitude of memories. As you read, I am sure you will appreciate why those fans in New York stood and applauded when, long after his playing days were over, they had the opportunity to salute Jean Béliveau.

– Montreal, July 1994

◆

INTRODUCTION

Tuesday, December 13, 1949, had dawned grey and snowy in Victoriaville, Quebec. But inside the kitchen of our semi-detached house, right next to the church of Les Saint-Martyrs Canadiens on Rue Notre-Dame, the town's main street, there was a feeling of warmth, of family.

I sat at the table enjoying one of my favourite meals, a thick, rich vegetable soup with a slice of crusty loaf and butter. Between spoons of soup, I would exchange a few words with my mother. This was a very difficult morning for her. I could see the sadness in every aspect of her body language, and hear the longing in her quiet voice.

On this morning, Laurette Dubé Béliveau must have felt much older than her forty-one years, and yet strangely young. We weren't alone in the house that day. From another room, we could hear the sounds of five-year-old Pierre and baby André. Mimi and Madeleine, my younger sisters, were absent at their classes, along with Guy and Michel, my younger brothers. They would arrive home shortly for lunch, as would my father, Arthur. My mother had borne him eight children in all, an average family in the staunchly Catholic and primarily semi-urban Quebec of the 1930s and 1940s. We had lost a sister, Hélène, when she was only two – struck by a car in front of this same house one fateful day ten years before.

Now, Laurette Dubé Béliveau was preparing to watch her eldest son leave home, perhaps forever. After three long years of dreading this eventuality, she knew nothing she could say or do would prevent it.

Just three months past his eighteenth birthday, her eldest son was the picture of health, at six-foot-one and 180 pounds. Like all her children, I owed much of my size and well-being to the tall, buxom woman at the kitchen table. Today, however, she took no comfort in these facts. The powerful body that she had bequeathed me was, in fact, one of the reasons I would soon be gone.

At one o'clock that afternoon, I would board a bus to Quebec City, about sixty miles to the north-east, a journey I would have made several months before, had not the old Colisée de Québec burned down the previous spring. When we arrived, my team-mates on the Quebec Citadels and I would resume our season in the Quebec Junior A Hockey League. The Citadels had trained at the Victoriaville Arena and played the first two months of the 1949-1950 season there, but now it was time to return. On Thursday, Monsignor Maurice Roy, Archbishop of Québec, would bless the new Colisée, and we would play a split-squad exhibition game with the Quebec Aces of the Quebec Senior Hockey League, before opening the next night against the Trois-Rivières Reds.

An hour earlier, my mother and I had packed what few belongings I would take with me in the family's battered, black suitcase. It was a leather and cardboard affair that expanded to hold a ton of goods, but on this trip I would not strain its capacity. Three or four shirts, two pairs of pants, some socks and underwear, and a couple of ties went into it, not much more.

Helping me pack had brought home the finality of the move to my mother. Her eyes were moist as I carried the case downstairs, and left it beneath my prized sartorial possession, a brown car coat with a fur collar, that hung on a peg by the door.

A few moments later, a Shawinigan Water and Power truck pulled up outside, and Arthur Béliveau joined his son and wife for lunch. My dad was slightly smaller than me – about five feet, eleven inches, and maybe 160 pounds – but his large hands and coiled strength spoke of the thick cedar poles and huge rolls of wire he had erected and strung over hundreds of square miles of southeastern Quebec.

My dad also had enormous strength of character, as hockey and baseball scouts and executives had discovered over the last three or four years, as news of my athletic talents had begun to spread far beyond Victoriaville and the Bois-Francs region.

One after another, he had stared them down, waiting out their promises and ploys, until he received what he felt was right for his son, and his son's future. Around Victoriaville, Arthur Béliveau commanded great respect from everyone he met, and had taught his children many valuable lessons.

"Jean," he said, "no matter how people will approach you with money and gifts and offers that seem ridiculously easy, you must remember that nothing comes free in this life, and that hard work and discipline will make you who and what you are."

This was not the homespun wisdom of a man who failed to comprehend the temptations of big cities and the world beyond. Arthur Béliveau was quite sure I was on my way to a lifestyle vastly different than his had been, different than the rest of my family's would be. But deep down, he knew that the same values that had helped me as I grew up could stay with me and make my life better no matter where I went.

There at the kitchen table, I caught the meaningful glances that passed between my parents. They had obviously envisioned this scene many times, and little remained to be said. As it was, lunch seemed to end much sooner than my mother wanted, and my father and I grabbed our coats and prepared to leave. A last hug for my mother at the door, and we headed downtown to the arena, where our team bus was due to leave for Quebec City, about an hour's drive away, in fifteen minutes.

It was a five-minute ride from our house to the arena. We didn't say a word. My father was composed and confident. He knew the entire Citadels hierarchy, from coach Pete Martin and business manager Roland Mercier, to owner Frank Byrne and his brother Bill. My father had chosen the Citadels over everyone else who had come courting since my mid-teens – the Montreal Royals, Nationals, Junior Canadiens; the Reds, from my birthplace Trois-Rivières; and among many others. But he'd met the Citadels in his own back yard, and liked what he had seen. He knew I was in good hands.

When we arrived at the arena, only a few players were hanging around outside the bus. The snow was coming down much harder now and had driven most of them on board. The snow also meant that our drive to Quebec City might be longer and more difficult than usual, so everyone was eager to get underway.

My father reached in the back of his truck and swung out the suitcase. Conscious of my teammates peering at us through the fogged windows of the bus, he handed me the bag, took my right hand in his, and shook it once.

"Do your best, Jean," he said. "It will be enough."

He turned and got back into the truck, and, waving curtly at me, drove away. The snow meant problems with the wires that sang overhead in Victoriaville, and Arthur Béliveau, crew foreman, was on the job.

Moments later, my suitcase was stowed in the luggage compartment underneath the bus, and I was in my seat. As we pulled away, a cheer went up from my teammates. After all, they were going home.

I sat watching as Victoriaville blurred past my window, not taking part in the team's talking and joking. We reached the outskirts of town, and as my home gradually slipped behind us, I felt sad. But the excitement inside the bus was contagious and soon I felt eager to turn the page, to see what would happen next.

I

✦

THE MEMORIES

We are quite the pair, Louise Richer and I. Visitors to the Forum on Atwater and St. Catherine Streets in downtown Montreal are immediately struck by the contrast between my six-foot, three-inch, 215-pound body and her tiny, birdlike frame. We're an odd couple, to be sure, but we've been an effective team for almost a quarter-century. Now, on this day late in the summer of 1993, as we begin to pack up my office on the Forum's second floor, we occasionally have to pause to wipe away the tears.

It's not an easy task, sorting and cataloguing the paperwork and photographs of a lifetime, but Louise keeps me going. She knows how tough it is, but she is supremely practical, and as the time passes, we encourage each other to continue with what must be done.

Louise and I go back to the 1960s. When I was team captain of the Canadiens and needed to have a letter typed, I'd come upstairs to the second floor after practice to see her. At the time, she worked in public relations with Camil Des Roches, Frank Selke, Jr., and Albert Trottier.

When I retired from competition in 1971, the Canadiens' president David Molson and general manager Sam Pollock had asked me to join them on the second floor. "Who would you like as your secretary?" Sam asked.

"Give me Louise," I replied. "Camil is cutting down on his workload; I'm sure she can handle both his stuff and mine."

Louise immediately became my right hand at the Forum. I could call her at any hour of the day – except when she was attending to her religious obligations, caring for her aged mother in their little house in Ville St. Pierre, or off on one of her customary excursions, perhaps a brisk walk from her home, up the hill into Montreal West, and over to St. Joseph Oratory – a distance of at least five miles, and most of it uphill.

When, in the late 1980s, I first began to think about retirement from the corporate side of things, Louise had said, "When you go, I'll go." But as the months and years went by, we reconsidered. Her mother had meanwhile passed away, and Louise was involving herself even more deeply in church and community affairs. "There's no rush for you to retire when I do," I told her. I'd cleared matters with Ronald Corey, who had become the team's president in 1982. "It's your choice, whatever you want to do."

After mulling it over, Louise decided to stay one more year, until July 1994. The determining factor, I realized, was "Her Boys," the Canadiens Oldtimers – Dollard St. Laurent, Phil Goyette, Henri Richard, Jean-Guy Talbot, Réjean Houle, and the rest. Louise is the secretary of the Montreal Canadiens Alumni Association. She organizes its annual golf tournament, and in general takes care of the needs and wants of her flock.

They're always calling her for this or that. I don't know how they're going to manage without her. I've overheard her one-sided conversations through the open door many times. "Jean

Gauthier again! The last minute! You knew a week ago that you needed tickets." Somehow, magically, the tickets are found, just as they always have been. Clearly it's been a labour of love, with Louise like a mother to those guys.

I take down a black-and-white photograph from the wall, and stare at it for a long time. It's a picture of the 1957-58 Montreal Canadiens, perhaps the greatest team in the history of the game. Here they are, frozen by the camera at the height of their superiority, in the middle year of an incredible five-straight Stanley Cup run never to be challenged in our lifetimes.

I stand proudly in the centre of the second row, behind our captain Maurice Richard, who sits with the Stanley Cup at his knee. Senator Hartland Molson, the team's co-owner, is to the Rocket's left, and general manager Frank Selke on his right. I'm flanked by Tom Johnson and Dollard St. Laurent. To the far left in the third row, next to our trainer Hector Dubois, stands an unbelievably young Henri Richard. Can this be the same white-haired Henri who now looks back on the record eleven Cups he earned as a player in eighteen seasons in the National Hockey League?

Two players to Henri's left is Claude Provost; nine Stanley Cups. Claude, who used to unplug a scoring machine named Bobby Hull, was one of the first players in this group to leave us. I quickly do an obituary scan – and in the fourth row, directly above Claude, I see Doug Harvey's irrepressible grin. How long ago now since Doug passed away? Four years? Five? At the far right in the front row, secure behind his goalie pads, sits Jacques Plante, whose funeral I attended in Switzerland in 1986. On his left, resplendent in a snappy camel-hair team blazer, is Hector "Toe" Blake, the man who forged this disparate collection of individual stars into a solid team. Toe has suffered from Alzheimer's for the past five years, which pains his many friends. In the fourth row, between Jean-Guy Talbot and Bob Turner, stands Floyd "Busher" Curry, one of the most honest, hard-working players of his era. I worry about his health, too, after recent conversations with the Canadiens' medical advisers.

The current condition of these men intrudes on my reverie. At the same time, I realize death and disease should have no place in my recollections of these virile men who stare back at the camera with all the arrogance of youth and victory. They were the best in the world the moment the camera clicked, and they knew it.

My smile returns, when my eyes light on Marcel Bonin, top right of the third row, and on Bernard "Boom-Boom" Geoffrion immediately below him. With the trade of Bert Olmstead to Chicago for the 1958-59 season, I would centre this unlikely pair of wingers, and survive to tell the tale. People would ask me how I could keep a straight face with these jokers on my flanks. The answer is simple: it's easy to have fun when you're winning. Marcel would help us to win four Stanley Cups, Boomer six.

I gently lay the picture down on my desk. Gradually, the "silhouettes" – the ghostly squares and rectangles where framed photographs once hung – are starting to multiply on my office wall. This team photograph will return home with me to suburban Longueuil, as will an even older black-and-white shot of Jean Béliveau with the Quebec Aces' team president Jack Latter and team secretary Charlie Smith, taken in 1952 at centre ice at Le Colisée. I'm also taking a colour reproduction of my *Sports Illustrated* cover of January 23, 1956, and another black-and-white depicting a hockey team of yet another era, the Victoriaville Tigers of 1948-49. Other photos are destined for the Hockey Hall of Fame, to which I've already donated several items, including trophies, pucks, and equipment. Still others will be deposited with the Canadian Archives. A final batch will be packed away and put aside for my daughter and granddaughters to do with as they please.

I hand Louise a memento of her own – a photo of Ray Bourque in his Team Canada uniform. The Boston defenceman, a Ville Saint-Laurent boy, has always been a favourite of hers, despite the historic Bruins–Canadiens rivalry. We share the opinion that he would have looked great in the *bleu-blanc-rouge*.

I am to officially leave the Montreal Canadiens on my sixty-second birthday, Tuesday, August 31, 1993, after forty-five years in hockey. I don't have to go. Indeed, Ronald Corey has asked me on more than one occasion to stay. We are more than professional colleagues. We are friends. But in the end he respected my decision, because I have convinced him that growing fatigue and a desire to be closer to my family must take precedence. Nonetheless, he secured my promise that I will make a certain number of appearances on behalf of the team over the next three years.

My retirement date, in fact, had been determined in 1988, when I first raised the issue of retirement with Ronald. Back then he was as blunt as only a friend could be. "Jean," he said, "you can't go now. You're too young and you'll regret it. I'm not embarrassed to be selfish. Hockey is going to face difficult times in the next few years, and we'll need people like you here." He didn't know how prophetic he would prove to be, especially about the state of the sport. More immediately, he did succeed in talking me into a five-year countdown.

As my official retirement date loomed closer, Louise and I began sifting through my files. This proved to be a long, often thankless task, but a curiously impersonal one. Printed materials – letters, reports, memos – didn't seem to carry the emotional weight of the photographs, so we left those until the end.

Since 1971, my title on the Montreal Canadiens organization chart has read: Senior Vice-President of Corporate Affairs. For twenty-two years, this has translated into six- and seven-day weeks, fifty-odd weeks of the year – a full schedule at the office, followed, more often than not, by official functions well into the evening. In addition, I have maintained business contacts in the corporate world, including directorships on as many as eight boards, the Molson Companies, Carena Developments, Dominion Textiles, Acier Leroux, and the Canadian Reinsurance Association among them.

You can stay on boards until you're seventy. I don't intend to hide, but I plan to gradually taper off my involvements. Even now, I'm not as visible as I used to be. I don't preside over as many golf tournaments. I'm learning to say "no." At dinner, I don't want to be at the head table. I've had my share of that. Slowly, without hurting anybody, I'm trying to pace myself, to adopt a new rhythm. I have had more than my share of official functions. Now I want to be like anybody else.

When I would join a board, I would do so on two conditions – that I could be voted out after one year or, if I didn't like it, I could resign after serving one year, with no hard feelings. The boards, I must say, have been learning experiences. I was hesitant at first. I didn't know what I could contribute. Then I'd look around and see that the people on these boards were from all walks of life.

Being on boards means many so-called "free" evenings have been spent wrestling with complex information in preparation for one directors' meeting or another. Now I'd rather read a good book. Reading has always been one of my greatest pleasures. On my desk at home I have the latest book by Marvin Miller, former executive director of the Major League Baseball Players Association. I've been trying to finish it for months now, but whenever I pick it up, I think of something else that must be done.

This time, it really is time to go. I leave knowing full well how fortunate I've been to have spent my entire working life in professional sport, a privilege accorded to very few. My on-ice career was tremendously exciting, and the chance to build a second career with the most successful team in professional sports, after I put away my uniform in 1971, made it even more worthwhile. The greatest advantage of working in corporate and community affairs for the Montreal Canadiens in the 1970s and 1980s was that I could write my job description as I went along, at a time when sports franchises of every kind were beginning to recognize new responsibilities to their audiences and to the public at large.

Just yesterday, someone asked if I felt like any retiring forty-year employee with any other well-known Montreal institution, like Northern Telecom, the Canadian National Railway, or Alcan. Was it time to take the gold watch and run?

I am ambivalent. Like any lifelong employee, I feel great loyalty to my working family. At the same time, my job has been special – perhaps unique – and has brought with it a degree of recognition and other rewards that I could never have dreamt of in my youth. Not only was I accepted as a public figure, I also became a sort of internal ombudsman for the Forum family, often serving as mediator or adviser for this side and that. As awareness of my imminent departure spread throughout the building, the requests came in from several quarters. The Canadiens' employees wanted to get me something. What would I like? (A television set.) Molson, with which I was associated all along, including my eighteen years as a player, asked about a farewell party. (Yes, if it was kept to a few intimates.) The NHL inquired as well, as did a number of media outlets. I told everyone the same thing: "Low-profile is the key. I've received many honours in my life, and now that it's time to leave, I want to do so quietly among friends." Thus, when it came time to receive my retirement TV during a private reception limited to the Forum's regular employees, it was a very moving moment for all of us. My door had always been open to them. We had shared careers for so many years, and so many early-morning cups of coffee in the cafeteria.

Since assuming the Canadiens' presidency in 1982, Ronald Corey has played host each year to a dinner with the coaches, their wives, and the Molson family on the Monday before the season opener. On this occasion I'll receive two more mementos – a beautiful set of luggage and a 1993 Stanley Cup ring. Later, some-body will joke, "That's seventeen rings, Jean. Do you wear them on your fingers and toes?" Actually, the championship commem-orative ring is a relatively recent innovation. The teams who won five straight Cups in the 1950s never received them.

Perhaps my most difficult task in the past few months has been winding down an especially personal labour of love, the Jean Béliveau Foundation. On February 11, 1971, I had scored the 500th goal of my career, completing a hat trick against Minnesota's Gilles Gilbert, in a 6–2 win over the North Stars. I was only the second member of the *bleu-blanc-rouge* (along with Maurice Richard) to reach this number. What made it even more special was that it had come in what was to be my final year as a player. I had decided long before to hang up my skates at the end of the 1971 season.

About a week after the win over Minnesota, one of the train-ers approached me during a workout, and asked me to go upstairs to Sam Pollock's office. I assumed Sam wanted to discuss my pres-ence at a dinner or a similar public event. Having been the team's captain since 1961, I was often called upon to travel on the speak-ing circuit.

When I arrived at Sam's door, he immediately escorted me down the hall to David Molson's office.

"Jean, we want to give you a night to honour your 500 goals and your career," David began. "This is your final season, and with everything you've done for the team, both on the ice and off, we feel that we owe you this."

I was touched by his offer, but I knew that I would be very uncomfortable if this "night" turned out to be a sort of depart-ment store on ice where all sorts of appliances and gifts are pre-sented, only to be topped off by the *pièce de résistance*, a shiny new automobile, wheeled out by a slightly embarrassed friend as 18,000 onlookers ooh and aah.

"All right," I said, "but only under certain conditions. I don't want a car full of gifts. I'll accept a maximum of four souvenirs: something from my teammates; the traditional silver tray from that night's opponent; something from *La Soirée du Hockey*; and something from the Canadiens' organization. If there's any money involved, I don't want a penny for myself. Let me split it among four or five charities I've been associated with through the years."

David and Sam agreed, and mentioned something about a date in late March. I didn't think much about it after that. We were in the thick of a playoff race with Boston and New York, after having missed the playoffs for the first time in my career the previous spring. I wanted no distractions in my quest for a tenth Stanley Cup title.

Back then, a hockey team's public relations department generally confined itself to rather basic matters, such as the issuing of press releases and the like. No one was equipped to handle major promotions such as special nights for players, and a team's management usually went to a player's friends for advice. In this case, the Canadiens cornered two of the very best friends and organizers a man could wish for – Zotique Lespérance, a former broadcaster, columnist, and Molson's executive, and Raymond Lemay, a prominent Quebec businessman and president of Montreal's Blue Bonnets Raceway. They agreed to help, and scheduled my celebration for the night of March 24, 1971.

Shortly before that date, the three of us got together for a progress report. Zotique and Raymond had had less than a month to publicize the event. Meanwhile, Montreal had come to a virtual standstill for close to a week, as a result of a blizzard that had dumped huge amounts of unplowed snow on top of the garbage that had gone uncollected by striking municipal blue-collar workers.

"Jean," said Raymond, "I don't know what you have in mind, but the money that comes in for your charities might be a lot more than you think."

I was doubtful, and told him so. "You've lost a week in there because of the snow and the strike — so how much could it possibly be? If you pick up a total $25,000 or $30,000, at least each charity will get $6,000 or $7,000 apiece. I can't see it being any more."

"Maybe we should have a back-up plan, just in case," Zotique cautioned, and he suggested the creation of a foundation. That same afternoon, he called in Jim Grant, of the law firm Stikeman Elliot, to create the Jean Béliveau Fund, as it was first known.

When, on March 24, they presented me with an oversized cheque for $155,855 at centre ice, I could hardly believe my eyes. Thankfully, all that money had someplace to go. I later discovered that Zotique had enlisted the help of Molson's sales representatives in every region of Quebec, while Raymond had put his connections in the upper echelons of Quebec corporate management to excellent use, including a meeting with Jean-Louis Lévesque which resulted in our first donation of $10,000. Together, they did a fantastic job, and the foundation was off and running from the start.

Now, some twenty years later, we were closing the books. Zotique, Raymond, and Ron Perowne, the original trustees, were still on board, along with Marcel Lacroix, who replaced my friend Jacques Côté when he perished in a plane crash; Jean Bruneau, who took over from Sam Maislin when he passed away; and my daughter Hélène, who joined us for the final five years. In two decades, we'd managed to pass along almost $600,000 for charitable good works, and still had almost $900,000 remaining.

The extraordinary thing is that, after the initial $155,000 was presented to me at the Forum in 1971, we never again had to solicit money. I managed to raise a fair amount by presiding over golf tournaments and the like. I'd donate the honoraria that I would receive for personal appearances, and ten or twelve friends would send me $1,000 or so each year. But the largest donation we ever received was $25,000 from the estate of people I never met.

One morning, I got a call at the Forum from someone with an accounting firm in Mont-Joli. "Mr. Béliveau, I'm the executor of a will of an elderly couple from Priceville, a little town up past Matane. The wife died a year ago, and the husband just passed away. They left their estate of $200,000 to eight charitable organizations, and your foundation is one of them."

"You're sure there are no encumbrances? No long-lost cousin or nephew somewhere?" I didn't want any of our precious resources to go on legal fees in an expensive probate battle.

"No family. No children. Nobody. Everything is clear."

With this $25,000 from these wonderfully generous strangers, our bank account began to grow. In the end, we decided to transfer the foundation's entire assets – the remaining $900,000 – to the Quebec Society for Disabled Children, earmarking the money for its summer camp northeast of Joliette. The only proviso for the Society is that it follow our standing rule: buy equipment and materials, tangible items that directly benefit the recipients. No foundation money ever went toward salaries or administrative costs. Louise Richer would handle the day-to-day operations, making sure that I saw each and every request for funds. If the trustees okayed an expenditure, I would authorize the charity involved to make the purchase from a local supplier, and have the bill sent to me. That's the way it worked, for twenty-two years, and I like to think it worked out reasonably well.

In the almost five months it took to dismantle the foundation, my daughter Hélène was of tremendous help. My wife Élise and I have only one child – a resourceful young woman now, of course, and the mother of two beautiful daughters, Mylène, age ten, and Magalie, eight.

As the only child of a sports celebrity, Hélène had a life that was hardly typical. She too has a scrapbook, having been photographed almost from her birth, in April 1957, by the local media. She was only fourteen when I hung up my skates. But if either of us thought that leaving behind an eighty-game season and extensive road trips would automatically bring us closer together as father and daughter, we were wrong.

I plunged into my new duties on the second floor. The next time it seemed I had the opportunity to look closely at this very special young lady, she was twenty-one years old and heading out into the world on her own. I felt, in retrospect, that we had missed out on many things together. As a public figure with a heavy workload, there were many nights, even weeks, when I could not be with her. This was my choice, of course, but all too often I found myself watching from a distance as my daughter matured and became her own person.

This is one reason why Élise and I have sworn an oath to be doting grandparents to Mylène and Magalie. There's another reason as well, the result of the sort of calamity that seems to strike every family at one time or another.

That Friday in October 1989 began as simply any other working day – the usual slate of meetings and appointments. Moments after I arrived at the Forum, nothing in my calendar would matter any more.

Two police officers were waiting for me at the reception desk, and asked to speak to me privately in my office. Inside I found the chaplain of the Montreal Urban Community police department.

"Jean," he said, "Serge took his life this morning, at Station Twenty-Five." This downtown precinct was only a couple of hundred yards east of where we stood. My son-in-law Serge was a police constable, a twenty-five-year veteran on the force, and the father of Mylène and Magalie, who were then five and three years old.

Despondent, in part, because his marriage, his second, was going through a rocky period, he had succumbed to these and other pressures. Too few people understand the daily stress that law enforcement officers must bear. It takes a strong mind and even greater strength of character to experience what they do, and emerge unscathed. In the end, it all proved too much for him.

I cannot adequately convey the feeling of devastation our family suffered. As I spoke with the chaplain and the other officers, it was apparent to me that perhaps the toughest job of my life awaited me: I would have to let Élise, Hélène, and the children know. Apparently, an acquaintance had heard a report of a police suicide on the radio and had phoned Élise at home, but could not provide any specific details. Because of this, however, Élise was filled with foreboding and half-anticipated my news when I called.

I returned home, the same home in Longueuil that we had purchased for $18,000 in 1955, and together Élise and I drove to St. Lambert to tell Hélène and the girls. Magalie accepted the news as well as could be expected of a three-year-old, but her older sister was devastated. Although Hélène and Serge had experienced marital difficulties, he had always been a dutiful father. Now he was gone, and the winter of 1989 was going to be especially dark and cold, as we would have to struggle to make sense of his death and to comfort one another.

Hélène went into therapy shortly after Serge's funeral. About a year later, she became involved with a group called Suicide Action, which counsels and supports those people whose loved ones have taken their lives. She quickly realized that the group was doing her considerable good, and she eventually joined it as a volunteer. She's remained involved to this day, and I believe that she has found her true vocation. Recently she told her mother that, while Serge's death was a terrible tragedy, it gave her the opportunity to find a way to help others, which, in turn, has brought new meaning to her life.

This came as a revelation to me, because I'd suspected that

Hélène might have been spoiled while she was growing up. But she was always very much her mother's daughter, imbued with a strong sense of character and a knowledge of who she was. Only that firm foundation could have helped her survive such an ordeal, and I give Élise full credit for that. She was always there for her daughter and they developed an extremely close relationship. As Hélène's father I can only marvel at the woman who has emerged from this traumatic experience, and I know that the strength that enabled her to survive it will be passed down to my granddaughters.

Like me, Hélène's passion for the Canadiens is a long and deep one. Hélène was only five years old when I first began to take her with me to the Forum on Saturday nights. I'd drop her off at the usherettes' room at 6:00 p.m. and they would take care of her. When she was older, they had a special usherette outfit made up, and she surprised me with it one game night in 1968 as the cameras clicked away. She went for years without missing a game, and still attends often, while Élise and I happily babysit the girls.

Late in the 1993 playoffs, in fact, Hélène wore one of my sweaters, complete with a captain's "C" on the front and the number four and "BÉLIVEAU" on the back. A couple of fans came up to her before the game, figuring that the sweater was a castoff from a father or an older brother, and suspecting that she might not even know who "BÉLIVEAU" was.

"Miss, this guy doesn't play anymore," one of them informed her.

Hélène pointed up to the twenty-three Stanley Cup banners that hang directly overhead. "I know," she said. "He's one of the ghosts." For some reason, other teams, especially the Bruins, truly believe that the Forum is haunted by the spirits of Canadiens past.

The fan turned to his friend and said, "Great answer! She's smarter than us; we should have thought of that and worn older sweaters."

As I've said, while our daughter was teaching the fans a lesson, Élise and I were playing the proud grandparents on babysitting detail. Our family is very closely knit, and we're bound and determined to be there for the girls whenever we possibly can. They come to swim with us in our pool each Sunday. It's their day. In fact, every day is their day, if they want it, because the time is not that far distant when they too will expand their horizons and their interests and begin to make their own way in the world. If we spoil them a bit, as they say in French, *tant pis*. I am secure in the knowledge that I am doing only what every grandparent would do if he or she could.

My pride in our daughter, and in her daughters, is also a reflection of the love I have for my wife. When we got married, I had a pretty good idea the direction my life would take, if not a grasp of its details. There would be hockey on the ice, of course, and hockey-related activities and interests elsewhere, and these would consume the greater portion of my time and energy, if I was successful. I remember saying to Élise when we first came to Montreal in the fall of 1953, "You take care of the house; I'll take care of the outside." Forty years later, we can look back in the satisfaction of two jobs well done.

However, I'm conscious of the fact that by retiring and cutting down on my outside interests I'll be infringing on her territory. I hope I don't become one of those newly retired husbands who's suddenly underfoot from morning till night, and vegetates in the corner. At least I'm assured of well-nigh perfect health. One of the first items on my retirement countdown was a complete medical examination, conducted by our team physician Douglas Kinnear. He gave me the works – scanners, X-rays, everything he could think of. The tests took up a lot of the summer of 1992, but I finally passed with flying colours.

In fact, there isn't very much chance of my sitting around the house. Today, I reviewed my week. The previous Saturday, I attended a sports-card show in Chicago with Maurice Richard, then flew back late and had Sunday to catch my breath. Monday is to be taken up by interviews and clearing out my office. Tuesday morning, I'll stop in at Molson and at the Forum before taking a two o'clock flight to Toronto. There's a Molson dinner there that evening, leading up to a general board meeting on Wednesday morning and a committee meeting in the afternoon. I'll fly home at six, and the next evening I'll attend a gala dinner sponsored by a Montreal daily. On Friday, there's a private luncheon hosted by my friend Raymond Lemay, and on Saturday I fly to Halifax.

Perhaps one man's retirement is another man's accelerated work load.

A friend asked the obvious question a few days ago: "How's retirement treating you?" Élise started to laugh. "You should see his agenda," she said. "He's on the road almost as much as before."

Back in the office at the Forum, Louise and I are almost through with our sorting. In front of me is a stack of special mail – the best wishes of fans I've never met; the goodbye messages of acquaintances and friends acquired over the years. Louise hands me a letter from Bob Gainey, whose team, the Minnesota North Stars, is in transit to Dallas, where it will emerge as the Stars. Bob has christened them the Interim Stars, and created a logo for their letterhead. I have a great deal of admiration for Bob, both as a player and captain during his sixteen years with the Canadiens, and now as a coach and general manager elsewhere. I read his kind words, and Louise makes a note to send him back our thanks.

The next letter comes from one of my greatest fans, a man in Windsor, Ontario, who has christened his newborn son with the first name Béliveau, and has enclosed a copy of the birth certificate to prove it. "They'll probably call him Bel for short," I reflect. It could be worse.

It's the squares and rectangles on my office walls, however, which represent the real milestones of my forty-five years in hockey, forty-one of them with a single team.

"This is my second retirement from the Canadiens," I muse. "It should be easier than in 1971."

But it isn't.

2

THE TOWN

It was a crisp winter day, the snow so brilliantly white it was blue, and so hardpacked that the crunch of heavy boots seemed to echo for miles. In 1943, there was no such thing as a wind-chill factor. Television and its temptations were still a generation away. With nothing to drive or lure us indoors on frigid Sunday afternoons, adults and children alike revelled in the 25-below-zero-Fahrenheit temperatures.

I was twelve years old, and sat with Guy, my eight-year-old brother, at the kitchen table. Somehow, my mother had convinced us to take off our toques and jackets, which now lay in a pile by the back door. Under the table, scarcely denting the industrial-strength linoleum that covered the kitchen floor, were two pairs of skates, still attached to our feet. Minutes earlier, Guy and I had been skating on the rink that Arthur Béliveau built every winter in the family's back yard. Melting ice chips began to drip from our blades beneath our chairs.

Moments earlier, Laurette Dubé Béliveau had stood at the door and uttered the magic word "lunch." Now the entire family was gathered for sandwiches and steaming bowls of soup. After several hours of non-stop shinny, the players were steaming as well, eager to rejoin the game. From time to time, Arthur Béliveau would have to reach across and gently swat one of his impatient sons for a breach of etiquette. Usually, however, all it took from either parent was a warning look, and order was restored.

Outside, the sounds of a puck booming on makeshift boards and the hiss of steel on ice had us leaning imperceptibly toward the door as we ate. Our friends and neighbours – Raymond, André, and Gilles Ducharmes; Charles and Jean-Marie Dumas; Marcel Boutet; Joe Moore; and Léopold and Jean-Marc Côté – were continuing the game without us.

This was the beauty of marathon shinny. Whenever chores and staggered lunch hours called one or several of the regulars away, the teams would reform instantly and keep on playing. The only hitch in our weekend games would arise when duty called us to the church of Les Saints-Martyrs Canadiens. On Saturday morning, I or one of the older players would serve early Mass as an altar boy, usually at seven or eight o'clock, before adjourning to the Béliveau kitchen for breakfast and the Béliveau rink for hockey. On Sundays, especially once we'd become senior altar boys, we would generally serve High Mass at ten o'clock, and then return home for a late lunch.

I took these tasks very seriously. Both of my parents were religious, having come from rural backgrounds. The Dubés were clustered in and around Charette, halfway between Shawinigan Falls and Trois-Rivières; the Béliveaus in the Saint-Célestin area, near Nicolet.

My father's family traces its roots back to Antoine Béliveau, who settled in Port Royal, Nova Scotia, on the Bay of Fundy, in 1642. Port Royal, now Annapolis Royal, was once the most fought-over place in Canada, the site of several eighteenth-century skirmishes between Britain and France which culminated in the great displacement of the Acadiens in 1755. When some 10,000 of them refused to swear fealty to the British Crown, they were expelled and fanned out in many directions. Some went back to France. Others journeyed to Louisiana, where they would become "Cajuns." Still others headed for the northeastern United States or toward Quebec. I've even heard that some of them decided to travel as far away as possible, and ended up in the Falkland Islands, off the coast of Argentina.

Our particular branch of the family settled in the Boston area for a while, before making its way back to Canada in the mid-1800s. Like many Acadiens who'd spent a generation south of the border, they may first have thought of settling in a French-speaking enclave in the Madawaska Valley of New Brunswick. But when they heard that the Quebec government was offering arable land in the Saint-Grégoire area, on the south shore of the St. Lawrence River near Trois-Rivières, they applied for and received a land grant, and stayed. At least, most of them stayed.

Around the time of the First World War, when my father was still a boy, four of his older brothers came to the same conclusion that had sent so many young French-Canadian males scurrying across North America: Quebec's family farms simply could not provide a living for most of its grown sons. Large households were the norm then, and eight to ten children – including five or more boys – might reach maturity. A farm could possibly be subdivided to accommodate the eldest two or three sons, but the rest would have to marry into families short of male offspring, or move to the nearest city in search of work.

My father was barely in his teens when his brothers prepared to go to western Canada for the fall harvest. He wanted to join them, but his mother called a halt to the great adventure. She had good cause. After all, it was a rough trip to the wheat fields, sometimes clinging atop a railway car. Several young men from their region had lost their lives en route. Perhaps my grandmother sensed something else about my uncles' trip that the rest of the family didn't, something that only time would prove right. And, in fact, the three months that her sons were supposed to be gone eventually stretched into many decades.

I finally met three of my uncles almost fifty years after they'd journeyed west. In 1959, Molson, the firm which employed me, purchased a number of breweries in western Canada, and I was asked to tour them in the summer of 1960. Élise and I started out by car from Montreal and drove across Canada. In Wolseley, Saskatchewan, about seventy miles east of Regina, we met Antonio Béliveau. He was retired, and his children had taken over the family farm. His brothers Ernest and Armand were in Saskatchewan, too, having settled down and raised families to the west of Regina, in Moose Jaw and Ponteix. Sadly, none of them could tell me what had happened to the fourth brother, who had seemingly vanished many years before in the interior of British Columbia. Perhaps a surprise awaits me in the form of long-lost relatives there!

The sixth and youngest Béliveau brother, Louis-Philippe, was not quite as adventurous as his older siblings. In the 1930s, he moved to Montreal, where he was to work for the Canadian National Railway for some forty years. When it came time to retire, he returned to Saint-Célestin and lives there still. He is eighty-six now, and I try to visit him whenever I can. As well, he attends our annual family reunion, which takes place each January.

The Béliveaus who stayed in Quebec tended to congregate near Saint-Céléstin, then began to spread out toward Quebec City and Victoriaville. Like his brothers before him, my father eventually had to leave the family farm. During the Great Depression, he was hired by Shawinigan Water and Power, then one of the province's largest private utilities. It later became part of Hydro-Québec.

Arthur was stringing electrical line in Trois-Rivières when he met Laurette Dubé, the only daughter in an uncharacteristically small family of only two children. Shortly thereafter, a wedding took place, and on August 31, 1931, Arthur and Laurette's first child, christened Jean Arthur Béliveau, arrived – just as the Great Depression reached its nadir.

Because my father was busy wiring much of the Bois-Francs region, we followed the hydro poles a fair bit in my earliest years. When I was about three years old, the family moved to Plessisville, but resettled in Victoriaville shortly after my sixth birthday. There I began elementary school at École Saint-David, before being taught by the Sacred-Heart Brothers at L'Académie Saint-Louis de Gonzague for grades five through nine, and then at the Collège de Victoriaville for grade ten.

My childhood was in no way remarkable. It was a typical French-Canadian Catholic upbringing, one hinged on family values, strict religious observance, hard work, conservatism, and self-discipline. We certainly weren't well-to-do in material terms, but in the 1940s, you could raise a family on a workingman's salary if you stuck to the basics, which, of necessity, we did. Our home was small and very old. Shortly after my family moved to a new house across town in 1952, it was demolished to make room for a larger yard for the neighbouring presbytery. Despite our reduced circumstances, we always had food on the table and clean clothes to wear. We had a back-yard vegetable garden, raised rabbits in the summer, and heated the house on the "Shawinigan Water and Power Company Plan." Sometimes when those cedar hydro poles were blown down by windstorms or knocked over by reckless drivers, my father would "harvest" the casualties and bring them home. Then he and I would spend hours sawing and chopping them down to size for burning in our furnace and kitchen stove. I'll always remember the aroma of cedar that permeated the house, and I believe that hewing all those logs helped build me up physically during my teen-age years.

We all worked hard in those days, and after our chores were done, both at Les Saint-Martyrs Canadiens and in the Béliveau household, we got to play our favourite sports. Summertime meant baseball from dawn to dusk. In winter, the family rink was barely free long enough for my father to flood it.

The wonders and distractions children experience today were, of course, unknown in the 1940s. Forget video games and Walkmans and rock concerts. At the same time, the pastimes we did have were never over-organized by well-meaning adults. We simply were left to our own devices. As a result, shinny at the Béliveau Forum may have been technically inefficient, singularly devoid of positional play and five-on-five chalk talk strategies, but we got to concentrate on the basics, learning how to skate, stick-handle, and shoot.

Our rules were few, but then so were our disputes. The score was secondary to enjoying ourselves. We kept score, of course, and often called our own play-by-play as we went along . . . "Richard goes around Milt Schmidt, holds off Bob Armstrong, leans low and sends a screaming backhand into the top corner. He shoots, he scores!" But, just to keep things interesting, the teams would change every ten minutes or so. There were no losers, and we were scrupulously fair in maintaining an equilibrium.

We learned by doing, and by holding onto the puck. The bigger, better boys were obviously more adept, and would control the play for long moments, while their younger opponents attempted to check them. When the younger boys grew larger and more proficient, they, in turn, began to dominate the game, daring the newcomers to challenge them. Today's sports psychologists might call this Darwinian hockey, survival of the fittest. We called it fun.

Until I was about twelve years old, I never played for a "real" team with sweaters, coaches, and scheduled games. The idea of sitting back and waiting for someone else to clear the rink was unheard of in our crowd. Our version of power skating involved getting behind a scraper and plowing a path through foot-high snow until the ice appeared. And yet, without all of the trappings that kids today have come to expect, I somehow learned to play the game, as did boys all over Quebec and throughout the rest of Canada.

The next stage in my hockey development occurred under the auspices of the Brothers of the Sacred Heart at L'Académie. The first "real" rink I ever set skates on, with a more or less regulation ice surface, proper lines, and boards and goals, was erected in the schoolyard each November, and would remain busy until the thaw of the following March.

At L'Académie, we played together after school in a four-team house league. The Brothers also formed an All-Star team that played on Saturday mornings at the Victoriaville Arena. Victoriaville was a relatively small town in those days, with perhaps no more than 10,000 residents, and was fortunate to have such a fine structure. The reason for the building's existence was simple: Victoriaville was the centre of the Bois-Francs region, an important farming area, and the arena was home to the summer agricultural exhibition every year.

Thanks to both the Sacred-Heart Brothers and an accident of geography, I was able to play on weekends against a wide range of hockey talent. We didn't have clear-cut divisions such as peewee or bantam; things weren't sufficiently organized for that. But our All-Stars often would face off against teams that were sponsored by local businesses and composed of factory workers. These players were much older and stronger than me and my schoolmates. Twenty-year-olds would sometimes be on the ice with kids of thirteen and fourteen. With the exception of myself and a boy named Cloutier, the academy All-Stars were pretty small, and our lineup of Ducharme, Patry, Côté, Boutet, Houle, Métivier, and Filion intimidated no one. Still, we had our share of successes, and learned a great deal in the process.

My hockey career took another step forward when, at fifteen years old, I went on to the Collège de Victoriaville for grade ten. That year I played for both the Collège and the Victoriaville Panthers, a team in an Intermediate B league that included teams from Athabaska, Princeville, Plessisville, and Warwick. Now my winter weekends began to be occupied by travel to and fro.

Ironically, it was baseball, not hockey, that almost took me away from my home and family. During the war years, an electrician named John Nault was known as "Mr. Baseball" in Victoriaville. He was what we call in French "*mordu*" – "bitten" by the game – and couldn't do enough for any boy who showed an interest. He organized leagues and wired the park to permit night games. When I was fourteen, he packed four or five of us into his car for a Sunday excursion to Boston's Fenway Park. We couldn't understand a word of what was going on around us, but we needed no translation when Ted Williams hammered the ball more than four hundred feet, deep over the right centrefield fence.

It was a gruelling twenty-hour round trip, but I've never forgotten it. All the way back to Victoriaville through Massachusetts and Vermont, a carload of wide-eyed young French Canadians dreamed of playing for the Boston Red Sox, digging in against Allie Reynolds and other New York Yankee aces.

On other Sundays, yet another professional ballpark was even closer to hand – about a hundred miles away in Montreal. We sometimes went to Delormier Downs to watch the Royals play, and I saw stars like pitchers Tommy Lasorda and Jean-Pierre Roy, as well as Chuck Connors, a towering first basemen who later became an actor, and starred on television in *The Rifleman*. The only Royals player I don't remember seeing was perhaps the most famous of them all – the inimitable Jackie Robinson.

I loved watching the big hitters because I myself was a pitcherinfielder with a big bat who knew the thrill of sending the ball out of sight. By the time I turned fifteen, my ever-increasing size had added several miles per hour to my fastball, and thirty or forty feet to my occasional home runs.

That spring, after school was out at four o'clock, John Nault and I would sometimes drive to Trois-Rivières, where I would warm up with a senior team that played in the Canadian-American League. I didn't actually play in the games, but I had the opportunity to pitch to guys who were twenty-five and older, and the local baseball scouts began to take notice.

One scout was so impressed by my size, pitching arm, and hitting skills that he tried to sign me to a Class C or D contract. Unfortunately, this meant that I'd be placed with a team somewhere in Alabama. The discussion didn't get too far. Needless to say, *maman* responded with an unequivocal "no."

The following summer, however, I did leave home, to play in a setting that was about as familiar as Alabama to a sixteen-year-old from Victoriaville. In 1948, Val d'Or, Quebec, was still a rough, tough frontier town – the haunt of gold miners, prospectors, and lumberjacks. Long, hard winters meant that the townspeople prized their summertime pursuits, which included hunting, fishing, and, above all, baseball. Val d'Or competed in the flourishing Abitibi Senior League, where each league squad was in the habit of importing players from elsewhere in Quebec and northern Ontario to bolster its fortunes. When the Val d'Or team lost a player through injury that summer, and went looking for an instant replacement, one of the guys from Victoriaville said he knew of a young prospect back home who might be able to help them out.

"How young?" he was asked.

"I'm not sure – maybe sixteen. Plays with my kid brother."

"We can't hire him at the mine, then. He's too young. Can you think of someone else?"

"Nobody as good as him. He's a good relief pitcher – plays the corners and hits the ball for distance."

"Hmmm. Maybe the city needs another kid to cut grass in the parks."

Which is how, a couple of days later, Jean Béliveau became a summer employee of the city of Val d'Or and a regular on the baseball team. I mowed by day and pitched in the evenings for maybe seven weeks. What I remember most – not in this order – were the unpaved streets, the wooden sidewalks, and the tremendous kindness I was shown by everyone I met.

Later, of course, I would meet many great hockey players from the area. Dave Keon, Jacques Laperrière, and Réjean Houle were from Rouyn, Quebec, while Christian, Jean-Paul, and Paulin Bordeleau hailed from nearby Noranda. Ralph Backstrom, Dick Duff, Bob Murdoch, Larry and Wayne Hillman, and Mickey and Dick Redmond were just across the provincial border in Kirkland Lake, Ontario, while Timmins was home to Frank and Peter Mahovlich. After spending a summer there, I always wondered what a winter in that wild country would be like. I know for a fact that the players who graduated from the northwestern junior leagues were well-schooled, and made for rock-solid professionals. Toronto and Montreal often fought tooth-and-nail to identify and sign them.

Val d'Or was my first extended period away from home. All of my subsequent departures would be brought about by hockey. When I was thirteen or fourteen, I'd seen the Victoriaville Senior Tigers play at the local arena. One of their players who quickly became a favourite of mine was a defenceman named Roland Hébert. Roland wasn't tall, nor was he particularly wide, but he had great hockey sense and a lot of heart, throwing himself in front of pucks at every opportunity. I revered him, as did many of my friends, but I had no idea that he would help send me further down the road toward my chosen career.

In 1946, Roland was invited to referee a game played between our college team and one sponsored by Victoriaville Furniture. The brother who coached our team played me the entire sixty minutes on defence, and I managed to score three or four goals, many on rink-long rushes. Roland was obviously impressed by my performance and size (by this time, six feet even, and almost 180 pounds). After the game, he asked me how I felt about a career in hockey. "The Montreal Junior Canadiens will be interested in hearing about you," he said, but I don't remember us pursuing the subject any further – perhaps because I couldn't believe he was serious.

Later that winter, however, one of the directors of the Senior Tigers, a man named Parenteau, invited me to practise with them. This proved especially beneficial, although the seniors came as quite a culture shock to a boy who had been playing Académie hockey just a year before. On the ice with me were veterans such as Roland Hébert, Dick Wray, and Phil Vitali. Lucien Dechêne, a former player with New Westminster of the Western Hockey League, was in nets. In those days, team practices amounted to glorified scrimmages, and I found myself on the same ice as experienced former professionals and doing a lot better than I realized, or so it seemed.

One day after practice, a man came by and introduced himself to me. His name was Jack Toupin, and he coached the Trois-Rivières Reds of the Quebec Junior A League. He was also a scout for the Toronto Maple Leafs.

"You're good enough to play with my team right now, Jean," he said. "All you have to do is give me the word, and I'll sign you. Besides, it would be exciting for you to play in your birthplace." I almost flew home that night. Barely sixteen years old! Junior A in Trois-Rivières, where I was born and my parents had been married! And close to the Béliveau and Dubé clans in Saint-Céléstin and Charette! What could be better?

This time, it was my father who said no. "Not yet, Jean, you're

still a bit too young," he counselled. "Your schooling is important. I want you to continue your studies at the college. If you have
the talent these people think you do, the hockey world won't
forget you just because you choose to stay in Victoriaville another
year or two." Case closed.

The following season, I joined the Victoriaville Panthers as an
intermediate. Unlike the situation today, which is strictly con-
trolled and highly regimented, young men in the 1940s played
more or less where they were capable of playing. Talent, not age,
was the determining factor. Intermediate hockey in particular was
a place where players in their mid-twenties or even thirties, who
were a step too slow for the senior leagues, could find a berth. But
these guys knew what they were doing, and there was a whole lot
more physical contact.

The special thing about playing intermediate hockey was that
the whole community got behind the team. One of our biggest
boosters was Adélard Morier, who owned a hardware store and
sold sporting goods. One day, out of the blue, he walked up and
gave me a pair of brand new skates. Considering our family's
finances, these were a luxury, and I always remembered that very
generous gesture. But Mr. Morier was not alone. Several other
local businessmen took it upon themselves to help out "their" Panthers in many ways.

That single season as an intermediate was an important spring-
board for my career. First and foremost, I became acquainted with
a wide range of people in the community, including its leaders,
whose kindness made life easier for the team. Second, I scored
forty-seven goals and added twenty-one assists – the first yardstick
of my progress in organized hockey. Third, I learned a very valuable lesson – to always reach for the next rung on the ladder.
When you're the best in your small corner, you can become too
satisfied. You may achieve success for a while, but you won't
progress or grow. Stand still, and you'll lose ground. Move on,

and you'll continually test yourself, proving your worth anew.

At the same time as I was coming to this understanding, hockey's jungle drums were beating messages up and down the province of Quebec. All the coaches and managers throughout the intermediate, junior, and senior leagues in the province aspired to move up in the hockey hierarchy, and the best way to do this was to ensure that the Montreal Canadiens knew what was happening in their back yard.

This sort of competition picked up steam in 1946, when Frank Selke joined the Canadiens as general manager. He immediately began to organize and encourage Quebec hockey (and hockey in other provinces as well) at every level. Before Monsieur Selke arrived, the NHL's scouting system had been a hit-or-miss network of hot tips and tall tales. All that changed upon his arrival, and Montreal's farm-club network became a production line, sending its output one-way to the Forum. Time and money were no objects to Selke. He never hesitated to fund or create teams, sometimes intervening to increase the size of a particular league. He was patient, working always toward long-term results. To do this, he needed a constant flow of accurate information. A coach's or manager's reputation improved if he was the source of this intelligence.

My father was right, of course, to keep me back for a year – but when my season with the Panthers ended, Roland Hébert himself brought me to the attention of the Canadiens organization. His friend, a veteran goaltender named Paul Bibault, happened to marry Frank Selke's daughter. At their wedding, Roland took Monsieur Selke to one side, and mentioned my name. He saved the best news till last. After recounting my scoring feats and describing how I'd fared in scrimmages with the senior players, Roland added the clincher: "And he's still growing."

And so the parade to Victoriaville began. One Sunday afternoon, after finishing a game of baseball, I was walking home when I was approached by two men. One spoke English only, the other acted as his translator. The man who appeared to be in charge introduced himself as Mickey Hennessey and stated that he worked for Frank Selke and the Montreal Canadiens. He invited me into a snack bar "to talk a little business," and ordered us soft drinks. When we'd sat down, he said: "If you sign a C Form with the Montreal Canadiens, I am authorized to give you a hundred dollars cash money, right here and now."

He extracted twenty ten-dollar bills from his wallet and fanned them out on the table. This was serious money, a lot more than I was used to – more, I think, than I'd ever seen before at one time. I used the translator to slow down the bargaining process, asking him to clarify certain points and repeat others. It took me a while to grasp that the C Form – a standard (and legally binding) document in those days – would link me directly to the Canadiens themselves, not to a junior team, although Montreal would have the right to assign me wherever they chose. I kept on asking questions, buying time, and trying furiously to think about what to do next.

With each hesitation, another purple ten appeared on the table-top, until $200 sat inches away from me. Belong to the Montreal Canadiens? Play on the same team as Richard, Blake, and Lach? And get paid for it? At least I was smart enough not to tell these rather intimidating men that I would probably do it for free!

Believe me, I was ready to go, lock, stock, and barrel – until, that is, I thought of the reception I'd get at home. Arthur Béliveau demanded respect and obedience from his children. If I was unwise enough to go behind his back, I'd strike out on both counts. Summoning up all my courage, and trying desperately not to look at the money, I finished my drink and told Hennessey, "Please talk to my father. I can't sign any agreement without his approval."

Hennessey took me at my word, and visited our house. Later, several other representatives of the Canadiens, including Émile "Butch" Bouchard, the team captain himself, would pay visits.

And, one after the other, my father turned them down. "My son will not sign something which gives someone else control over his life," said Arthur Béliveau, and he meant it.

Finally, however, an acceptable offer did arrive, albeit from another quarter. Sam Pollock's Junior Canadiens sent along a consent form – a totally different document which, if signed, meant only that I would report to their training camp for the following season, and nothing more. I was free to go my own way afterward, whatever happened at the camp. My father and I signed this consent on the recommendation of Roland Hébert, and returned it to the team by mail.

That seemed to settle the matter. However, my father and I were unaware that Lucien Dechêne, the Tigers' goaltender, had meanwhile contacted a friend of his elsewhere in junior hockey – Roland Mercier, the business manager of Frank Byrne's Quebec Citadels. Mercier had been Lucien's coach in Junior B between 1941 and 1944. The problem was that Dechêne wasn't sure of my first name. He knew me only as "the tall boy with the blue toque." As a result, Mercier had a hard time at first trying to find me, but succeeded at last. Three weeks before my seventeenth birthday, I received a document similar to the one that I'd already signed and returned to the Junior Canadiens, accompanied by a letter inviting me to the Quebec Citadels' training camp.

Had both invitations arrived simultaneously, there was a strong chance that I would have gone to Quebec City. After all, the provincial capital was closer to Victoriaville, and not quite the daunting metropolis that Montreal was. However, scant weeks before everyone's training camps began, Frank Selke changed the rules overnight by funding a drastic expansion of Quebec's junior league, almost tripling its size. One of the expansion centres that received a conditional franchise was Victoriaville, which suddenly found itself with both Senior and Junior Tigers, the latter being coached by none other than Roland Hébert.

Hébert immediately went to work on Selke: "Release Béliveau from the Junior Canadiens and let him play in his home town. We're going to need all the help we can get to be competitive as an expansion team, and a local star will fill the rink. Besides, Sam Pollock has enough talent in Montreal already." Selke agreed, and Hébert came to me with the news that I could join the Tigers.

We didn't sign right away, though, figuring Roland Mercier's Citadels and Jack Toupin's Reds surely would submit counter-offers when they discovered that the Junior Canadiens had relinquished their claim. But these were not forthcoming, and I signed with Victoriaville three days before the season began. Only later did my father and I discover that Selke's release had been delivered to Hébert in secrecy. Neither the Citadels nor the Reds knew anything about it. Frank Selke did not build a hockey dynasty by letting players get away.

Before I signed, however, my father had a long conversation with Roland Hébert. "Jean will sign to play for you for one season only," he said. "But after that, his rights revert to me."

"That's not how it works," Roland countered. "Players become the property of the team they sign with, unless they are traded or released."

"Not Jean Béliveau," my father replied, and we didn't sign the contract until that clause was added. Roland Hébert sensed my father's determination. Being from Victoriaville himself, he knew that, while Arthur Béliveau would be scrupulously fair, he would stick to his guns when he felt he was right. After the season ended, I would be a free agent. End of discussion.

So it was that, when play in the Quebec Junior A Hockey League began in October 1948, I was wearing the gold-and-black of the Tigers. Like most of the other expansion teams, it was a diverse crew of castaways and newcomers. Still, we had some decent players, among them Denis Brodeur and André Belhumeur in nets, with Rémy Blais, Gordie Haworth, Roger Hayfield, and me up front, along with Gildor Lévesque and Marcel Chainey on defence.

The name Brodeur will be familiar for many reasons. Denis went on to play goal for the Montreal Nationals at both junior and senior levels. He also represented Canada in Olympic hockey competition; fathered Martin Brodeur, the superb young netminder of the New Jersey Devils; and later became one of Montreal's foremost sports photographers.

(The elder Brodeur's most difficult assignment came on Wednesday, December 8, 1993, when Martin, the same kid who used to tote Denis' equipment as a teen-ager, led his team against Montreal. There is nothing like a Forum "homecoming" for Canadiens' legends; behind the Devils' bench were two familiar names, head coach Jacques Lemaire and defensive assistant Larry Robinson. Of course, Martin earned the first star in a 4–2 win over the Canadiens, and Denis' lenses were fogged for all three periods.)

Very few local boys made the Tigers in 1948, besides myself and Paul Alain. The majority of players had come from far and wide. "Since you're living at home and you don't have to pay room and board, your salary will be $15 a week," said Hébert. I wasn't overwhelmed by his logic, figuring that on-ice performance, not my sleeping arrangements, should determine how much I was worth. Team management soon saw it my way: by Christmas I had as many goals as the rest of my teammates combined, and a raise in pay to $35 a week. In those days, by the way, $35 a week could comfortably raise a family of four.

My season began promisingly enough with a 4–3 victory over the Verdun-LaSalle Cyclones. Roger Hayfield and I scored a pair of goals each against a fire-hydrant-shaped goalie named Lorne Worsley. At first, the Tigers did quite well for an expansion team, playing slightly less than .500 hockey through the fall as we approached a big game against the mighty Quebec Citadels on November 25. Going into that game, Quebec had fifteen wins and one tie for thirty-one points to lead the Southern Division, thirteen points more than the second-place Nationals, and nineteen more than us, stuck in fourth place with six wins and nine losses.

That night proved auspicious for two reasons. It was my first starring role in Quebec City's Colisée, and my introduction to a goaltender who would share a big part of my hockey career. I ended the game with two goals and an assist, having scored one of these goals and the assist in overtime, helping to upset the Citadels 4–2.

We had opened the scoring on a goal by Rémy Blais early in the second period, but the Citadels responded with a pair before the middle period was finished. My goal midway through the third had sent the game into extra time.

Back then the rule was a full, ten-minute overtime period, not sudden-death. About three minutes in, I fed a pass to Gérard Théberge, who one-timed it into the Quebec goal. Several minutes later, the puck was cleared out of our zone and toward the Quebec goal. I took off after it, with no one in close pursuit. The Citadels' netminder, who I'd heard was infamous for his wandering ways, decided to come out after the puck. Just as he reached to poke it away, I managed to get my stick on it. The goalie sprawled at the Citadels' blueline while I swung around him and tucked the puck into the open net.

In later years I had many opportunities to kid Jacques Plante about the night I "deked him out of the rink and ruined his streak" – but the true star that night was our netminder Denis Brodeur, who stopped thirty-nine shots to keep the contest close.

My first experience with Junior A hockey was quite different from that of the majority of my teammates. I was living in my hometown, continuing my education, maintaining a hectic schedule even then. I was a regular eight-to-four daytime student at the college, which also required that we attend study hall on Monday through Thursday evenings between seven and nine o'clock.

However, the Tigers held a practice at four o'clock, and played their games at eight. On game nights, I'd make a token appearance in the study hall, flash my special hockey player's pass, and receive permission to leave. Brother Fernand was in charge of the hall, and as I flew past him he'd usually say something like, "Boy, you're in a hurry to avoid your studies." I never knew whether he was upset because I had dispensation to play, or if he was only kidding.

Many years later, after I had joined the Canadiens, I was playing in Boston and I got a call at my hotel room. It was Brother Fernand, looking for a ticket. I got him one and sat him right behind our bench. After the game, he waited for me, and we reminisced about the tall student hot-footing it by him at the study hall door. He had to admit that my "studies" had gone fairly well.

Grade ten at Collège de Victoriaville had three streams: business, technical, and science. I was enrolled in technical, in pre-electrical studies. I'd thought that perhaps I would follow my father into the power company. But a year later, worn out by one too many five-in-the-morning returns from a road trip, I had to put an end to my formal schooling.

The Tigers and I got off to a slow start that debut season. By early December, I was well back in the individual scoring statistics, with twenty-one points on thirteen goals and eight assists. Frankie Reid of Trois-Rivières was well in front with fifty-one points, three ahead of the Nationals' Bernie Geoffrion, with forty-eight. By season's end, Reid still led on points, but I had a league-leading forty-eight goals, which earned me dual honours as "rookie of the year" and "most promising professional prospect."

As the season had progressed, it appeared that the Tigers would not make the playoffs, but we squeaked in when Roland Mercier reported that a Citadels player named Marius Groleau had been playing with false identification, namely, his dead brother's birth certificate. Groleau was ruled ineligible, and Quebec had to forfeit all the games in which he'd played. This moved us out of last place and into a best-of-five divisional semi-final. But our luck didn't hold. We were eliminated 3–1, and, although I didn't know it yet, my hockey career in Victoriaville was over.

After the Tigers were bumped from playoff action, my father and I began to negotiate with the Quebec Citadels for the following season, 1949-50. Thanks to my father's insistence, I was a free agent, able to deal with anyone we chose. We met Roland Mercier, the Citadels' general manager, at a hotel in nearby Princeville, and discussed contract terms. A few days later we reconvened, and came to a general agreement. It looked as if I'd be headed for Quebec that autumn, barring unforeseen snags with the league or the Tigers.

In the meantime, however, Roland Hébert's excellent work in Victoriaville had not gone unnoticed. He accepted the post of head coach and general manager of the Chicoutimi Saguenéens of the Senior League and he attempted to have the Junior Tigers declared an official Chicoutimi farm team. When this proved impossible under the league's by-laws, Roland rescinded Victoriaville's junior-league concession, and all of his players became free agents along with me.

Or at least that's the story as I've understood it for more than forty years. But while I was preparing the manuscript of this book, I had occasion to review these events with Roland Mercier, who revealed for the first time that other moves were taking place behind the scenes.

In fact, I was never a free agent, and had belonged to the Citadels since November 1948. Without going into the fine print of league by-laws and hockey contracts, it seems a player who'd signed with a given team (in my case, the 1948-49 Victoriaville Junior Tigers) could sign with another team (in my case, the Citadels) on one of three conditions. I would have had to obtain a release from the first team, which the Tigers wouldn't have granted. I would have had to be an over-aged junior, which I wasn't. Or, the first team would have had to cease operations – which the Tigers in fact did; but nobody knew they were going to until it happened.

This means that, despite my father's best intentions, the contract we signed with Roland Hébert could have been contested by the league, or by any other club. The clause that we added sounded fine, but had no real validity.

In any event, Roland Mercier took his first step toward signing me with the Citadels that fall – immediately after the game during which I scored on my friend Jacques Plante. Roland went straight to the Tigers' dressing room, and concluded a deal which sent Leonard Shaw to Victoriaville for $100 and "a player to be named later" – with "later" meaning the 1949-50 season. Roland felt no need to mention that the player he had in mind was me.

When the Tigers ran into financial difficulties a couple of months later, Roland returned their $100 cheque, and informed them that he would waive the usual $100-per-game fee that the Citadels – a major draw – would receive for playing in the Victoriaville Arena. The Tigers were surprised by his generosity, and asked him to name at last the player he wanted to complete their deal.

When he uttered the name Béliveau, the Tigers' directors were up in arms, and threatened to renege. Roland calmly pointed out that the deal had been transacted in front of several witnesses, and that he intended to hold them to it.

This also explains why, after the Old Colisée burned down, the Citadels took up temporary residence in Victoriaville. In effect, I was Citadels' property, loaned to the Tigers for the duration of the season – which few people other than Roland Mercier have ever known.

None of which really matters, I suppose, because the rest of the story unfolded exactly as I've told you. I played those first two months with the Citadels in Victoriaville, waiting for construction to be completed on the new, improved Colisée.

In all my conversations with Roland Mercier and Frank Byrne, they were very explicit as to why they wanted me on the team. The old Colisée had been a glorified exhibition barn. Its replacement would be state of the hockey art. "Our building opens sometime in December," said Byrne, "and it is more than twice as big as the Old Colisée. We need a star to fill those seats. We believe that star is you."

3

✦

LA VIEILLE CAPITALE

June 26, 1993, comes into the world – or at least to those of us who are enjoying an eight o'clock breakfast on the Dufferin Terrace of Quebec City's Château Frontenac – as a radiantly sunny day. It is a Saturday, almost midway through what amounts to a holiday week throughout the province. Many people choose to vacation between June 24, Saint-Jean Baptiste Day, and Canada Day, on July 1. Despite the early hour, the terrace is already bustling.

In hotels and motels all over town, muscular young men, most of them between the ages of seventeen and nineteen, have been up for hours, having spent a night of tossing and turning with visions of twenty-six different National Hockey League uniforms dancing in their heads. Later today, starting at one o'clock, they will gather at Le Colisée to find out whether the NHL thinks each is good enough to gain employment in the sport he loves. There has never been a more varied geographical mix: these young men come from Russia, Latvia, Belarus, Kazahkstan, Slovakia, the

Czech Republic, Norway, Sweden, Finland, the Ukraine, Poland, Switzerland, Germany, the United States, and even Canada.

By the end of the 1993 NHL Entry Draft, ninety-three defence-men, seventy-three centres, thirty-seven right-wingers, forty-six left-wingers, and thirty-six goalies will have to have been selected, for a total of 285 players. Hundreds more will return home in shock and disappointment, their dreams turned to nightmares.

The afternoon will belong to these young men, those selected and those not. But this beautiful morning, here in the city where it all began for me, belongs to Élise and Jean Béliveau, and we're not sharing it with anybody.

The Dufferin Terrace provides a view I consider second to none. It's the equal, certainly, of Hong Kong's Victoria Peak. Today we can see clear across to Ile d'Orléans, to Levis-Lauzon and the shipbuilding yards. The view is so special in part because of its familiarity. Élise was born and raised in Quebec, we met and married here, and I spent four tremendous years here early in my career. I've always said that my experiences in Quebec gave me the foundation upon which I built my professional career.

Familiarity means having come to know the Château Frontenac staff, especially those in the downstairs coffeeshop. Back in my days with the Citadels and, later, the Aces, I'd often wait until the lunch crowd had thinned out, then I'd spend a leisurely afternoon with them, eating and chatting about the previous night's game. We all started out together in the hopeful post-war period, and we've all reached retirement age at the same time.

This morning, Élise and I walk to the Slide, where in winter toboggans go careening downhill on the Dufferin Terrace. I have a painting of this scene, done by Iacurto, one of Quebec's leading artists. It was presented to me by the Kiwanis Club in 1956, when he was known only locally. Today I dropped into an art gallery in the Château, and saw another of his paint-ings hanging there. It was very expensive. Iacurto's fame has spread, and my gift has proven to be as valuable as it is beautiful.

I was glad when they repaired the Slide in 1992. It had been closed for several years, and it's nice to see such an important part of Quebec City's history brought back into use. If Élise and I had more time, we would have continued our walk, down the long flight of steps to the Citadel. I last was there with the late Honourable Madame Jeanne Sauvé, Canada's Governor-General. The Governor-General traditionally spends a month or two in residence at the Citadel, and Mme. Sauvé invited me to a gala reception.

I look off the Dufferin Terrace with sadness, too, because the opportunities to visit this city, my second home, are fewer and further between. I'm constantly on the road to other places, drawn by other duties. Every bit of "down time" is precious. An infrequent day off is a day to be spent at home, with granddaughters and family.

I am retiring officially from the Montreal Canadiens in two months because I need the rest. But Élise and I have promised each other that Quebec will be on our itinerary in coming years, even though many of our friends from our Quebec days – Frank Byrne, Jack Latter, Charlie Smith, Émile Couture, Saint-Georges Côté, and Punch Imlach – have passed away.

It is doubly ironic that, on this day for young men, an old man sees the beauty of his past and laments the years speeding by. When you're eighteen or nineteen, as I was when I first came here, I would often refer to my "old uncles" in their sixties. But I'm the "old uncle" now. From twenty to sixty seemed like an eternity then; the middle years would never come. But when you reach forty or sixty and you look back, you realize that the chasm that loomed in front of you was just a tiny step, especially if you were always running and active, with something to do each day.

That is never more true than for the athlete, whose stock in trade is youth. My father put it into perspective for me long ago: "Jean, when you're in your forties, time passes at forty miles an hour. Then, in your fifties, it goes fifty miles an hour." I stand on the Dufferin Terrace, looking out over the St. Lawrence River, looking back on my life. Suddenly, I'm sixty-one years old, sixty-two in nine weeks. My father was right, and I fully expect that the next eight years will disappear at sixty miles an hour, unless I can find a way to slow them down.

Two nights ago in this city, I marked one of the greatest moments of my life with close and valued friends. Forty years earlier, at eleven o'clock in the morning of June 27, 1953, I married Élise Legaré Couture at St. Patrick's Church on the Grande-Allée. Our "official" fortieth anniversary is tomorrow, and we'll return home after the NHL draft to a quiet celebration with my daughter Hélène and her two girls. But on Thursday night, we met for a commemorative dinner with people who had been with us on our wedding day.

Hélène had wanted to organize a much larger party for all my friends, but that's not my style.

"You're not going to go around asking everyone for $50 or $100 so they can send us on a trip or buy us a special present," I told her. "Your mother and I don't go for that sort of thing."

"You've done it for others I don't know how many times," she replied.

"That may be, but we don't want it for ourselves. With all of the official functions your mother and I have attended over the years, we've come to appreciate the peace and quiet of a small, private gathering."

That's why, on Thursday, our group was quite select – Élise's sister, Rita Proulx; her husband Jean; Jean's sister, Simone Couture; the widow of Élise's brother, Georges, who passed away a year ago; Rose Lafond, who came to work for the Couture family and has stayed with the family all her life; and Roland Mercier, one of my closest friends for close to forty-five years. He's seventy-three now, and we speak at least once a week. Hockey has always been his life. He once served as chairman of the board of the Canadian Amateur Hockey Association, and his interest hasn't dimmed one bit. Sometimes, when I'm at home in Longueuil, watching a game on television, and something out of the ordinary happens, it's a safe bet the telephone will ring seconds into the intermission. Élise will look up and say, "That will be Roland," and it always is.

On Thursday night, as the saying goes, "We told a few lies and wiped away a few tears," and had a marvellous time. This was eminently better than several hundred people in a room, with Élise and me on display at the head table, awaiting the arrival of the inevitable cake.

Our original plan for this June had been to come to Quebec on Thursday afternoon, attend the anniversary party with our friends, see to some Hall of Fame Players Selection Committee business (I'm retiring from that, as well), then head back to Montreal on Saturday morning. But these plans changed when, on the previous Thursday, I was in New York for the Canadian Society of New York's annual hockey dinner. The CSNY brings together all the Canadians who live and work there. Once a year, right after the Stanley Cup playoffs, they have a night and honour a former player. I had been honoured by them in 1987, and wanted to pay my respects to Marcel Dionne, who'd been named the recipient for 1993. I was in my hotel room getting ready for the dinner when a call came through from the president of the Quebec Nordiques. I've always admired Marcel Aubut and his prodigious energy. He was the force behind the Rendez-Vous '87 All-Star series with the Soviet Union, and I believe that the Nordiques could not have entered the NHL without his presence.

Marcel had called to ask me to remain in Quebec throughout the day on Saturday, until the draft selection had been completed. "We're going to have this little march from the Arsenal to the Colisée," he explained. "And who better to lead it than the man who built the Colisée in the first place?"

Marcel is well versed in hockey etiquette, and took care to use the words "march" and "procession," not "parade." There is only one parade in professional hockey each year, and that parade features the float upon which the Stanley Cup is proudly displayed. I didn't have to remind Marcel Aubut that this parade had taken place about a week earlier, in Montreal.

Marcel went on to explain that the top ten draft choices would ride in individual horse-drawn carriages, each player accompanied by a Hall of Famer or other high-profile veteran. The Stanley Cup itself would probably travel in one of the calèches as well. And, because the 1993 NHL meetings and the expansion and entry drafts represented the birth of the league's two newest teams, Blockbuster Video's Florida Panthers and Disney's Mighty Ducks of Anaheim, there was a chance that Mickey Mouse himself might be along for the ride.

Thus, on this sunny Saturday morning, instead of driving back to Montreal with Élise, I myself am taking a carriage ride with Alexandre Daigle, a handsome young man from the Montreal suburb of Laval who will be drafted Number One by the Ottawa Senators, moments after the Colisée's doors swing open and the entry draft begins. He is well-dressed and polite, almost shy, a credit to his parents. The hopes of several million Québécois ride with him. They have seen too few of their numbers selected high in the Entry Draft by NHL scouts in recent years.

En route, Alexandre and I sign what seem to be hundreds of autographs. The pads, pieces of paper, magazines, and hockey cards are thrust at us from all directions, as we travel the four-mile route. We're barely able to exchange a few words.

"You started here, Mr. Béliveau?" he asks.

"Yes."

"Were you the first draft choice that year?"

"No, the draft didn't even start until I'd been in the league more than fifteen years." This observation provides another poignant moment for me, another reminder that the clock is running fast. I retired from playing almost four years before Alexandre was born. A few days ago, the Ottawa Senators had announced it had signed this young man to a contract which will pay him $12.5 million over four years, not including a unique revenue-sharing arrangement on his promotional and endorsement earnings.

Alexandre's eyes seem to widen, and I can almost hear the unspoken question: "Well, then, how *did* you negotiate your entry into the NHL?"

Had he asked the question, my answer would have been: "We had ways, Alexandre. We had ways."

The bus ride to Quebec City from Victoriaville on December 13, 1949, took a little more than three hours – twice as long as usual, because of snowbound roads. We went directly to the Colisée and unloaded our equipment. Actually, we went directly to the old Colisée and stored our equipment there. The previous spring's fire damage had not extended to those dressing rooms, while the rooms at the new Colisée, about a hundred yards away across the grounds of the Exposition de Québec, were not completed. For the first month of our season, it had been decided we'd get dressed, pick up our skates, and walk or take a shuttle bus from one building to the other. Intermissions were to be spent in a brand-new but very gloomy room reeking of the smell of fresh concrete and containing only a few bare planks on which to rest our weary behinds. When the game ended, we'd return to the old Colisée for a shower and a change back into street clothes.

When we arrived that Tuesday afternoon, coach Pete Martin and Roland Mercier offered a few words of welcome, then we were off in various directions to our billets.

Milt Pridham, Dave O'Meara, and I had been assigned to the Paquette family's boarding house on St. Cyrille Boulevard

Above: Here I am (second from left, top) with my fourth-grade class-mates in Victoriaville. *Below:* Five years later: I'm in grade nine at L'Académie Saint-Louis de Gonzague. You can spot me in the top row, third from left. (*Studio Bedard, Victoriaville*)

Hockey, of course, was a popular winter time sport at my school. Here I am (second from right, back row) with some of my Académie teammates in 1945.

Here's what I looked like at age fifteen.

I played my first organized hockey with the Victoriaville Panthers. Here I am in the team uniform at age sixteen

Showing my batting and
pitching style at, respectively,
age fourteen and sixteen.
I loved playing baseball.
When I was a teen, I spent
part of a summer playing and
pitching for Val d'Or in the
Abitibi Senior League.

Above: A picture of me (back row, seventh from right) with my teammates in the Panthers, taken at the end of the 1947-48 season. *Below:* The next year I played with the Tigers of the Quebec Junior League. I'm standing in the middle row, behind the coach. (*Studio Bedard, Victoriaville*)

LES TIGRES Jr. DE VICTORIAVILLE -:- 1948-49

Fall 1946. *Above:* With my younger brothers Guy and Michel.
Below: We had a rabbit hutch in the backyard of our Victoriaville
home. I'm with my brothers Guy, Pierre, and Michel.

In 1949 I joined the
Quebec Citadels and
played with them for two
seasons in their new arena,
the Colisée. In 1951 I
moved up to the Quebec
Aces (below) and played
in the same building.
(*David Bier Photo Inc.*)

Above: Here's a team picture of the Quebec Citadels. I'm on the far right end of the front row. *Below:* I spent two happy seasons with the Quebec Aces of the Quebec Senior Hockey League. Punch Imlach (left) was my coach, and an awfully good one. (*David Bier Photo Inc.*)

Much to the relief of general manager Frank Selke (left) and coach Dick Irvin (right), I finally signed my first NHL contract with the Montreal Canadiens in October 1953. (*David Bier Photo Inc.*)

between Salaberry and Turnbull streets in Upper Town, not far from the National Assembly. Our rooms were small, but they were all we needed. Our lives would be taken up by hockey for the next five months.

I think that the billeting arrangements were handled by Roland Mercier. Placing me with two English-speaking players was his way of accelerating my second-language instruction. At that time, I could manage *Yes* or *No*, and several simple phrases, but that was it. All of my schooling, and, of course, every conversation at home, had been French only. Milt and Dave were literally my first English teachers. The following year, I would room with Gordie Haworth and Bruce Cline, who did their part to make me conversant with unfamiliar nouns and verbs. Roland Mercier knew that English came in handy in the NHL. He wanted to expose me to it now – another sign that the people in my growing hockey family were convinced that I was going on beyond the junior ranks.

The Quebec Citadels of 1949-50 were a solid, tough team, led by Dave O'Meara and Marcel Paillé in goal. Spike Laliberté, Gordie Hudson, Bernard Lemonde, and Jean-Marie Plante were on defence. Up front with me were Roger Hayfield and Gordie Haworth, my former teammates from Victoriaville, plus Rainer Makila, Pridham, Cline, Jean-Marc Pichette, Jules Tremblay, Roland Dubeau, Russell Tuer, Norman Diviney, and Gaston Gervais.

We had plenty of offensive power, but we played in a league of strong offensive teams. The Montreal Nationals counted Bernard Geoffrion and Skippy Burchell among their ranks, and Sam Pollock's Junior Canadiens were spearheaded by Dickie Moore. In my first season with the Citadels I had fewer goals (thirty-five), but more assists (forty-five) than in previous years. But my eighty total points were to rank second only to "Boom-Boom"'s, and I was glad to see the scoring responsibilities spread among my Citadels teammates.

As it turned out, we finished the regular season in second place, and beat the third-place Nationals four straight in the semi-final, winning the last game 6–5 in overtime. It was an extremely close and clean game, with both teams skating full tilt from the opening face-off. This spoke well for the Nationals, who trailed 3–0 in the series on our home ice, but refused to fold. We were down 5–4, when my second goal of the game at 19:06 of the third period sent the teams into overtime. I netted a hat trick with a breakaway goal at the forty-eight-second mark of extra time. The victim of all three goals was my former Tigers' teammate Denis Brodeur.

Our semi-final victory was marred by an incident which bothered me and my teammates for several days. With the completion of the new Colisée and the continued success of our team – remember, the Citadels had been a first-place club during my year in Victoriaville – the crowds began to swell. We played before more than 10,000 fans every night, and this enthusiasm was shared throughout the league. Trois-Rivières, Verdun, and the three Montreal teams all drew capacity crowds. But with the increased attendance came increased rowdiness in the stands. Sometimes real idiots would emerge "from the woodwork" in each city.

When I scored a third-period goal against the Nationals in game four, it prompted both a standing ovation and a shower of debris which littered the ice surface and delayed resumption of play for several minutes. Most fans threw rolls of toilet paper, streamers, or cardboard, but someone thought it would be a good idea to toss a bottle from the upper seats. It struck a Nationals player on the head, and the Colisée fell silent as he was carried off on a stretcher. Fortunately, he was all right, but the episode was a disturbing one and several of our players made angry gestures at the crowd.

Still, the Nationals series could be viewed as a fairly clean encounter compared to the league final against Sam Pollock's Junior Canadiens. It was all-out war. Sam's not-so-secret weapon was Dickie Moore, one of the fiercest competitors I've ever met. Dickie stood maybe five feet, ten inches tall, and weighed 170 pounds soaking wet. I was five inches taller and almost thirty pounds heavier, but every time we played the Baby Habs, he was in my face. My coach, Pete Martin, would put another man on against him, switch lines, double-shift me, or sit me out for a while, but Dickie didn't care: whenever I came out, he'd be in front of me, always taking shots.

With the notable exception of Eric Lindros, many bigger hockey players today are faulted for failing to take advantage of their size, for hesitating to use their bodies to lean on smaller, but highly aggressive players. I heard that often enough during my junior career. I was continually dubbed a "gentle giant." It didn't bother me, because I knew where my true strengths lay. Moreover, when we played the Junior Canadiens, it wasn't true – because Dickie and I were running each other all the time. The high-sticking, cross-checking, elbowing, and roughing went on relentlessly, and I'm not ashamed to admit that on certain occasions, Dickie wore me down. I wasn't a fighter – mostly by choice, because I didn't like it and recognized my obvious limitations in that area. But I tended to make an exception for Dickie, and he got as good as he gave. He was a wild man, and on more than one occasion went up in the stands after long-distance tormenters. But you could never find a better teammate, as I would discover in a few years.

Dickie aside, what made playing against the Junior Habs of 1950-51 so difficult was Moore's formidable supporting cast: Bill Sinnett, Dave McCready, Donnie Marshall, Herb English, Ernie Roche, George McAvoy, Kenny Rocheford, Billy Rose, and Art Goold. These boys could skate like the wind, pass beautifully, and frustrate the opposition with both their forechecking and control of the defensive zone. If you did manage to get past a defenceman like Kevin "Crusher" Conway, you would have to contend with either Charlie Hodge or Bill Harrington in nets.

Our best-of-seven series was deadlocked at two hard-fought wins apiece when Frank Selke decided to muddy the waters, with some remarks that beat Mario Puzo's *Godfather* to the punch by almost three decades. "When this season is over, I'm going to make Jean Béliveau an offer he can't refuse," he told the Montreal media. He went on to say that the Canadiens' weak spot that season was at centre, where Elmer Lach, the Old Reliable, wasn't getting any younger.

"I know that Jean Béliveau is only eighteen, but he is a big boy, and other boys of that age have broken into our league. I think that he has demonstrated all the right qualities to be able to do this, and to be a star in our league for a long, long time."

Naturally, Frank Byrne and Pete Martin were angered by this. It was galling enough that Papa Selke had told them in no uncertain terms that he was going to come and get me (with a year of Junior eligibility still to go, which was akin to tampering). But Selke's announcement also had the effect of painting a bull's-eye on my back for any Junior Canadien who wished to make his mark.

Most observers felt that our series would not go the full seven games, and that the Saturday–Sunday home-and-home series on March 25 and 26 would settle matters. They were right. The Canadiens came out with all guns blazing on Saturday night. They followed Sam Pollock's script to perfection, and Rocheford scored on a goalmouth pass from Donnie Marshall at 5:20. Then Herbie English set up Ernie Roche a scant two minutes later.

We began to return, urged on by an impatient crowd, but lost momentum when the penalty box was filled to bursting after a scrap erupted between (no surprise) myself and Dickie Moore. Still, we managed to get one back before the period ended, on a screen shot by Gordie Hudson, and had the crowd back on our side midway through the second period when Gaston Gervais and Jean-Marc Pichette set me up for the equalizer. It wouldn't be enough.

A knee injury to Bernard Lemonde hurt us on defence, and the Canadiens stepped up their relentless attack, with Herbie English putting them ahead to stay with less than two minutes remaining in the period.

We were hanging on by our fingertips when Dickie Moore decided to put us out of our misery, setting up Roche for his second goal at 12:17 of the third period. Milt Pridham brought us back to within one in the eighteenth minute, prompting Pete Martin to pull Marcel Paillé in favour of an extra attacker. Pridham took the face-off deep in the Montreal zone and I was at the point, ready to let go with my best shot. The puck went behind the net and up to Moore. He passed to Roche, who went one-on-one with me. I never was an NHL-calibre defenceman, and even less an NHL-calibre goalie. Roche backed me into our net and easily put the puck behind me, and the Junior Canadiens were one win away from the title.

The following night at the Forum, they came out firing on all cylinders, taking a 3–0 lead by the 13:10 mark on goals by Bill Sinnett, Art Goold, and Billy Rose. We replied with markers from Rainer Makila and Jules Tremblay, but Rose added two more in the middle period, to one of ours by Gervais, our best player in the final two games. Another two in the final period gave Sammy Pollock a 7–3 win and his first-ever junior league title. Later that spring, Dickie, Donnie, and company went on to defeat St. Mary's of Halifax, then the Guelph Biltmores, and finally the Regina Pats to win the 1950 Memorial Cup.

The 1950-51 season had been wonderful for me, even though the first few months in Quebec were tough for a newcomer. I was lonely, making a difficult adjustment to life away from home and family. I couldn't continue my high-school studies in the technical course I'd begun in Victoriaville, because the hockey schedule placed far too many demands on my time. I felt isolated, and my natural shyness inhibited me from meeting people my own age, outside the rink. I was pretty much a loner that year, reluctant to initiate social contacts. I seemed to spend a lot of my newfound spare time reading or walking all over Quebec City. If it wasn't too cold, I would walk for miles – along St. Jean Street and past Salaberry, Turnbull, Park, and Fraser, all around the Cartier Street neighbourhood.

Rue Cartier in Upper Town is still a very popular street. In those days, there was a drugstore with a lunch counter and a soda fountain on the corner of St. Cyrille Boulevard, and another one further up, where constables from the RCMP office on Grande-Allée and Cartier would eat lunch daily. I used to boast that I was the best-fed and best-protected hockey player in Quebec. My RCMP buddies would watch over me, and Mr. Laroche, the lunch counter's owner, would give me a free steak each time I scored three goals. I would eat a lot of Grade A beef in my second year in Quebec.

That summer I returned home to Victoriaville for the last time, living with my family and working days at the Fashion Craft plant for $15 a week. Evenings were spent hitting home runs for the firm's team in a commercially sponsored softball league. It sounds like an ideal life, but there were one or two problems. I worked in the shipping and receiving department, and the warehouse wasn't air conditioned. Since Fashion Craft's winter coats were manufactured in summer, we had to wrestle with huge boxes and mountainous piles of thick, bulky material, often in ninety- or hundred-degree-Fahrenheit temperatures. I put on weight that summer, all of it muscle in the back, shoulders, and upper arms. As fall approached, I was anxious to get back to Quebec City.

First, however, there was a stop in Montreal where I'd been invited to attend the Canadiens' training camp. I enjoyed my three weeks there, did not receive "an offer I could not refuse" from

Frank Selke, and returned to Quebec in late September. I felt reasonably comfortable playing with the Canadiens in intra-squad games, and against senior league opposition in exhibition contests, but I was determined to return to the Citadels for my final junior year. I had had several conversations with Roland Mercier and Frank Byrne in the off-season, and they'd assured me that the Citadels would be a serious challenger for the 1951 Memorial Cup.

Mind you, Montreal hadn't given up hopes of luring me there. The prospect of seeing Geoffrion, Moore, and Béliveau – three of Canada's most highly touted junior stars – in the same uniform had set Canadiens' fans and Montreal sportswriters to salivating. While I was skating with the big team, Frank Selke's emissaries had fanned out to both Victoriaville and Quebec City, but to no avail. The Canadiens offered the Citadels some of their top junior talent in exchange for me, but Arthur Béliveau and Frank Byrne stuck stubbornly to their agreement.

There was another factor, too. Frank Byrne had told me, before I left to attend the Canadiens' camp, that money was not an issue. "Whatever they offer you, Jean," he said, "we'll match or better. Just don't sign anything." Frank had reason to worry. The Citadels had attracted record crowds the previous season. An over-capacity 13,714 paying customers had marched through the turnstiles for our fourth game against the Junior Canadiens in the league final. Quebec sportswriters such as Louis Fusk, Guy Lemieux, and Roland Sabourin regularly described Le Colisée as "Château Béliveau," and the pressure was on for me to return to the provincial capital to help the Citadels' drive for the Canadian championship. Deep down, however, most Quebec fans and media personalities felt that I would yield to Frank Selke's overtures, and that, in fact, I had already played my final game for the Citadels.

What these people weren't considering were the lessons that Arthur and Laurette Béliveau had taught their children – although Frank Selke, a deeply religious and fair-minded man himself, no doubt respected our stand, and secretly approved. "Loyalty is another form of responsibility," my father had often told me. "If you feel that you owe something to someone, no matter what the debt, it behooves you to pay it. Sometimes, those very people will do or say something to indicate that they are discharging the debt, but only you will know what the best policy will be. Your good name is your greatest asset."

Call it loyalty or a debt of gratitude, I was determined to return to Quebec, and nothing Mr. Selke could say or do in the late summer of 1950 would alter my decision.

When I arrived in Quebec, I soon discovered that Frank Byrne had kept his end of the bargain. The Citadels had lost a number of valuable veterans, most notably Spike Laliberté, Milt Pridham, Jackie Leclair, Jean-Marc Pichette, and Jules Tremblay. But we had managed to retain a strong nucleus, including goalie Marcel Paillé, defencemen Gordie Hudson, Jean-Marie Plante, and Bernard Lemonde, and forwards Rainer Makila, Gordie Haworth, Norm Diviney, Gaston Gervais, and Bernard Guay. Newcomers included left-winger Claude Larochelle, who would go on to become the dean of Quebec City sportswriters, Copper Leyte, Camille Henry, who would win the Calder Trophy as NHL Rookie of the Year in 1954, defencemen Neil Amodio and Jean-Paul Légault, and back-up goalie Claude Sénécal.

Frank Byrne had promised performance, and we delivered, exploding out of the blocks as a team and scoring tremendous numbers of goals.

A promise of off-ice employment turned out to be a public rela-tions job for the Laval Dairy, at $60 a week, which was a lot of money at that time. At age nineteen I was earning about $6,000 a year with the Citadels – a competitive NHL salary – and another $3,000 or so from Laval, where I began to pick up the off-ice skills that would help me later in life.

Part of my job was to co-host a Saturday morning children's

program on radio station CHRC. We had all the ingredients for a successful show. After a cowboy story, we'd go live and mobile, taking the show to the kids by broadcasting from one of three locations – the Durocher Centre in Lower Town, La Canardière Centre in Limoilou, and a Knights of Columbus Hall in Ste-Foy, near Laval University. It was amateur radio at its best, and our weekly draw for ice cream products, hockey sticks, and tickets to Citadels or Aces games was wildly popular. The first week, a couple of hundred kids came by to watch. Four weeks later, we had an audience of more than one thousand.

Later, my popularity with the younger generation of Quebec hockey fans reached record heights, when I became the Laval Ice Cream Man. The dairy built a cooler which fit into the trunk of my car, and filled it with all sorts of goodies. My duties were simple: whenever I came across a group of kids, I'd pull over to the curb, open the trunk, and pass out free ice cream. The 1950s were a far more innocent time. Somebody who did this today might risk arrest.

Of course, these activities were rudimentary at best in a meet-the-public sense. But you have to start somewhere. I was always – and I suppose still am – an introvert, something I believe I inherited from my mother. The idea of making a speech had always bothered me. But when you're introduced to 500 people in a hall who are there to hear you say something, and then a microphone is shoved in front of you, you learn quickly enough, even though it's a form of shock therapy for the habitually shy.

At least Laval Dairy was a family business, and treated me like family. It was owned by two brothers, Jules and Paul Côté. Jules enjoyed our Saturday show so much that he'd often get up and start dancing. Paul was more reserved, but he always came to the broadcasts as well. Each of them had a son: Pierre (Jules) and Jacques (Paul). Jacques and I became particularly close. The two elder Côtés were ideally matched in temperament to run the company together, as would their sons later on, when Jacques took over the production side while Pierre handled administration. They made an excellent team – and one of the saddest days of my life came twenty years later, in 1971, when news arrived that Jacques Côté had died in the same plane crash that claimed the life of Roger White, the harness race driver. Jacques owned several pacers, and the two men were en route to southern New York from a Fort Erie race track when their plane went down.

What began as a professional relationship quickly became a series of lasting, enriching friendships. The Côtés were dedicated family men, and when Paul's wife passed away, he was desolate. I was playing in Montreal at the time, and I remember Jacques called me from Quebec.

"Jean, we have to do something for my father. He's completely lost without my mother and we need something to pick him up and get him going," he said. I managed to find a pair of Canadiens' season tickets, and for years after, Paul never missed a game. In August, when the upcoming season's schedule would be published, he'd go to a travel agency and make an entire season's worth of reservations for the Quebec-to-Montreal train, as well as room reservations at the Queen Elizabeth Hotel if he had to stay overnight. If we played, say, on Thursday night, he'd come to Montreal in the afternoon, return to Quebec Friday morning, and come back to Montreal on Saturday for that night's game. He was in motion almost all the time.

That first year, the only two tickets I could get were down at one end of the rink. This was before the NHL asked teams to raise the height of the protective glass. One night, a puck flew over the net, and Paul had just enough time to raise his arm. For weeks afterward, he brandished the broken wrist in a cast and happily bragged to friends and acquaintances, "I got hit by a puck in the Forum."

While I may have been a star hockey player and a budding media personality, Quebec City in 1950 was a simpler, gentler place. I never thought to demand a luxury penthouse as a signing bonus. That second season I roomed in a boarding house run by three older ladies, the McKenna sisters. One of them worked for the Red Cross, the second at Anglo-Canadian Pulp, while the third managed the boarding house day to day. I had a small room on the third floor and a further opportunity to practise my English, although all three sisters were perfectly fluent in French.

Many of my friends and acquaintances in the neighbourhood had become familiar with my daily jaunts all over the *quartier*, and I think that some of them despaired of a tall, young man whose only pursuits seemed to be playing hockey and reading a book wherever he could sit down. Among my friends were the Gagnon family, who lived around the corner on des Érables. They were regulars at our games, and I often met them during my walks.

One Monday night, with several off days before my next scheduled game, they said, "Jean, you should come out with us on Wednesday. We have a nice girl we'd like you to meet."

Since they wouldn't take no for an answer, two nights later we were on our way to the Manoir St. Castin at Lac Beauport, north of the city, as part of a group of ten or eleven. (It's a small world: forty years later, the Manoir was bought by a group of Quebec City investors including Marc Tardif, my teammate with the Canadiens in 1970 and 1971.)

I met Élise Couture that evening. I think what impressed me the most about the pretty, bilingual blonde was that she knew absolutely nothing about hockey. She'd never been to a game before and had no idea what all the fuss was about. It would be several months before she dared to tell her mother that we were going out, because Mrs. Couture, whose maiden name, Mahon, reflected her Irish ancestry, had little confidence in hockey players.

We didn't dance much, because I'd never really learned how, but we did spend a lot of time talking. It didn't take long for me to realize that this was a strong-willed lady, with clear convictions and opinions, and that I would like to get to know her better. That winter, as our relationship slowly developed, she taught me how to drive her family's Studebaker – a timely lesson, as I would soon discover.

On the ice, my career was accelerating at a breakneck pace – so much so that, in a three-week period in late November and early December of 1950, I played games at three different levels of hockey. On Sunday, November 26, I joined the Quebec Aces for a game at Le Colisée against my former coach Roland Hébert and his Chicoutimi Saguenéens. I played on a line with Dick Gamble, who would join the Canadiens before the season was out, and we both scored a pair of goals in a 4–4 tie.

Twenty days later, Bernie Geoffrion of the Nationals and I made our NHL regular-season debut with the Canadiens in a 1–1 tie against Boston. Boom-Boom scored Montreal's only goal, but I had nine shots on net, earning me the game's first star and scaring the heck out of Frank Byrne, who remained daunted by the possibility of my deserting the Citadels. As one Montreal columnist wrote the following week, "Mr. Byrne was here to watch the boy make his debut in National League company, sharing the Selke box for the occasion. He declined Selke's invitation to visit the directors' room for a sandwich and a cup of coffee after the game. 'I can't say I blame him,' said Selke. 'He must have suspected he'd be under a lot of pressure if he'd come in here.'"

Six weeks later, with both Billy Reay and Maurice Richard ailing, Boom and I joined the Canadiens once again, along with Dick Gamble of the Aces and Hugh Currie of the Buffalo Bisons. Teamed with left winger Claude Robert, Boom and I each scored a goal and an assist against veteran netminder Harry Lumley in a 4–2 win over Chicago, a team that had gone winless in nineteen previous games. Then, another two weeks later, I played for the Aces in a special exhibition game against the Detroit Red Wings in Quebec City, but that would be the last NHL competition I would enjoy until late in 1952.

As it turned out, this hiatus did not bother me in the least, because the Citadels were firmly atop the league standings. I was enjoying my most productive season ever, locked in a struggle for the scoring championship with Boom-Boom and his Nationals' linemate Skippy Burchell. Late in the season, Boomer was summoned by the injury-riddled Canadiens and left having totalled ninety-six points, ten more than his league-leading eighty-six the previous season – an amazing figure, considering that he'd played only thirty-six games. As luck would have it, Burchell and I came down to the last game tied at 122 points, an all-time junior league record.

The Nationals jumped on us quickly, taking a 4–0 lead on a pair of goals by Burchell and Bert Scullion, but we got two back before the end of the period when Gordie Haworth scored at 15:40 on a pass from Camille Henry, and I racked up my sixtieth of the season on a penalty shot. Gordie made it 4–3 midway through the second period, and Ray Goyette added still another. As the minutes passed, it appeared likely that both the Nationals' lead and Burchell's scoring championship were safe, especially after Pete Larocque collided with me in the second period and I went off with a charley horse, seemingly finished for the night.

I sat in the dressing room for the rest of the period and into the intermission. A large ice-pack did very little to alleviate the physical pain, and nothing to ease my emotional anguish. The scoring title had eluded me. We'd beaten the Nationals in seven of nine previous games, and clinched first place much earlier in the season, so only my personal satisfaction was at stake. Or so I thought.

Pete Martin and special adviser Kilby Macdonald filed in with the rest of the team during intermission. Outside, the fans were despondent. The Citadels were losing, but for them this seemed secondary. The local star had fallen behind his Montreal rival in the scoring race, and was condemned to finish second for the second straight year.

"Jean, nobody in this room will think you selfish if you go out there and try to tie Burchell," said Martin. "I don't have to tell you how everybody feels about Larocque's hit, either." In fact, I hadn't thought that Larocque had caught me with a bad hit, but every subsequent whistle from referees Déziel and Saint-Armand had been greeted by a chorus of boos.

There was a tremendous cheer when I came out for the third period, limping noticeably. Camille Henry joined Rainer Makila and me for the final period, replacing Bernard Guay on left wing. That added offensive punch to our line, and gave the Nationals something else to worry about. During the entire third period, two games were being played, neither of which had anything to do with the score. Our checkers were doing their utmost to shut down Burchell whenever he was on the ice, while the Nationals' checkers did the same to contain Camille, Rainer, and me.

Even though the Nationals won the game, 5–4, our side won the scoring joust. With the teams playing four a side, Makila broke out of our zone, one on one with a Nationals defenceman, with me trailing. He drew the Montreal defender to him and laid a perfect pass onto my stick. I had plenty of net to shoot at, and my first (shared) scoring championship. After the game, an army of photographers gathered around Skippy Burchell and myself as we posed for a study in contrasts – his five-foot, seven-inch David to my six-foot, three-inch Goliath. We'd both wound up with 124 points, mine on a league-leading sixty-one goals and sixty-three assists, Burchell's on forty-nine goals and a league-leading seventy-five assists.

We would meet the second-place Junior Habs in a best-of-nine semi-final, while the Nationals, Verdun, and Trois-Rivières would play a six-game round robin to determine the other finalist. This format made little sense, but we were grateful for an opportunity to avenge our 1950 loss to Montreal. The 1951 edition remained a formidable group, with Moore, Sinnett, English, McCready, Nadon, and Marchesseault returning from the previous year, and joined by two promising newcomers, forward Scotty Bowman and goalie Charlie Hodge. We had come out ahead in our ten-game season series by the narrowest of margins, 6–4, and the nine-game playoff promised more of the same.

I went into the playoff opener hoping that my charley horse had cleared up, and scored two goals and an assist, while Makila popped two and added three assists in the 5–3 series opener. After four games, with the series tied up, I had a double charley horse and wasn't feeling so well. I'd been out for a week, missing the third and fourth games, when Frank Byrne and Sam Pollock began a spat over the scheduling and site of the fifth game. The fourth game had been played at the Forum on Sunday night, and the next one was slated for the Colisée on Tuesday. Unfortunately, for some reason or another, the Colisée was unavailable for that day, and Buster Horwood, the league president, ordered that the game be transferred back to Montreal.

"We are obliged to finish our Quebec playoffs by April 1, so the winner can go on to the next level," he said. "We cannot have four-day breaks between series games if the championship is to be completed in time."

Frank Byrne got his Irish up and kept the Citadels in Quebec that night, claiming that we'd won home-ice advantage throughout an arduous season, and would not yield it at a bureaucrat's whim. Horwood threatened suspension, forfeit, and fine – but when he saw that Byrne was determined, he relented, scheduling a Thursday night encounter in Quebec, followed by a sixth game in Montreal on Sunday.

At the same time, Horwood could not resist a parting shot at what he thought was Byrne's real reason for not playing in Montreal. In an official statement released by his office, the president stated that: "It is most probable that the Citadels are acting this way to give Jean Béliveau time to recover from an injury."

Whatever the case, we won the fifth game 4–0, and went on

to win the series, too – but not before Dickie Moore became embroiled in a penalty-box scuffle with two Quebec City policemen that prompted his teammates to swarm over the boards when the fighting spread into the nearby stands.

A week later, with a four-game sweep of the Trois-Rivières Reds under our belts, we patiently awaited the representatives of the Ottawa and District Hockey League. One day after practice, Roland Mercier and Émile Couture mentioned that the team wanted to express their gratitude to me with a special presentation before an upcoming home playoff game. Would I mind? Figuring that I was in line for a nice watch and a couple of well-wishing speeches, I said okay and thought no more about it, largely because we were busy defusing the Inkerman Rockets, 9–0 and 16–4, in the first two games of our best-of-five eastern Canadian series.

On Tuesday, April 10, 1951, immediately after dignitaries from three levels of government had saluted the teams in a pre-game ceremony, a 1951 Nash Canadian Statesman de Luxe was driven onto the ice. The licence plate was 99-B, in honour of my number 9. Flabbergasted, I took possession of the keys and tried hard not to fall down on the spot. My teammates and I were so dazzled by this remarkable show of appreciation that we went on to demolish the hapless Rockets 13–0, to sweep the series in three straight games, and move onto the semi-finals.

Up next were the Barrie Flyers of the Ontario Hockey League, a powerhouse coached by the venerable Hap Emms with five future NHL stalwarts in its ranks: Jim Morrison, Leo Labine, Réal Chevrefils, Jerry Toppazzini, and Doug Mohns, the last a Junior B call-up for the series.

The Toronto newspapers began to promote the series as Béliveau versus the world. After we lost the first two games at a sold-out Maple Leaf Gardens by 6–2 and 6–4 margins, the press shifted gears, writing both me and the Citadels off as the stuff of an inferior league.

We weren't convinced. Returning home, we promptly tied the series with 7–2 and 4–2 wins. Then yet another dispute over venues broke loose.

Many people will be surprised to learn that it would be Frank Selke who would take much of the responsibility for our failure to win the Memorial Cup that year. In those days, a junior team competing for the Cup could pick up one or two last-minute star players from other teams. This year, Frank Byrne had asked Dickie Moore if he would join the Citadels, and Dickie had said he'd be happy to oblige.

Much later, Dickie told me what happened. "I was a Quebecer and I would have loved to stop an Ontario team for a third straight year," he said. By this, he meant that he'd helped to win the two previous Cups — first with the Royals, then with the Junior Canadiens.

"But Frank Selke stepped in. The year before, he'd broken up the Royals and directed most of their talent to the Nationals. I went and signed with Sammy Pollock and the Junior Canadiens, which didn't please Selke one bit. When I told him I wanted to play for the Citadels in the Memorial Cup, he said, 'Over my dead body.'"

Hap Emms had heard a rumour that Moore would join the Citadels for the Flyers series. He thought the rumour might be true when he ran into Dickie at Le Colisée, early on the day of game three.

"What are you doing here?" Hap asked.

Dickie laughed at Hap's discomfort. "I'm playing for Quebec, if we can find a way to kill Frank Selke."

Selke lived, however, and Dickie wasn't able to supply us with his awesome competitive skills. Prior to the series, the Barrie Flyers had argued long and loud that at least one game should be played in their home rink fifty-five miles north of Toronto – a tiny little bandbox with very few seats and very little on-ice room to manoeuvre, especially for visitors who were unfamiliar with its nuances. We'd argued just as long and loud against this un-welcome scheme. It was accepted practice in those pre-television days for Memorial Cup games to be played only in large-capacity arenas, such as Maple Leaf Gardens, the Forum, or the Colisée. As well, smaller towns like Barrie were not readily acces-sible by train or plane, making the back-and-forth travel of a seven-game series frustrating and time consuming.

Unfortunately, we lost the argument, and left Quebec City on a Rimouski Air Lines flight at 4:30 in the afternoon, flew to the Camp Borden army base, then caught a bus to Barrie. We walked into the Barrie arena at 9:00 p.m. and took the opening faceoff thirty-two minutes later. The Flyers were waiting for us. They scored four powerplay goals in the first thirteen minutes, and we took a 10–1 shellacking. We tied the series back in Quebec City, but lost 8–3 in game seven at Maple Leaf Gardens, having survived yet another adventure in early Canadian passenger aviation. It was only fitting that a team named the Flyers won that series. To give them their due, they played well, and were very well-coached. In fact, they went on to defeat the Winnipeg Monarchs for the Memorial Cup.

With that my first two years with the Citadels were at an end. Summertime would be a decision time for me. Where would I play that fall: Quebec City or Montreal?

4

✦

THE TUG-OF-WAR

In 1991, Eric Lindros shocked both the National Hockey League hierarchy and most of the population of Quebec when he refused to report as ordered to the Quebec Nordiques. This highly talented six-foot, five-inch centre, who weighed in at 235 pounds, had been dubbed "The Next One" in his early teens. His progress through the ranks of minor hockey had been closely monitored by the media, just as they had earlier kept a breathless watch on Bobby Orr, Wayne Gretzky, and Mario Lemieux. There's always a "Next One" waiting in the wings keeping the sports media busy.

I watched each episode of this soap opera as it unfolded over two years with more than passing interest and more than a little sympathy. I'll return to Eric in a later chapter, when I deal with the purely financial side of the present-day NHL. For the moment, let me say that, despite our superficial similarities, his situation and mine were curiously reversed. If he was "The Next One" of the

71

1990s who wouldn't *go to* Quebec City, I was "The Next One" of the 1950s who seemingly wouldn't *leave.*

With the 1951–52 season looming, Frank Selke was determined to sign me to a professional contract, and as quickly as possible. My two games with the Canadiens in the previous season had whetted the appetites of Montreal fans, the city's media, and the club's management. Having not won a Stanley Cup since 1946, they had convinced themselves that they simply had to have me.

Why did I stay in Quebec? Let me list some of the answers: Élise Couture, the Côtés, Roland Mercier, a 1951 Nash, Le Baril d'Huîtres, the Château Frontenac, Émile Couture (no relation), Chez Gérard, Punch Imlach, the McKenna sisters, St. Cyrille Quartier, La Porte St-Jean. Also, I was barely twenty years old and Quebec City had come to feel like home.

The first time I thought seriously of staying was the afternoon of our third game against the Inkerman Rockets, when the Citadels presented me with my first car, that big Nash sedan. I felt an overwhelming obligation to the people of Quebec that day. Shortly after our playoff loss to the Barrie Flyers, I was chatting with Élise and Roland Mercier. "What can I do to thank the fans and the city for these two great years? I was treated like a king here."

I answered my own question in a flash. "The best way to show my appreciation is to play another year." In deciding to remain, I also decided to take a step up from junior ranks, to the Quebec Aces of the semi-pro Quebec Senior Hockey League.

If Frank Selke was frustrated by his inability to sign me after my first year with the Citadels, his frustration mounted on June 8, 1951, when my father and I worked out an agreement with Aces coach Punch Imlach and club treasurer Charlie Smith, who came to Victoriaville to visit us. A couple of weeks later, the news was made public – but yet another stumbling block appeared.

The NHL and the Canadian Amateur Hockey Association had reached a tentative agreement that, if initiated, would bring about two major changes. The on-ice change concerned games played at the senior level; it replaced the two-referee system with one referee and two linesmen. The second change became known as the "Béliveau Rule," because it was very specific, and seemed to be targeted directly at me.

In essence, it stipulated that every player whose name appeared on an NHL team's negotiating list had to sign a contract to play with that team before he would be eligible to play in the QSHL. For example, if I wanted to play with the Aces, I'd have to sign with the Canadiens first. They would then assign me to the Aces, but only if both parties agreed to the deal. If the Canadiens wanted me in Montreal, I would have to play there.

Not surprisingly, Jack Latter, the owner of the Aces, had voted against this rule, but he was in the minority, and it looked as if nothing could halt its ratification at a future CAHA session.

I don't know to this day precisely what happened next – but apparently telephone calls were made by highly placed persons to NHL headquarters in Montreal. The rule was never ratified, and I would spend the next two years in an Aces uniform.

The extreme rivalry that then existed between Quebec City and Montreal will be familiar to present-day fans. But some will have a hard time grasping the way that Quebec politics and business intruded into sports in the 1950s. Let me try to explain just a little bit.

First, I'll mention money, and, *en passant*, the name of Eric Lindros. Perhaps the major difference between the Lindros situation and mine is that the 1990s Quebec Nordiques, a full-scale NHL franchise, could not, finally, successfully compete for his services against other teams in larger, wealthier American markets. In my case, the Aces were relatively "backwoods," part of the QSHL, a semi-professional league. Logically, they should have been out of the bidding for my services when the Canadiens came calling. But they weren't.

The Aces, in fact, won out for several reasons. First, I wanted to stay in Quebec for personal reasons, and would have considered any offer that the Aces happened to present. Further, they could, in fact, match or better any Canadiens offer because they were owned by a large company, Anglo-Canadian Pulp and Paper. Indeed, the name Aces was an acronym of Anglo-Canadian Employees Association. (Later, when nationalist sentiments were on the rise, this was changed to the As de Québec.) Just as the Citadels had been determined to outbid the Junior Habs, the Aces wanted me on hand, and had money in the till. They knew they'd make money, too: in Quebec, senior hockey didn't take a back seat to the professional ranks, and the Colisée was filled to capacity night after night.

Thus, financially at least, I had nothing to lose by staying in Quebec City. In my first year with the Aces, the 1951-52 season, I was paid $10,000. By contrast, the going rate in the NHL was $100 a game, or $7,000 a year, for a seventy-game season. Each September, when I left to attend the Canadiens' training camp, the Aces offered to meet whatever figure Frank Selke might come up with – a repeat performance of my experience with the Citadels.

How serious were they to have me stay in Quebec? I found out when it came time to sign my next contract with the Aces, this one for the 1952-53 season. This time the government became directly involved. You may remember that Maurice Duplessis – *le Chef* – ruled Quebec as premier with an iron hand between 1936 and 1939 and again from 1944 until his death in 1959. His right-hand man, the man with his fingers on the purse strings, was Gérald Martineau. He had two favourite sports, politics and hockey, and was involved for a long time with the Quebec Frontenacs junior team.

In preparation for my second season with the Aces, I met with Jack Latter and Charlie Smith and agreed on a raise to $15,000 – not bad by NHL standards. The day before I was to sign, I got a call from Latter.

"Jean, would you mind if we go to Mr. Martineau's office to sign the contract, instead of at Anglo-Canadian?"

I was somewhat mystified by this, but told him it didn't matter to me.

The following day at eleven o'clock, we went to Martineau's office and found the contract on the table. As I moved toward it, Martineau said: "Jack, you're making money with Jean. Give him $5,000 more."

Martineau was the bagman for Maurice Duplessis. Anglo-Canadian Pulp had lumber concessions in Forestville. Jack Latter had to go through Martineau to get them. In other words, Martineau's comment wasn't a suggestion, it was an order.

I sat there, my eyes getting wider by the minute, as Jack Latter, one of Quebec City's top executives, meekly agreed that Mr. Martineau was "probably right." Which is how twenty-year-old Jean Béliveau became a $20,000-a-year semi-pro hockey man, at a time when the NHL base rate was barely a third as much. Indeed, for a short time, I was making more than Gordie Howe and Maurice Richard.

All that having been said, it wasn't the money that kept me in Quebec, even though by staying I was conducting a rather subtle negotiation strategy with the Canadiens, whether I fully realized it at the time or not.

In Montreal, meanwhile the media were forever speculating that I was remaining in Quebec because I had a fragile psyche, and was lacking the confidence needed to make it in the big time. After all, Bernard Geoffrion had gone straight to the NHL from junior, they argued. Dickie Moore had spent a short half-season in senior before moving up to the Canadiens. And here was Béliveau, hiding out in Quebec City while the world passed him by.

It goes without saying that these commentators didn't know me. My decision to stay put was only partially about hockey. I stayed in Quebec City, first and foremost, out of a sense of obligation to the people. As for Boomer and Dickie, they were city boys, born and bred, whereas I came from a small town. The extra time in Quebec, as it turned out, helped me acclimatize to the demands of city life and to grow up more normally – or at least more gradually and in a more orderly fashion – than I would have had I been a twenty-year-old Montreal Canadien.

Looking back on my career, it was perhaps the wisest course I chose. I've seen the almost insane demands that were placed on teenagers such as Lindros, Gretzky, Lemieux, and Guy Lafleur. I didn't envy them the sudden loss of their youth. By contrast, I was able to mature both on and off the ice, at more or less my own pace, surrounded by what we'd call today a support network of close and reliable friends. As a result, the Jean Béliveau who finally did sign with Montreal in 1953 was much better prepared for the demands of NHL stardom.

Quebec City was an idyllic place to be in the early 1950s, especially for a young francophone hockey star who was making excellent money, had met the lady of his life, and who was taking his time growing up. It was still the pre-television era, and we made our own fun, in the many boîtes, bistros, clubs, and restaurants in and around the city.

What follows now might appear to be a travelogue of Quebec in the 1950s, the equivalent of showing slides of your vacation to a captive audience. But this period shaped who I was, and who I was to become. Many people have complimented me on my comportment during my career with the Montreal Canadiens. I'm flattered – but if I behaved well, it stemmed from lessons learned in *la vieille capitale*.

I plunged into the social whirl of a young and vibrant provincial capital, with a large group of people my age and slightly older who frequented places like Chez Gérard and La Porte St. Jean, two night clubs run by a very convivial Gérard Thibault. Artists from both Quebec and France were regulars in the clubs, among them

Patachou, Charles Trenet, and Carlos Ramirez. We enjoyed live entertainment, perhaps because anyone could afford to go out and enjoy it. By doing this, I gradually developed my social skills and conversational abilities, and I started to come out of my shell.

Roland Mercier introduced Élise and me to the club scene; he worked for the federal revenue department where he ensured that foreign artists were paying tax on revenue earned in this country. Gérard Thibault was a Quebec City institution, the subject of a fascinating biography. He brought Charles Trenet to Canada, and I remember the famous *chansonnier* sitting on the wharf near the Lévis ferry writing songs. Élise and I had a regular table at La Porte St. Jean, and a semi-private entrance through the side door. (The door's still there. We saw it the night we celebrated our fortieth wedding anniversary.)

Another regular haunt was a famous restaurant on St. Joseph street in Lower Town called Le Baril d'Huîtres – the Oyster Barrel – owned by Adrien Demers and Raymond Comeau. The Baril gang and some young Jewish boys whose families owned stores on St. Joseph Street used to play pick-up hockey games at the Old Colisée on Monday nights, while Phil Renaud, my teammate on the Aces, and I would referee. After the games, both teams would retire to the Baril for oysters and beer. It and Pat Mercier's Tavern on Dorchester were the closest things we had to sports bars in those days. The crowds from both places were fanatical Aces fans and would follow us all over the league, especially to games in Chicoutimi, a 150-mile drive. Every time we played the Saguenéens, a convoy of thirty cars or more would form behind our team bus. After the game, we'd all turn around and come back home again, stopping at L'Étape, a restaurant and gas station complex in the middle of Parc des Laurentides that provided both good food and the only restrooms that were open en route at that hour of the night.

Sometimes we'd crawl along the highway in the midst of a

terrible snowstorm, barely making it to L'Étape for beans and *tourtières* at three in the morning, only to continue on our way when daylight broke and we could follow a snowplow. One night the bus's fuel pump failed in twenty-five-below-Fahrenheit weather. The police came out to rescue us, and ferried us to L'Étape in their cruisers.

By this time, Élise was starting to attend hockey games. Once she accompanied Jacques Côté and his wife Claire to see me play in Chicoutimi. Having seen fans at other games ringing bells in the stands, she wanted to join in the fun and took a little dinner bell from her mother's silverware set. We played well that night, and the tiny bell got a real workout – until, that is, a disgruntled Chicoutimi fan grabbed it and disappeared out the nearest exit. As I mentioned earlier, Élise's mother did not have a high opinion of hockey players. "How am I going to tell her that the bell is gone?" she moaned after the game.

"Well," I said, "you'll start by forgetting to mention the circumstances under which it disappeared."

Chicoutimi was well and good, but perhaps the best trips were to Montreal, where the QSHL would stage those memorable Sunday afternoon contests at the Forum. In later years, Camil Des Roches and I would often recall these games. At the time, he'd have to march out onto St. Catherine street and tell people to go home, because the Forum was sold out.

"I never did that for Canadiens games," he said. "Only for senior league games, and especially when the Aces came to town to play the Royals." Busloads and trainloads of Quebec City faithful would go to Montreal for those games, and it wasn't unusual to have fifty or sixty per cent of the crowd cheering for Quebec. Nowadays, when I hear people cheering for the Nordiques at the Forum, it's nothing new for me.

There was one other special trip, in December 1952. I was called up by the Canadiens for another three-game trial, my first return to the NHL in more than a year. I would play in Montreal Thursday night against the Rangers, and follow that up with a home-and-home series with the Bruins, at the Forum Saturday night, and in Boston on Sunday.

The gang at the Baril d'Huîtres was crazed with excitement. They quickly organized a private car on the two o'clock train to Montreal on Thursday afternoon, and one of the Jewish guys went ahead on Wednesday to scare up some tickets. When the train pulled into the station, he was waiting with enough tickets for everybody. He'd gone all over town, picking up pairs wherever he could find them – in factories, restaurants, offices, and hotels – and I don't think he'd had the luxury of too much sleep. That night I scored three goals, and the Baril boys hooked up their private car to the midnight train and celebrated all the way home. With fans like that you can see why I was more than happy to remain in Quebec City.

I have to credit one more person who helped convince me to stay. His name was Émile Couture, and everyone assumed, once I began going out with Élise, that she and he were sister and brother. In fact, they weren't related in any way.

Émile worked for Calvert's Distillery, which used to award a trophy to the junior league's most valuable player. He was a happy-go-lucky boulevardier who loved the good life and knew the best spots in town. He also knew many people in the Aces' organization, and acted as a sort of intermediary between it and myself. He came to all the hockey games, and I was always pleased to see him. I'd known him back in Victoriaville, and his family owned a restaurant and hotel in Laurierville called La Maison Blanche, where all the professional wrestlers on the circuit would stop in on their trips between Montreal and Quebec City.

Few people knew that Émile's name also was known around the world – at least, by a select group of international military personnel. During the Second World War, Winston Churchill,

Franklin Roosevelt, and Mackenzie King met in Quebec City in 1943, to discuss plans for the European theatre of operations in the following year. Destroyers and mine sweepers patrolled the St. Lawrence River below Cap Diamant, warplanes of three nations flew overhead, and heavily armed soldiers cordoned off most of the city centre, erecting checkpoints on all the major roads and at the railway station.

The most secure place in town was the Château Frontenac, where the three leaders stayed and held their meetings. And yet Émile Couture managed to walk out of that building with plans for the Normandy Invasion, Operation Overlord, tucked underneath his arm.

Émile at that time was a sergeant in the Royal 22nd Regiment of Quebec on quartermaster duty. It was his task to provide all the stationery for each session. He also had strict orders to destroy anything that was left on the tables after the meetings ended each night. On the second-last day of the conference, he was asked to remove the desks of several participants who'd completed their presentations. He did just that, but, when he looked inside one of the desk drawers, he found a sheaf of papers in a red binder. If he'd stopped to think, he'd have destroyed it then and there. But he didn't. Instead, he returned to his quarters at Lac Beauport. Later that night, out of idle curiosity, he took out the binder and began to read.

In his hands were plans for the 1944 invasion – who, what, when, and where; how many planes, ships, and men. He read some more, and tried to go to sleep but he couldn't. At dawn, he returned to the Château, where the belated discovery that the binder had gone missing had headquarters in an uproar. Émile tried to report his find to a succession of top brass, all of whom were too panicked to pay attention.

Finally, after several hours had passed, he prevailed on the commander of the military district to listen to his story. Within minutes, Émile was surrounded by military investigators. After the authorities were convinced – and very relieved to find – that the binder hadn't fallen into enemy hands, the question became: what to do with Sgt. Couture?

His background was impeccable, his military record spotless, and they couldn't very well lock him up. First, he'd returned the materials of his own volition. Second, a jail sentence might arouse suspicion within the community – the Coutures were widely known – which in turn might somehow alert the enemy.

For months, Émile was kept under strict surveillance. Finally, after the invasion had taken place, he was off the hook – on the condition that he wouldn't publish the story without permission. *Life* magazine approached him at least once, but as far as I know, his tale never appeared in print. I learned about it because he and I were so close, but as a rule Émile never really liked to talk about it. After the war, however, he was awarded the British Empire Medal, a very important decoration. When people would ask him about the B.E.M., Émile would smile innocently and reply, "Who knows why they give these things out?"

This, in short, was life off the ice. On the ice, I'd moved up into faster company, in every sense of the phrase, the minute I put on an Aces uniform. The QSHL was the stomping ground of former NHL and American Hockey League players who had been looking for a congenial place to spend the latter stages of their careers. They were shrewd and experienced, and I was fortunate to be among them. They taught me a great deal. In my first year with the Aces, one of my linemates was Gaye Stewart, recipient of the Calder Trophy as NHL rookie of the year with the Maple Leafs in 1942. Jack Gélineau, our goalie, had won this honour with Boston in 1950.

Other veterans included Ludger Tremblay, Gilles' older brother; the infamous Frank "Yogi" Kraiger; Joe Crozier, formerly of the AHL Cleveland Barons; Claude Robert (my linemate on my first call-up with the Canadiens in 1950); Jackie Leclair, another former Canadien; and Marcel Bonin, who would travel with me to Montreal via a circuitous route.

Yogi Kraiger deserves a book unto himself. He was tough as nails, when he wasn't into the sauce. When he was, he was truly spectacular. Sometimes he would get so smashed that he'd forget where he'd left his car, and have to ride, horribly hungover, all over town on Quebec Transit buses looking for it.

During my first November with the Aces, we had a light schedule and five or six days off. Our coach, George "Punch" Imlach, hated the idea of us getting stale, so he'd organized an exhibition game in Cornwall. We were returning the next morning by bus up Highway 2, the main link between Montreal and Toronto before they built the 401. We'd just reached the old Soulanges Canal, and I suppose that the water turned our conversation to swimming.

Yogi wasn't the shy, retiring type, even when sober. In this instance, however, he'd found a source of liquid inspiration in Cornwall. We'd become accustomed to his self-promotions. It was impossible to escape them. Simply put, as only he could put it, old Yogi was the finest athlete ever, in each and every department – gymnastics, track and field, basketball, and so on.

Swimming, however, was a recurring theme, and (by his telling) Yogi's personal best. Never mind if he could sink hundreds of three-pointers in basketball for a week without sleep, or throw the javelin a mile. If you were foolhardy enough to question his aquatic exploits, Yogi was bound to take exception. This would not have been a desirable turn of events. Yogi was a very impressive physical specimen, whose idea of a limbering-up exercise was doing chin-ups by his fingertips off the top of the door frame.

Yogi had made a career of upsetting Punch Imlach, and by the time we hit the canal that day, Punch was on the boil.

"I've heard enough of this B.S.," he announced to the team in a loud voice. Then he turned his attention to the driver. "Next bridge we come to, stop the bus. Yogi can't even swim the canal from side to side. All this B.S. about swimming for miles in Lake Superior is crap, pure and simple, and I'm going to prove it, I'm bettin' fifty bucks he's full of it."

Have I mentioned that this was late November, and that the summer sun had ceased to warm the canal's waters months ago? There were even a few chunks of ice around the edges.

This didn't faze Yogi. "For fifty bucks, I'll do it," he said. However, as usual, he was dead broke. A quick plea to his teammates to stake him yielded instant results. Dollar bills rained throughout the bus, and the action in side bets demonstrated team unity at its best. Per instructions, the driver stopped the bus at a convenient bridge, and team trainer Ralph McNaughton got out a couple of blankets for our Polar Bear Club inductee.

Everybody hopped off the bus, and admired Yogi's strip-tease down to his boxer shorts. With barely a pause, he dove into the canal, losing his shorts in mid-air. He then proceeded to swim the canal buck naked, as Ralph walked along the opposite bank with a blanket, awaiting Yogi's arrival.

As you can imagine, the sight of twenty or so young men peering anxiously into the cold, stagnant canal was a red flag for passing traffic. Cars and trucks came to a screeching halt, and a crowd of people gathered to gawk at what they plausibly assumed was an awful accident.

Instead, they were greeted by the sight of Yogi climbing onto the opposite bank without a stitch. Ralph wrapped him up and they quick-stepped back across the bridge and onto the bus. The team followed and we continued on our way. Naturally, all this exercise had aroused a powerful thirst in Yogi Bare. When we hit the outskirts of Montreal, near Vaudreuil, he said to Punch, "You'd better get me a gin to warm up, or I'll have a cold for the rest of the winter."

Once again Punch stopped the bus, and we all trooped into the Vaudreuil Inn at eight o'clock in the morning so Yogi could have his gin. We never did recover his boxer shorts.

Punch, of course, was dumb like a fox. He knew that he could use this sort of nonsense to strengthen team harmony, even if it meant that the players bet against him. For fifty dollars, Yogi's little dip was a bargain in morale-building.

Another famous character on the Aces was Marcel Bonin, whom I'd played against in junior and would meet again in Montreal in the late 1950s. Marcel loved to show up for practice in November with his hunting outfit on, and two or three rifles and shotguns under his arm.

"Hey Punch, make it a short practice today," he'd say. "Marcel is going hunting in Dorchester County, and the light goes early at this time of the year."

Punch knew better than to quibble with an armed man, especially a marksman like Bonin. Besides, thanks to Marcel, the Aces had acquired a taste for venison.

Marcel was a tough guy like Yogi, and made his way into the NHL thanks to an exhibition game we played against the Detroit Red Wings in February 1952 on behalf of the Federated Charities. He got into a scrap with Terrible Ted Lindsay, and raised eyebrows by holding his own. Then, and I can't recall how it happened, he ended up in a penalty-box brawl with Vic Stasiuk. Somehow, Marcel's thumb got wedged in Vic's mouth and Marcel used it as leverage to pick Stasiuk up and repeatedly bang his head on the concrete wall at the back of the box. Stasiuk was biting down to save his life, but nothing could stop Marcel from pounding him senseless.

People said that Marcel used to wrestle bears for a living, and perhaps it's true. In any case, the Red Wings were impressed by his fisticuffs. Not long afterward, they purchased Bonin, and he went on to terrorize the opposition in a similar fashion, before joining the Canadiens in 1957-58.

I mentioned earlier that Claude Robert had played with me in my very first call-up with the Canadiens. When I joined the Aces, he was already with the team. He was a burly man, very strong, who eventually would join the Montreal police. He had a high tolerance for pain, too, as he proved to Punch the day we played, and beat, the AHL's Providence Reds in an exhibition game in Grand'Mère. During the contest, Claude took a major-league bodycheck in the corner along the boards, and flew into the air, landing awkwardly. He limped back to our bench, went right through the door, and directly to the dressing room. When Punch and the trainer followed him in, Claude said he was injured, and didn't think he could play anymore. In those days you played with pain, a lot of it, and coaches would do anything they could to get you back on the ice.

Imlach turned to Ralph. "Guess we'll have to freeze the leg. Get the needle."

As big and tough as Claude Robert was, like most big, tough hockey players, he was scared to death of needles. He would run a mile to avoid hearing the word.

"Uh, I'm okay. I can play," he said over his shoulder as he scurried out of the room and back to work.

He played in all our games for the next three weeks, but complained that the leg still bothered him. Finally, Punch relented and sent him to hospital to have it checked. X-rays showed a clean break.

Years later, when the media made a fuss about Bobby Baun playing on a hairline fracture for one game during the 1964 playoffs against Detroit, I immediately thought of Claude. It might be nothing more than coincidence, but Baun's coach that season was none other than George "Punch" Imlach.

For all his toughness, Claude was a natty dresser. He always looked good, because he managed his resources well and his money went a long way. Marcel Bonin, for all *his* toughness, loved to spend his money like water, especially on the necessities of his favourite pastime, hunting.

One evening I came upon them in the dressing room. Claude was coaching Marcel on fashion and budgeting. "Marcel, you could end up in the NHL one day, and they aren't going to let you wear lumberjack shirts or hunting outfits. You'll be in a shirt and tie and a suit," he said. Claude's locker looked like a high-class men's clothier. Extra suits in dry cleaner's plastic hung in a row. Shirts in their packages were stacked neatly on a shelf. There was even a tie rack, full of the latest looks.

"But," Bonin protested. "I don't have that kind of money."

"Yes you do, Marcel, but every time you get a dollar you spend it on another shotgun."

I left them deep in their conversation, convinced that Claude would have an uphill battle if he hoped to "beautify" Bonin.

At the next home game, we were amazed to see a spiffy Marcel Bonin strut into the room wearing a suit, dress shirt, and tie. Claude was the most surprised of all. "Marcel, those are *my* clothes," he declared.

"I know," Bonin answered proudly. "How do you like my budgeting?"

The QSHL was a remarkable training ground for me, and for other players. For example, I played with, and learned a great deal from, men such as Ludger Tremblay and Gaye Stewart. After his rookie year with Toronto, Gaye ended up playing with every other NHL team but one, Boston. He turned in 510 NHL games over nine seasons in the twelve-year period between 1941–42 and 1953–54, and finished up with 185 goals and 159 assists. Today's junior graduates will never have the opportunity to play with someone with this kind of experience, prior to moving up to the NHL.

The QSHL had a host of veteran forwards and defencemen, as

well as up-and-coming stars like Dickie Moore, Bob Fryday, Bob Frampton, Les Douglas, and Jacques Plante, all of whom played for Frank Carlin's Montreal Royals. Tommy Gorman's Ottawa Senators played out of the old Ottawa Auditorium and featured Neil Tremblay and Al Kuntz up front, Butch Stahan on defence, and the legendary Legs Fraser in nets. Valleyfield was coached by Toe Blake and included players such as my former junior team-mates Gordie Haworth and Bruce Cline, André Corriveau, Jacques Deslauriers, and Larry Kwong. Sherbrooke stars included Tod Campeau, Jimmy Planche, Bobby Pepin, and Jacques Locas. In Chicoutimi, they had Lou and Stan Smrke, Pete Tkachuk, Ralph Buchanan, Sherman White, Gerry Glaude, Marcel Pelletier in nets, and Georges Roy and Jean Lamirande on defence. They were coached by Roland Hébert, my former junior mentor in Victoriaville. Last but not least, the Shawinigan Cataracts rallied behind star netminder Al Millar, and included Jack Taylor, Erwin Grosse, Roger Bédard, and Spike Laliberté.

The QSHL was also home to many players who, for various reasons, never would or could make it to the NHL. One such player was Herbie Carnegie, a smooth-skating playmaker equally adept at centre and on a wing. Herbie had one drawback: he was black, or "coloured" as the expression went back then. When I was a youngster in Victoriaville, Herbie, his brother Ozzie, and a third black, Matty McIntyre, all played with Sherbrooke in the Quebec Provincial League. Herbie made it up one rung on the hockey ladder, but could go no further.

It's my belief that Herbie was excluded from the NHL because of his colour. He certainly had the talent, and was very popular with the fans, who would reward his great playmaking with prolonged standing ovations, both at home and on the road. Perhaps they suspected that his colour was an issue with the NHL, but it certainly wasn't with them.

I followed Herbie from a distance over the years. He did very well with Investors Syndicate, as I could see as a board member with the company. As well, I heard from mutual acquaintances that he was a major contributor to public service in the Toronto suburb of North York.

The Aces had their share of excellent players, too, forwards like Armand Gaudreault, Martial Pruneau, Jackie Leclair, Copper Leyte, Bob Hayes, and Murdo Mackay. Our captain Phil Renaud anchored a defence that included Joe Crozier, Yogi Kraiger, Jean-Guy Talbot, and Butch Houle. We had speed, quick hands, toughness, and determination, which enabled us to defeat both Chicoutimi, in our own league final, and then Peanuts O'Flaherty's Saint John Beavers, to capture the 1953 Alexander Cup, emblematic of the senior hockey championship of eastern Canada.

In my two seasons with the Aces, I won the QSHL scoring championship each time. Not surprisingly, this helped intensify the pressure in Montreal for me to sign with the Canadiens. The "Man Who Stayed Away" story made the rounds, kept in the forefront by hockey commentators throughout the NHL.

The *Toronto Star* went so far as to run a WANTED poster on me. It read: "Jean Béliveau. Age 20. 6'2". 195 lbs. Wanted by Canadiens to play NHL hockey. Reward $15,000 a season . . . and he turns it down. There's a reason. Jean Béliveau, star of the Quebec Aces, is hockey's highest paid 'amateur.' In addition, he picks up a few odd thousand a year as a public relations man and doing a daily radio broadcast." And so forth. A couple of months later, the same poster ran in the French media, but by then it was out of date: I stood 6'3" and weighed 205.

Rumour and speculative stories ran rampant, both in Canada and in the United States. Read one report from New York: "If Béliveau doesn't sign by his birthday (August 31), he will be removed from the Canadiens' negotiation list and then claimed by the team in the NHL basement (the New York Rangers)." Another version had me headed for Chicago, for a preposterous sum of money.

Meanwhile, every sports columnist in eastern Canada, it seemed, was negotiating my deal with the Canadiens for me. The most bandied-about offer was Frank Selke's opener: $53,000 over three years, $20,000 as a signing bonus and salaries of $10,000, $11,000, and $12,000 per annum over the length of the contract. Of course, we had turned that down. You'll remember that, thanks to Gérald Martineau, I was making $20,000 (not $15,000) annually with the Aces.

Of course, it wasn't my long-term ambition to remain in Quebec City forever, making more and more money each year. As my second season with the Aces progressed, I sensed it was time to move on, to test myself on the next rung of the ladder. Besides, if I'd stayed much longer, I might have started to pose a threat to Premier Duplessis, who remarked on my popularity when he himself fell victim to it. At that time, Quebec's leading radio personality was Saint-Georges Côté of CHRC, who frequently invited me to join him on his morning show. In 1952, he bought a well-known restaurant on Boulevard Ste-Anne called La Dame Blanche, and staged a grand opening complete with foot-long hot dogs and two special guest "celebrities" – Élise and myself. That same day, Premier Duplessis and a host of political dignitaries were busy inaugurating a new highway over the Pont de Québec. Very few people turned out. In the meantime, Élise and I were being swamped by a crowd of seven thousand hot dog lovers.

Élise Couture and I had become engaged at Christmas 1952, and we started to seriously consider what our lives held in the future. "This is going to be my last year in Quebec City," I told her. "I've always planned to play for the Canadiens, and next season will be the right time for me. After we get married in June, we'll head to Montreal and scout out some places to live."

Élise was the first to hear of my plan. I was in no rush to let Frank Selke know. I wanted to keep my bargaining power as high as I possibly could. Two scoring championships, an Alexander Cup victory, and full houses throughout the QSHL, and in the Forum, added to my credit column.

The negotiations also could wait for something else. On June 27, 1953, the only woman in my life became Mrs. Jean Béliveau a little after eleven o'clock in the morning in St. Patrick's Church in Quebec City.

While we were on our honeymoon, the QSHL franchises met in Montreal to debate whether or not the league would go professional. Punch Imlach (who didn't know of my decision, either) was not in favour of this, but when he arrived at the meeting, all of the other owners were lined up against him.

Punch began by asking them whether or not Jean Béliveau had filled their buildings over the past two seasons. Forrest Keene of Sherbrooke said that this wasn't entirely the case. Tommy Gorman of Ottawa answered that, by going professional, he'd be better able to control the destiny of his franchise, rather than having to depend on NHL and AHL teams to assign players to him each September. (Just by the way, Sherbrooke dropped out of the QSHL shortly before the 1953-54 season began; and Gorman's Ottawa Senators folded just before Christmas.)

Punch, with the wisdom of foresight, said that while both owners' points were debatable, only one thing was certain: if the QSHL went professional, I belonged to the Canadiens, who would claim me in five seconds flat.

Punch lost the vote, and I was on my way to the NHL.

5

◆

THE FANTASTIC FIFTIES

An autobiography must by definition be written in the first person, but the "first person" was never what my career was about, on or off the ice. Everything I achieved throughout my career, and all the rewards that followed, came as the result of team effort. If they say anything about me when I'm gone, let them say that I was a team man. To me, there is no higher compliment.

I had the God-given talent and immense good fortune to become a star on a team of stars who set a record that may stand forever. That record, of course, was five straight Stanley Cup wins. It seems doubtful that any team now or in the foreseeable future will be able to approach, match, or surpass this feat. Professional hockey has changed so much since the late 1950s – we've seen the expansions, the use of entry drafts to disperse talent among the neediest franchises, the rise in player salaries – that it's unlikely any general manager or coach, no matter how savvy, will succeed in putting together a bona fide dynasty team.

That's why I'd like to tell you now about my team, my equally talented teammates, and the reasons why the Montreal Canadiens surged ahead of the rest of the NHL in the late 1950s, and have stayed there ever since, although the Cup victories are fewer and further apart.

Let's get the numbers out of the way first, then I can describe more fully the many individuals who contributed to these remarkable sets of statistics.

In 1955–56, we finished first with 100 points on forty-five wins, fifteen losses and ten ties, twenty-four points ahead of second-place Detroit, and won the Cup with 4–1 series victories over both the Rangers and the Red Wings.

In 1956–57, we were in a three-team race during the regular season with Detroit and Boston. Detroit surged ahead at the end, finishing first with eighty-eight points, to our eighty-two and the Bruins' eighty. But we defeated the Rangers and Bruins 4–1 in both series to win the Cup again.

In 1957–58, we left the opposition far behind once more, ending the season with ninety-six points, nineteen better than the Rangers, then sweeping the Red Wings in the semi-final and defeating Boston 4–2 in a six-game final contest.

In 1958–59, we won the Prince of Wales Trophy once again, finishing twenty-one points ahead of runner-up Boston. We downed Chicago in six in the semi-final, and Toronto in five games in the final, for our fourth Cup.

In 1959–60, we won our fourth regular-season title in five years, earning ninety-two points to Toronto's seventy-nine. We improved on the previous year's playoffs by sweeping the Hawks, then the Leafs in eight straight games for our fifth consecutive world championship.

I signed my first contract with Montreal on October 3, 1953. Frank Selke was there, of course, smiling the biggest of smiles. And so was Dick Irvin, the team's coach. Later that same day, I played my first official game as a Montreal Canadien in the season opener against the NHL All-Stars. Between 1947 and 1965, it was traditional for the reigning Stanley Cup winner to host a collection of the best players from the five other teams. This evening I found myself on the ice with Gordie Howe, Ted Lindsay, Red Kelly, Alex Delvecchio, and Terry Sawchuk of Detroit; Fleming Mackell and Bill Quackenbush of Boston; and Bill Gadsby of Chicago, among other intimidating hockey greats. We had our own All-Stars in our lineup, of course, including Doug Harvey (a First Team selection), and Second Teamers Gerry McNeil, Maurice Richard, and Bert Olmstead. We lost 3–1, but, to be honest, I didn't feel out of place.

There was plenty of excitement at the Forum that night for several reasons. Since the Canadiens were the defending champions, the crowd was eager to see if they would maintain their supremacy. Moreover, everyone could sense that Frank Selke's patient cultivation of the dark, rich soil of Quebec junior and senior hockey was about to produce the first of many bumper crops.

No other NHL franchise had a list of young stars like those who had toiled in the minors for Montreal. Boom-Boom Geoffrion, Dickie Moore, and myself were the leaders of three successful junior teams, and all three of us had excelled in our NHL call-up games while still of junior age. Now we were finally in the Canadiens' lineup as full-time players, along with Jacques Plante. At the same time, the fans knew that Jean-Guy Talbot, Don Marshall, Phil Goyette, André Pronovost, Henri Richard, Charlie Hodge, Ralph Backstrom, and Claude Provost would be joining our ranks sooner or later. Top talent was waiting in the wings out west as well, including Bob Turner, Ab McDonald, and Billy Hicke.

If Montreal could add one or two of these young stars each year to a Stanley Cup team which already featured Doug Harvey, the league's premier defenceman, Maurice Richard, its top scorer and most exciting player, and veterans such as Tom Johnson, Bert Olmstead, Dollard St. Laurent, Floyd Curry, Gerry McNeil, and

Ken Mosdell, the betting was that the Canadiens should be at or near the top of the NHL standings for a generation.

All of which did come to pass, pretty much according to Frank Selke's plan, even though we'd have to wait two years after my arrival for our next Stanley Cup victory.

One reason for the "delay" was the presence of yet another dynasty, Jack Adams' Red Wings. Between 1947 and 1954 the Wings finished first for seven consecutive years and brought back four Stanley Cups to Motor City.

Another contributing factor was one of the most notorious incidents in the history of NHL hockey.

When I first arrived in Montreal, the Canadiens may have been managed by Frank Selke, but they were really Joseph Henri Maurice Richard's team. The Rocket was the heart and soul of the Canadiens, an inspiration to us all, especially to younger French Canadians who were rising through the ranks. He was man and myth, larger than life in some ways, yet most ordinarily human in others.

Maurice was not only first in the hearts of French Canadians, he was the first among his NHL peers: the first to break Nels Stewart's scoring record with his 325th goal, the first to reach the 400- and 500-goal plateaus, the first player to score fifty and then seventy-five playoff goals. Moreover, the timing of his contributions, from the war years through to 1960, coincided with that period in Quebec when a tidal wave of change was sweeping aside more than 300 years of history.

As players, however, we saw Maurice in simpler, more immediate terms. He embodied something which would rub off on many of his teammates, something which would carry us to five straight championships by the end of the decade. Quite simply, Maurice Richard hated to lose with every fibre of his being. Everyone picked up on this – his teammates, his opponents, the media, and the hockey public at large.

Headline writers in the United States borrowed from their national anthem to celebrate "The Rocket's Red Glare." North of the border, in a country that had been forged by steel rails, another metaphor held sway. Maurice was often described as a runaway locomotive, with a Cyclopian eye that rooted helpless goalies to the ice, or froze them into immobility, like deer caught in headlights.

For me, the best description of Maurice Richard came, fittingly enough, from a winner of the Nobel prize for literature, the American William Faulkner. This Southern novelist, who, not surprisingly, knew very little about the game, was commissioned to write a story on hockey for *Sports Illustrated* magazine. He covered a match between the Canadiens and the Rangers at Madison Square Garden, and was immediately captivated, writing that Maurice had the "passionate, glittering, fatal alien quality of snakes." When you think about it, the last thing that goalies would indeed see would be those mesmerizing eyes, microseconds before Maurice would strike.

Maurice Richard would be the first to admit that he was not the greatest skater in the world. Nor was he the best shot, stick-handler, or passer on our team, let alone in the entire league. What made him special was the way he could take his incredible, virtually unstoppable will to win, and mould it into an explosive charge that would be unleashed from the opposition's blueline toward their net. This awesome concentration of firepower was his trademark.

Every star has his critics, and Maurice Richard was not immune. It was said that he was a lousy backchecker, that he had little interest in the defensive game, and that this shortcoming drove his coaches to distraction. It was baloney, of course.

Admittedly, the kind of all-out run that Maurice would take at the opponent's net usually ended with him sprawled in front of the crease or over in the corner. He wouldn't be able to rejoin the play very quickly, especially if the other team made a rapid transition to offence. Even when he scored, he'd always have one or two guys all over him. The puck was in the net, and Maurice was flat on his back. Although truly spectacular to watch, the Rocket had to make sacrifices to play that way. He was a highly tuned, highly specialized hockey instrument, not a well-balanced all-round player. It's his particularity that made him great. The other elements of his game were there, all right, but perhaps they suffered by comparison.

His charges were doubly dramatic because he was a left-handed shot playing on the right wing. This allowed him to take the puck on his forehand and break straight for the goal, letting the puck go off-stride and catching many netminders napping. Add to this a lethal backhand off a straight blade, and you'll understand why a common reaction to one of the Rocket's goals was "I didn't see it coming."

Maurice was much more than a hockey player. He was a hero who defined a people who were emerging from an agrarian society in the post-war era and moving to the cities to seek their fortunes. I was just one of thousands of young hockey players who sat rapt by the family radio on Saturday nights, letting my imagination magnify the Rocket's epic feats on *La Soirée du Hockey*, then mimicking those same actions on the local rink on crisp Sunday mornings after Mass.

Later, as his teammate, this sense of awe remained. As an adult, the realization that Maurice opened it up for us – built it for us – was almost overwhelming. Even more impressive was the fact that he was rather shy, and very modest about his exploits. Back in 1952, when I scored three goals against New York in a call-up game, Maurice assisted on all of them, twice putting me in alone on Chuck Rayner with perfect passes. After that, about the only time we played together was on the lethal Montreal power play that changed the rules of hockey. (Nowadays, when a power-play goal is scored, the penalized player can leave the penalty box. This wasn't always the case. A player used to serve his full time, no matter what happened while he was off. The NHL was forced to change that rule, because the Canadiens would habitually rack up two, three, or sometimes four goals while the other team was short-handed.)

In the history of the National Hockey League, players have scored a grand total of well over 100,000 goals – but to my mind, they're all eclipsed by Rocket's goal in the 1952 playoffs. It is the stuff of legend.

The Canadiens were expected to win the Stanley Cup semifinal that year against the Bruins, but went into Boston trailing three games to two on Sunday, April 6. The Canadiens were saved by an overtime score from Paul Masnick, one of Frank Selke's Saskatchewan boys, and tied the series. The teams returned to Montreal for the deciding game two nights later – but things did not look promising for the Canadiens when the Rocket was knocked unconscious in the course of one of his spectacular rushes early in the second period of a 1–1 contest.

Maurice had swept past defenceman Hal Laycoe, when the other Bruins' rearguard, Leo Labine, moved across, using his defensive partner as a screen. Labine went low, and Rocket saw him at the last second. He tried to jump over the check, but it was too little too late. Labine caught him on the shins, Richard's legs were knocked straight up in the air, and he crashed to the ice head-first.

You could literally have heard a pin drop as Rocket lay unconscious in an expanding pool of blood from an ugly gash over his left eye. Trainers Bill Head and Hector Dubois brought him around with smelling salts, but when Rocket was escorted to the Forum clinic, not a soul among the 15,100 fans that night believed that he would return. Fading into and out of consciousness, Maurice stayed in the clinic for almost an hour, occasionally asking the medical attendant to update him on the score.

With five minutes remaining in the third period, Rocket made his way to the bench and sat down alongside his teammates. After checking Maurice out, coach Dick Irvin sent him over the boards with Bert Olmstead and Elmer Lach at around the sixteen-minute mark. As the teams faced off, every eye in the Forum was on Number Nine, who leaned over with head down, waiting for the puck to drop.

The puck went deep into the Montreal end, but Butch Bouchard got to it behind the net and passed it quickly across to Rocket, who was already building up a head of steam. If they'd been making a movie of what happened next, they'd have used slow-motion for dramatic effect. Rocket flew up the right-wing boards and cut in toward defenceman Bill Quackenbush. Holding him off with one arm, Maurice stormed toward Sugar Jim Henry in the Boston goal and jammed the puck into the net from the edge of the crease. The Forum exploded.

Afterwards, a dazed and bloodied Richard shook hands with Henry, who had two black eyes of his own from earlier in the series.

Three years later, Boston defenceman Hal Laycoe was involved with the Rocket in another spectacular incident that would culminate in the notorious Richard Riot. Laycoe, who had played with the Canadiens for four seasons between 1947 and 1951, was not a dirty player. Far from it: he had been Rocket's tennis partner in the off-season, and bore him no grudge.

Before I describe the events of March 1955, I must stress that, although he was arguably the game's greatest star, Maurice Richard had been forced to spend his entire career battling very tough players, hammer and tongs. His fights were almost as spectacular as his goals. He went the distance with Detroit's "Terrible" Ted Lindsay in a string of memorable brawls, pummelled Boston's tough Fernie Flaman, and ko'd the Rangers' Bob "Killer" Dill at Madison Square Garden.

The same held true for Gordie Howe and other 1950s superstars. The team "policeman" had yet to make his appearance in the NHL, and you were expected to take care of yourself, no matter where you stood in the scoring statistics. Fortunately, Maurice was gifted with his fists and had the temperament of an exploding mortar shell when aroused.

Several events earlier in the 1954-55 season paved the way for the riot. In a game in Toronto during the Christmas holidays, Maurice became embroiled in a fight with Leafs defenceman Bob Bailey. It was broken up, and the combatants were escorted to their respective dressing rooms. As Maurice approached our bench, Dick Irvin leaned over the boards and said something to the Rocket, who charged after Bailey for a second time. During this rematch, Maurice manhandled linesman George Hayes, but referee Red Storey did not assess an extra penalty, nor did he write up the incident in his game report. Later, the newspapers speculated that Maurice was incensed because he felt that Bailey had been trying to gouge his eyes during the original fight. As it happened, the Leafs had filmed both the fight and Irvin's intervention, and they sent the footage to league president Clarence Campbell.

No suspension occurred, but Richard and Frank Selke did receive a severe tongue-lashing at NHL headquarters. In its wake, the league decided to initiate a crack-down on violence. Later that season, when Ted Lindsay attacked a fan in Toronto, he was suspended for ten days, an indication that any further altercations involving officials or onlookers would be dealt with harshly.

On Sunday, March 13, we were in Boston, getting whipped 4–2 by the Bruins. The score was not sitting well with us, because we were involved in a close race with Detroit for first place, and a loss to the fourth-place Bruins would be frustrating in the extreme. Late in the game, I faced off with Olmstead and Richard on my wings, and we moved down the ice. Maurice closed in on Hal Laycoe at the blueline, and it just so happened that Laycoe got his stick up and cut him. I was standing only a few feet away, and saw Maurice take his glove off. He passed his hand over the cut, and it came away covered with blood.

Maurice immediately went after Laycoe, and everybody else on the ice dropped their gloves and paired off. I took Fleming Mackell up against the glass, and tried to follow the growing melee out of the corner of my eye. Apparently, as Rocket charged Laycoe, referee Frank Udvari and linesman Cliff Thompson got in his way. One version of the story is that Maurice was well under control by the linesman, but then Doug Harvey broke free of Fern Flaman and pulled the official away. Maurice broke free as well, then broke his stick across Laycoe's back, and was still going after him when Thompson intervened once more. Maurice later said that when Thompson grabbed him the second time, Laycoe was able to punch him unimpeded. After warning Thompson three times to let him go, Richard turned and punched the linesman, and was assessed a match penalty by Udvari. Dick Irvin was quoted in the papers to the effect that Maurice was so mad he was in a trance: "At this point, it was almost as if he'd just discovered the presence of the linesman. I still don't know whether Rocket recognized who he was." According to yet another story, Irvin himself handed Maurice a stick so he could go after Laycoe a second time.

This sort of thing was not about to pass unnoticed. The consensus was that Rocket would be suspended for the three games remaining in the regular season, and lose his chance of winning the scoring title. Nobody thought that he'd get off with impunity. However, when Clarence Campbell suspended him for the rest of the year, playoffs included, it struck most observers as far too harsh, both for Maurice and for the Canadiens.

I was sure that Campbell hadn't taken this decision on his own. To my mind, the other five teams had ganged up on the Canadiens. Frank Selke was quick to describe the rancour of his fellow managers: "All these gentlemen demanded that something be done to curb Maurice Richard, whose greatest fault was defeating their teams and filling their arenas to capacity."

French-speaking Montrealers were very resentful of Rocket's

suspension. For them, the action was simply another excuse to humiliate French Canadians by excessively punishing their favourite. Death threats and bomb threats were phoned in to NHL headquarters, and Montreal's Mayor Camillien Houde suggested that Campbell would be wise to avoid the upcoming game on Saturday against the Red Wings. Campbell, who had been a prosecutor at the Nuremberg trials of Nazi war criminals, said he would not back down in the face of any threat from any quarter, and promised to be at the Forum in his regular seat.

Despite the loss to Boston and Rocket's suspension, our fight for first place with the Wings was still on. When we played them that Saturday, we knew a win would put us out in front. Still, the suspension had unsettled us, and Detroit took advantage, going ahead 4–1 in the first period. Toward the end of the period, a young fan went up to Campbell and threw a punch at him. Others in the crowd hurled tomatoes, eggs, and smoke bombs. The action in the stands was heavier than on the ice.

We were craning our necks to see what was happening as we filed out to our dressing room at period's end. Even in the room, we could hear the mounting clamour. Just at the moment the racket outside was its loudest, Mr. Selke came into the room. "Boys, get dressed," he said. "The fire commissioner has ordered us to empty the Forum."

We showered, dressed, and emerged into a downtown that had become a battle zone.

Over my many years in the league, I came to appreciate and respect Clarence Campbell as a fair-minded individual who always had the NHL's best interests at heart. Still, I could not agree with Rocket's suspension, particularly since it smacked of a deal worked out among the board of governors. Nor did I think that Campbell was wise to make an appearance at the game.

On the other hand, what could he do? As league president, he couldn't hide or give the impression that he was hiding, especially since NHL headquarters were a short drive away. Maybe his pride was a factor. Maybe he felt he had to make a statement by attending. Besides, even his absence might not have made a difference.

Whatever the case, Campbell hurt both Maurice, who lost the scoring title, and the team, which lost first place in the final week of the season and went down to defeat in the Stanley Cup playoffs against the Red Wings. I would have liked our chances against them, had Rocket been in the lineup. Maurice rose to the occasion during any playoff, and scored many important goals.

Rocket's suspension also affected the league scoring race, which, of course, continued on without him. Boom and I were right behind him in, respectively, second and third place that season when he was suspended, and the idea of going ahead of him while he couldn't play was not appealing to either of us. The team had to finish ahead of the Red Wings to secure home-ice advantage for the duration of the playoffs, but Boomer was worried. For all his laughter and shenanigans, Boom was a sensitive guy. He was concerned about his image. He wanted to be liked by the fans.

"Jeez, Jean, if we go ahead of the Rocket, those people out there are going to come down on us as traitors," he said, just prior to our final regular-season game against the Red Wings at the Forum.

Doug Harvey was sitting nearby. "We're goin' for first, Boom," he said, with the finality of an ice general who would have your stripes if you weren't giving your best. "There's no question of shootin' wide of the net."

I agreed with Doug. "Boom, if it's there, you have to score. The fans will understand."

I was wrong, and Boom was right. As it turned out, the team wound up in second place, two points out of first. Boom scored one more point than the Rocket, and two more than me, as we finished one-two-three atop the scoring list. I hit the post twice in that final regular-season game.

A few days later, just before our first home game against Boston

in the semi-finals, Maurice was introduced to the crowd, prompting a standing ovation that seemed as if it would never end. Minutes later, when Boom was presented with the Art Ross Trophy
for winning the scoring race, the fans booed and littered the ice
for almost as long as they had cheered the Rocket. Boom-Boom
remembered this episode for a long, long time. Try as we might
to convince him that the crowd's reaction had everything to do
with Maurice, and nothing to do with him, Boomer was incon-
solable. Still, he and I each managed to score a goal in a 2–0 win
that night, and he was our leading scorer with eight goals and five
assists in twelve games, as we took Detroit to seven before finally
losing the Cup.

While I was still in my first year with the Aces, Elmer Lach was
quoted by a Montreal paper as saying that, when Béliveau got to
town, it would signal his swan song with the Canadiens. This was
a strange comment, coming from a man who continued to display great strength at his position even in his later years. For four
seasons, he'd teamed up with the toughness of Toe Blake and the
spectacular scoring of the Rocket to form the Punch Line, one of
the league's top trios. When Toe broke his leg and retired, Elmer
carried on with the Rocket and a succession of left wingers,
including Bert Olmstead, a player who was very similar to Toe in
the corners.

When I joined the Canadiens in 1953, Elmer was still there,
contributing both on the ice and off. Just as Punch Imlach had
tried to improve my quickness by having me work out with teammates on the Aces, Dick Irvin assigned Elmer as my tutor during
my first season with Montreal. We would practise a variety of techniques together. He was especially skilled on face-offs, and I picked
up a lot of very useful tricks. I'd always tried to put my stick down
just as the puck hit the ice, but Elmer told me not to wait, to be

in motion as the puck was dropped. That split second gained meant a lot of face-offs won, and winning face-offs has always been one of the most significant factors in a victory.

Elmer was also one of the finest passers around. He could give you a quick, soft pass that would nestle on your stick; it just seemed to settle on the blade without a bounce. In addition, he was a very smooth and very shifty skater. Although his shot wasn't particularly heavy, his quick release made him dangerous. He would use defenceman to screen the goalie, especially when he got to within fifteen or twenty feet of the net. If Maurice and Toe were covered, Elmer could take the netminder by surprise. If a goalie tried to look around his defencemen for Elmer's shot, that wonderful passing ability would come into play, and one of the wingers would find himself with an easy score after the puck appeared as if by magic on his blade. I knew that I would have a long career in the NHL if I could learn to pass only half as well as Elmer.

Another veteran who shaped my game in my first years with Montreal was Bert Olmstead, the hard-rock left winger who could hammer an opponent senseless, and seconds later chew you out on the bench because you were three inches out of position on a play. The best years Boom and I ever had – and remember that we won back-to-back scoring championships in 1955 and 1956 – was when Bert was on our line. He never let us relax or gave us a minute's rest. He was always after us . . . pushing, pushing, pushing.

Often, Bert would be banging away in the corner with two or three opponents draped all over him, and I'd be waiting and waiting out in front of the net. Instinctively, I might drift over to help him, but he'd scream, "Get the hell out of here! Get back in front, and stay there!" More often than not, he'd come up with the puck, Boom or I would receive the pass, and we'd find ourselves staring down the goalie, unopposed.

Pity the defencemen who faced us in those days. If you played on the right side, Dickie Moore and Bert Olmstead would be pounding on you shift after shift. If you were on the left, you had Boom-Boom and the Rocket to contend with.

When I joined the Canadiens, Émile "Butch" Bouchard was on his last legs, both at our blueline and as our team captain. I only played with Émile for two years, and in that last year he didn't play all that much. Still, he was well respected throughout the league for his strength. One night, a fracas started in Detroit and he went right to the Red Wings' bench, opened the door, and chased a player through it – unheard-of behaviour then, as now. Nobody on the Detroit team dared do anything, and they certainly had their share of tough customers. The only other defenceman of that era who matched Butch in terms of strength was the late, great Tim Horton of Toronto.

Butch lived in Longueuil, not far from me, and in his final season we often drove in to the Forum together. Like many large, strong men, he was somewhat reluctant to demonstrate physical prowess, believing that a kind word and a smile went a lot further than brute force.

Butch also holds another interesting distinction. Although I played with several brothers – the Richards, the Mahovlichs, the Rousseaus, and the Plantes – Butch was the only player whose son would become a teammate in my later years (in my last season, in fact). Pierre Bouchard, "Butch Junior" to his friends, had his father's strength and easy laugh. Unlike many hockey fathers, however, Butch Senior didn't bring his son to the Forum very often when Pierre was growing up. He must have learned his lessons back at home.

As a captain, Butch Senior took great pains to listen to everyone's opinion on any issue, and served as a model for my stint as team captain in the 1960s.

Besides Bouchard, the other influential veteran on the Canadiens when I joined them was Doug Harvey. Doug was a one-man Welcome Wagon. If a rookie needed anything, he could go to Doug, who would take the time to help him. Doug was a team man on the ice, in the dressing room, and on the road.

Oh, and lest I forget, Doug Harvey was also the best NHL defenceman who ever lived. No exceptions. I'll talk later on about Bobby Orr, and how he single-handedly changed the game.

Offensively, of course, there's no comparison. Orr was so fast that he could take chances in an opponent's zone, then rush back to his blueline if his sortie didn't work out. That said, Bobby Orr could not do all the things Doug Harvey could – a judgment shared by Doug's teammates, his opponents, and anyone who had the good fortune to marvel at his on-ice abilities.

Defensively, Harvey was far superior to Orr – thus, to anybody he faced. Indeed, he was probably the finest natural athlete ever to play our game. Scouts and sports organizers argued endlessly about his abilities in baseball, football, and hockey. Many people in the Snowdon and Notre-Dame-de-Grâce districts might say he missed his calling, and should have settled on another sport, where he'd have done even better. In the 1940s, he was recruited by Ottawa's AA baseball team, and won the batting championship. A couple of years later, he played for Montreal in the Quebec Rugby Football Union, then part of the Canadian Football League. In a game against Toronto, he played all sixty minutes as both running and defensive back.

His stamina was something to behold. If the team had lost two or more players to injury, especially in the middle of a road trip, Doug would play all night. If he needed a rest, or thought the game was getting too frisky for his liking, he'd simply slow it down.

How could a single player dictate the tempo of a game? Doug could. He would control the puck and defy any and all comers to take it away from him. Forecheckers were reluctant to go all-out against him because he could handle them physically, or embarrass them with a sudden move. When someone got careless, he'd let go with a long pass that would spring a teammate into the open for a breakaway. Even at the end of his career, when he came up with St. Louis for the 1968 playoffs thirty pounds overweight and barely able to skate, he was still controlling the game in smaller ways.

When Doug was on the ice, you played his way or you didn't play at all. Many sports fans like to indulge in a round of "what if" speculations – wondering how players from my era would fare if they time-travelled into today's NHL. Doug Harvey would fare very well, unlike a number of today's wingers, who have the habit of hanging around the boards at their own blueline, waiting for the breakout pass from a defenceman.

Doug used to tell our forwards: "I won't give you the puck if you're not skating. If you're standing still, if you park yourself near the boards and wait for a pass from me, it won't come. You'll die of old age standing at the boards. If you want the puck, you'll get it on the fly."

We skated, and he got us the puck. And, for his efforts, Doug won every Norris Trophy as top defenceman between 1955 and 1962, the only exception being 1959, when it went to his team-mate, Tom Johnson. Only Orr, with eight trophies, has surpassed Doug's magnificent record.

How good was Doug Harvey? Good enough to call his shots.

We were going for our fifth straight Cup in March of 1960, and had opened the series against Chicago with a 4–3 win at home. It had been a surprisingly hard-fought contest, given that the Hawks were without Stan Mikita and Bobby Hull. Two nights later, we were sitting on a slim 3–2 lead when Billy Hay stole the puck from Doug at our blueline and scored with a minute to go in the third period. We sat in the dressing room glumly contemplating overtime.

"Well, boys, I owe you one," Doug said, very matter-of-factly. And at 8:38 of the fourth period, he walked in on Glenn Hall to keep his promise. Nor did he relax his vigilance in subsequent games. The Hawks never scored again in the series, as we dumped them 4–0 and 2–0 back in Chicago to move to the final. Jacques Plante received much of the credit for the back-to-back shutouts, but it was Doug's inspired play which made the goalie's work much easier.

That Chicago series was one of the very few times when I didn't see Doug displaying his almost perpetual grin. He was a non-stop joker, a happy-go-lucky guy who could always be counted on to lighten the tension during a vital game. When a game didn't count for much in the standings, he'd keep us all in stitches. Once, at an exhibition game in Sudbury against the Wolves of the Ontario Senior Hockey League, he went right over the top.

Sudbury was Toe Blake's hometown, and he wanted his home-coming to be a memorable one. Thanks to Doug, it was. We were leading 5–0 in the third period, just coasting along, when the Wolves suddenly managed to score.

Something special happened every time the local team put the puck in the net. An effigy of a wolf would fly out from behind a curtain at one end of the rink, and float above the ice surface on a guy wire, while a tape recording of a howling wolf resounded in the arena. Naturally, the crowd would start to howl along, and the whole arena would sound like the world's largest wolf pack had come to call.

Doug was so taken with this that several moments later, he acci-dentally-on-purpose put the puck past a flabbergasted Jacques Plante.

When Doug returned to our bench, Toe Blake was howling mad. "Are you nuts? This isn't a practice where you can fool around, this is a game." He was tomato-red and a vein was throb-bing prominently on his temple.

Doug flashed his trademark Little Rascals grin. "Sorry, Toe, but seein' that wolf again was worth it."

Much, perhaps too much, has been written about Doug's other side – the drinking and carousing that coloured his post-

Canadiens career and diminished him in some people's eyes. I'd like to say a couple of things about this. I hope they reflect an understanding of his plight, and convey a sense of the person whose many great qualities remained unaltered, even toward the end.

Doug had come out of a hard-drinking, harder-working blue collar neighbourhood in the 1940s. That background, and the Snowdon Tavern, never left him.

I have been asked many times: "What could you have done to help him? Did you as players see him heading in this direction?"

In fact, there was very little we could have done. It wasn't our place to dictate his behaviour. Doug was older than us, one of our leaders. Besides, his drinking didn't affect his play. He never showed up for a game the worse for wear.

Yes, the weekends were rough, and Doug would celebrate a victory, or drown the sorrow of a loss. But he wasn't alone in this by any means. Just like players today, we'd all have beers after a game. You could lose four to five pounds over three periods of play, and your first priority afterward would be to replace the lost liquid. A player isn't hungry at 11 o'clock, just thirsty. And what's open at 11 o'clock at night, especially on the road?

Doug enjoyed his parties, but he never hurt anyone, with the possible exception of himself. On the contrary, he was always ready and willing to help. Once, after his playing days were over, he called me at the Forum from a charitable organization's summer camp, somewhere in the Eastern Townships, where he was building a walk-in freezer.

"Jean, we're running short on wood. Is your foundation able to help?"

"Sure, I'll provide equipment and materials. How much do you need?"

"I think with $500, I'll have enough to finish the job."

"Okay. Tell them to send me the bill. But what are you doing? How long have you been there?"

"A little more than a week. Jean, it's just beautiful here. We're building the freezer now, having a few beers, a few laughs."

I always felt that some part of Doug never grew up. Life was there to enjoy; and life was short, so he made the most of it. He lived to show generosity and kindness to everyone.

After we lost to Chicago in the 1961 playoffs, Frank Selke sold Doug and Albert Langlois to the Rangers in return for tough guy Lou Fontinato. Doug became New York's player-coach, but lasted only a year. He had an eye for the game, and was a very good judge of talent. But he couldn't stand the loneliness of coaching, the invisible barrier that separated him from his teammates, and gave it up after a single season. Besides, his methods were unorthodox. He'd raised eyebrows in the Rangers' executive suite when he called his first team meeting in a bar. Doug left New York in 1964, and kicked around the minors for a while – as a player-coach here, a scout there – and finally ended up with the Quebec Aces, coached by his former teammate Boom-Boom Geoffrion.

The Aces were heading off on a road trip, and rather than come into town to catch the bus, Doug asked to be picked up at a spot on the highway, near his home in Lac Beauport. This was on an ice-cold winter's day. The bus came by, and there was Doug, warming his hands over a fire he'd lit in an old oil drum – a fine example of self-sufficiency for the rest of the team.

When Doug went to New York, Frank Selke came in for a good deal of criticism. People said he'd banished Doug because of his activity on the executive of the National Hockey League Players' Association. Selke had already traded Dollard St. Laurent to Chicago for apparently similar reasons. Perhaps these accusations were true, but it wasn't like Frank Selke to run with the pack. I always thought that, by sending Doug to New York, Selke was offering him the chance at a second career. If he'd stuck with coaching, he could have done well – but only if he got his personal life under control. Remember that Doug was a few months shy of his thirty-seventh birthday at the time. His playing days were coming to an end, one way or another.

I've said it earlier in this book, but it bears repeating here. Of all the stars on the 1950s Canadiens – thirteen of whom have been inducted into the NHL Hall of Fame – the most ferocious competitor was Richard Winston Moore. Dickie and I knew each other intimately by the time I joined the Canadiens, having taken turns at wreaking havoc on each other throughout junior hockey. When I was with the Citadels, we hated each other with a passion, and proved it night after night, because Dickie wouldn't have had it any other way.

If you were on an opposing team, especially if you were one of its leading players, you could expect to find Dickie in your face. He attempted to crack the Canadiens' lineup after graduating from junior hockey in 1951, but was sent down to the QSHL Montreal Royals for seasoning, which afforded him yet another opportunity to make my life intolerable as by that time I was with the Aces.

Dickie did not last too long in senior, however. When Maurice Richard was plagued for most of the 1951–52 season by a nagging abdominal tear, the Canadiens summoned Dickie to their ranks on December 15. He scored eighteen goals and fifteen assists in the remaining thirty-three regular-season games, and appeared to be on his way.

Unfortunately, the injury bug bit him, just as it had the Rocket, and as it would me in my NHL debut season. Dickie would play only thirty-one games in the next two seasons. In his third (my first), we got to know each other even better, but under much more agreeable circumstances than we had shared in junior. Our newfound good will, however, did little to cheer him up. That year, a knee injury limited him to a mere thirteen games during the regular season, although he came back to lead us in the playoffs with thirteen points in eleven games. Often, we'd sit there nursing our wounds together. I missed twenty-six games of my own with a variety of ailments, including a cracked ankle.

Dickie's knees were arguably worse than Bobby Orr's. Late in his career, Dickie would walk into a room, and you'd know who it was without looking up, by the telltale "click, click" sound.

How tough was Dickie?

Well, he won the scoring championship in 1957-58, playing most of the season with a broken left wrist. Before doing so, he convened a meeting to ask his linemates if they would continue to play with him, because he was afraid of hindering Henri Richard's attempt at the scoring championship. Dickie was fitted with a special playing cast, and Toe Blake switched him over to the right wing on our powerplay to protect it. Never a big scorer in junior, Dickie ended the season with thirty-six goals and forty-eight assists, edging out the Pocket Rocket by four points. A year later, he successfully defended his Art Ross Trophy, with forty-one goals and fifty-five assists for ninety-six points, a league record which lasted six seasons until Bobby Hull totalled ninety-seven points in 1965-66.

An even dozen of the 1950s Canadiens remained with the club for all five Stanley Cups: Maurice and Henri Richard, Boom-Boom Geoffrion, Dickie Moore, Jacques Plante, Tom Johnson, Don Marshall, Claude Provost, Bob Turner, Doug Harvey, Jean-Guy Talbot, and myself. Part of that period could very well be subtitled: Life with Boom. We had a lineup full of players who absolutely refused to accept defeat, incredible competitors all. We also had our share of flakes, but Boom was a blizzard all by himself.

In 1959, we went into Chicago for the playoffs, and Boom was reading the TV listings at the breakfast table. "Jean," he said excitedly, "look at this. What a movie! *Job in Chicago*. I bet it's gangsters and cops with lots of shooting and tommyguns."

Of course. What else, in Al Capone's hometown?

Boom's bass tones became even deeper as his enthusiasm grew.

"It's on at 10:30. We'll get back to the room early, so we can watch it." During the day, he mentioned our rendezvous over and over again, to make sure I wouldn't forget. Boom was a peaceful man, but he loved his bloodthirsty gangster movies.

At 10:30, we were ready. The TV was tuned to the proper channel. But when the show appeared, *Job in Chicago* had become *Jobs in Chicago*.

The dialogue was uplifting and informative: "Job Sixty-Six, company in Oak Grove needs a plumber. Call this number and specify Job Sixty-Six." And so on, through every service industry and building trade. The only sign of gangsterism was the announcer's "machine-gun" delivery.

Boomer went nuts, swearing in *bon Québécois* for half an hour.

In the mid-1950s, Kenny Reardon, a former Canadiens defence-man and a member of the Hall of Fame, was the team's assistant general manager. He had been known for an unorthodox skating style in his playing days. During a practice, as Kenny watched from the boards, Boom-Boom did a perfect imitation of Kenny's tip-toe run, caromed off the boards on either side of the rink, cut across behind a defenceman, braked hard in front of the net, and sent the puck way up into the whites, the Forum's highest tier of seats.

Boomer was half of our Class Clown tag-team act – I'll tell you about his partner in a minute – but his love of a joke very nearly killed him in 1958. We were at practice and he seemed to brush against André Pronovost. There was no collision but, suddenly, there was Boom, rolling all over the ice. Our reaction was predictable: we thought he was fooling around, so we let him entertain us for a while. Then I skated up to him, and he said through clenched teeth, "Jean, I'm not joking!" I motioned for trainer

Bill Head to come out and they whisked him off to hospital.

Boom had a ruptured spleen, and underwent emergency surgery moments after his arrival. The doctors said the attack could have happened while he was walking down the street. (Boom enjoyed good health as a player, but he's had his problems lately. In 1993, both he and his wife Marlene, the daughter of Howie Morenz, underwent surgery in their adopted home city of Atlanta, Georgia. Marlene had an eight-hour triple bypass operation, and Boom was treated for prostate cancer. I'm happy to say that both of them have since recovered fully.)

In addition to his comedic talents, Boom fancied himself a singer and, truthfully speaking, he did have enough of a voice to be asked to appear on television in both English and French. On the road, we'd occasionally go for a few beers in a club that featured live entertainment. We'd barely have time to get settled in our seats, when Boom would climb on stage and commandeer the microphone. Nowadays everybody does it. It's called karaoke. Back then we had another phrase for it – Big Ham.

Perhaps Boomer's most celebrated vocal appearance occurred on *Juliette*, the popular variety program on CBC television. He changed the words in the song "C'est Magnifique" to suit and celebrate himself. When he wasn't doing Maurice Chevalier, Boom would fall back on Dean Martin tunes. As a vocal impersonator, he was well ahead of his time.

Boom, of course, had his serious side, and always played to win. In 1961, he was shooting for the Rocket's fifty-goal single-season scoring record, and netted the magic goal against Toronto's Cesare Maniago on March 16, in a 5–2 win over the Leafs at Montreal. It was Boom's sixty-second game of the year, the team's sixty-eighth.

Throughout my career, I'd heard complaints that I passed the puck too much, but I shrugged them off because I'd always enjoyed making plays. I think I got assists on thirty-seven or thirty-eight of Boom's goals that season, which cut down on the complaints.

He finished first in league scoring with ninety-five points, five more than me. When they presented him with the Art Ross Trophy at the Forum, nobody booed.

Boomer and I had several set plays. Back then, most defence-men tended to be stocky and slow. A good stickhandler was usually given the blueline, and I was able to use my long reach to advantage. If I went to the right, I would try to hold onto the puck until the defenceman committed himself. If he came at me, I'd flip it to Boom and he'd blast it. If the defender backed in, we'd take the puck right into the crease.

When you're on top of the world, which the 1950s Canadiens were, a certain arrogance will surface on occasion. Boom could sneer with the best, as I saw one Sunday night at Madison Square Garden. We had beaten the Rangers 6–0, and New York coach Phil Watson was so angry that he waited until the stands cleared, then took his team right back onto the ice for an eleven o'clock workout.

Boomer and I were among the last players to leave our dressing room. As we walked along the aisle beside the rink, we were greeted by the unusual spectacle of weary Rangers sweating out stops-and-starts under the watchful eye of Fiery Phil.

Boom put his nose right up against the glass, and yelled at a group of players that included Andy Bathgate, Wally Herge-sheimer, Dean Prentice, and Gump Worsley. "Skate like hell, you bums!" he cried. "Keep it going! Keep it going! Try to get it right!"

The Rangers stared back at him with glassy-eyed resignation. This was their second straight beating in an hour.

Character that he was, Boom finally had nothing on Marcel Bonin, my former Aces teammate who found his way to Montreal from Boston in 1957.

You'll remember that Marcel was fond of hunting and bor-rowing other people's clothes when the occasion demanded. He could also walk on his hands as well as he could on his feet. Sometimes, while we were going about our pre-game preparations, we'd look up to discover a stark-naked man, wandering around the dressing room upside down. That could relax you before an important contest.

So could Marcel's habitual pre-game questions. "Who are we playing tonight?" he'd ask. "Who are their tougher players? Marcel is feeling strong!" All of this would be accompanied by a lot of flexing of very thick biceps. To drive home the point, Marcel would occasionally snap off a piece of a drinking glass with his thick fingers, pop it into his mouth, and grind it to powder inside one cheek, just like a chaw of tobacco.

Marcel was always good for something new. Once, we were sitting in the room, getting dressed before a big game with about five weeks remaining in the season, when Marcel made a strange announcement. "Jean, starting tonight, Marcel is going into a slump," he said.

"What?"

"A slump."

"What are you talking about?" Goals were hard enough to come by in the NHL, and I'd never heard of a player who wouldn't score on purpose.

"Fifteen goals, that's my usual production. I'm already there. If I score twenty, they'll ask me to score twenty-five next year, and I can't. So for the next seven or eight games, I'll be the playmaker. You score. Marcel is going into a slump."

In fact, in his five years with us, Marcel Bonin never did score more than seventeen goals a season – although, when he was on the line with Boom and me in 1959-60 and 1960-1961, he put together fifty-one points in each of those seasons. Maybe he could have done even better, but decided to slump after he'd hit the half-century mark.

Marcel was a very helpful guy to have on your side when the

going got rough. One night we were involved in a brawl in Boston. Boomer was grappling with Jack Bionda, a big, tough defence-man, and Marcel was off in the corner with somebody else. When the fight broke up, everyone skated back to their benches, or to the penalty box – all except Bionda, who sat exhausted at centre ice, shaken by his scuffle with Boom.

Marcel spotted Bionda just sitting there, out of gas, bothering no one. As a sort of afterthought, he casually paused in front of him, leaned over, and *whang*, knocked him out cold with one swat, then continued to our bench. Needless to say, the clans gathered, and once more fights broke out all over the rink.

Another time, we were playing in Chicago Stadium on a very warm night. Elmer Lach had taught me not only to have my stick in motion as the puck was dropped, but to be the last man in on the face-off. I'd set up for it as usual – but when I could see that the linesman was ready to drop the puck, I'd pull back, glance around to see where everybody was, and then move in again. That night, I looked over and spotted Marcel, talking cheerfully to someone in the stands.

I stepped back again and skated over to him. "Marcel, what's going on?"

He nodded at the fan. "Jean, this guy just dropped a glass of beer down the back of my neck. You know how hot it is. I was telling him that next time, he should tell me, and I'll turn around, so he can put it here." He gestured toward his throat.

Everybody was cracking up. What could I do, or say?

"Okay Marcel, let's get rid of this game and we'll go for a beer after."

In those days, we could afford to act like that. We were winning all the time.

After he retired from hockey, it seemed only natural that Marcel gravitated to police work, joining the force in Joliette, about thirty miles northeast of Montreal. He was off duty on the afternoon of a robbery at a hardware store. A silent alarm alerted the police, who trapped the robbers inside. But the crooks were armed, and shots were exchanged. When the police chief got there, he gave the order: Send for Marcel.

Since Marcel was hunting that day, it took a while to get in touch with him. An hour or so after the drama began, Marcel showed up, armed to the teeth. By this time, the press photographers had arrived as well.

Marcel told me the rest of the story. "Jean, I'm moving along, hugging the wall, and trying to get to an opening where I could say something to the guys inside, when I hear this 'Psst' behind me. It's one of the photographers from Montreal, a guy I knew really well at the Forum.

"He says, like we're taking a picture of me in a hockey uniform, 'Marcel, move the shotgun out from your body a little bit; I'll have a better picture.'

"I turned around. 'Are you nuts? Where do you think you are? These guys are shooting bullets, not pucks!'

"But he wouldn't listen, he wouldn't leave me alone until he had the picture he wanted."

I could understand the photographer's confusion. This was probably the first time in his life that Marcel was asking him, or anybody else, to be serious. (The crooks surrendered peacefully in the end, which was just as well. Marcel was a sharpshooter; he could hit a target behind him, shooting back over his shoulder, by aiming at its reflection in a diamond ring that he held in front of him.)

These then were some of the major contributors to our 1950s success. I'll talk later on about Henri Richard, Claude Provost, and Jacques Plante who, while present in the 1950s and 1960s, can more properly be dealt with when we reach the 1960s. I realize that I've omitted several important names, including Tom Johnson, Bob Turner, and Dollard St. Laurent, three remarkably consistent performers. Tom, for example, played 857 games in thirteen seasons. When he first joined the team, he was paired with Butch Bouchard and they became very close friends. Later, he played a lot with Jean-Guy Talbot. Like Johnson, Bob Turner was a westerner, a very good skater who joined the team in 1955-56, and therefore had a share in Stanley Cup victories for his first five years in the NHL. But everyone on the team – and throughout the Canadiens organization – made a contribution of their own. It was a decade to remember, and to be proud of always.

At the same time, the 1950s was not a decade entirely free of pain and distress. My beloved mother was diagnosed as having cancer and passed away at age forty-nine in 1957, the year my daughter was born. My father remarried, and Mida, my stepmother, helped him with the task of raising my younger brothers and sisters.

Perhaps I should mention here another event that anticipated the problems I would face in the 1960s. As I've said, Élise and I had been prepared for the glare of the celebrity spotlight by our time in Quebec City. We had learned to cope with media demands, but these intensified when we moved to Montreal. Every week, or so it seemed, a newspaper or pictorial magazine was knocking on the door, seeking fresh insight into the lives of the Béliveaus. We were posed in pictures of domestic bliss – cooking, eating meals, reading, enjoying music. Our fans expected this sort of coverage, and we were usually happy to oblige.

But there is always another side to the coin. In 1955, a rumour spread that we were experiencing marital difficulties. This story originated in Quebec City, where Élise was frequently seen without me. In fact, her mother had fallen ill that year, and Élise was visiting her more frequently.

The rumour was very quickly embellished to include a rival, the professional wrestler Jean Rougeau. There was only one drawback to this juicy scandal: Élise had never met him in her life. Journalists were dispatched to investigate the story, but when it was denied by all concerned, the gossip eventually died down.

At the time, however, it was upsetting, and gave mean-spirited persons an excuse to add fuel to the fire. One night, Élise answered the telephone, and found herself speaking to a woman who'd been in the habit of calling with lurid descriptions of my infidelities.

"You think you're so smart, Madame Béliveau," she said, "but you should see where your husband is."

This woman knew that, given my busy schedule, the chances were that I'd be away from home when she made her calls. This night, however, Élise could indeed see where I was, since I was sitting right next to her. She informed the caller of this, and we heard no more from her – but the whispers about my or Élise's imaginary carryings-on persisted for quite a while.

We got through this period thanks to the support we received from our families and our mutual love and respect. We were never threatened by the gossipmongers, because there was no basis for their speculations. The trouble is that a wounding story can strike in many directions. Several years later, I had occasion to meet Jean Rougeau, who said he felt very badly about what had happened. He too had a wife and family, and the gossip had had a similar effect on his household.

Winning the 1959-60 Stanley Cup brought the 1950s to a satisfying close. Entering my second decade of play would be a ten-year roller-coaster ride that would bring fresh triumphs and unaccustomed troubles, while ushering in a whole new chapter in the unfolding saga of the *bleu-blanc-rouge*.

6

✦

THE NEGLECTED
SIXTIES

Sam Pollock has called the 1960s the "forgotten decade" in the history of the Montreal Canadiens. In the course of the endless debate over "which team was greatest" – the 1950s Canadiens or the 1970s edition – even the most meticulous Hab historians tend to overlook the men who won four Stanley Cups in five years, five in seven years, if (like me) you consider the 1970-71 Canadiens as essentially the 1960s lineup.

Only two other NHL teams – Toronto between 1944-45 and 1950-51, and Edmonton between 1983-84 and 1989-90 – have ever won five Cups in seven years. And yet, for reasons that escape me, the 1960s Canadiens get little recognition and even less respect.

At the time, nobody doubted our abilities. Along with the Maple Leafs (in the first half of the decade) and the Chicago Black Hawks (by its half-way point), we were recognized as the force to be reckoned with. By the end of the decade, people were using the word "dynasty." Then along came Lafleur, Shutt, Gainey, Ken

Dryden, and the rest, and we found ourselves relegated to a high, dusty shelf at the back of the hockey library.

On the personal side, I can honestly say that my second decade with the Montreal Canadiens was more eventful than the 1950s. It came as a rude awakening, after our previous successes. The shocks were both physical and mental – potentially career-ending injuries, scoring slumps, the wholesale trades of All-Star teammates, league expansion, the boos of my home fans, and almost never-ending speculation about my apparent imminent retirement.

I wasn't young any more as I started the decade. Indeed, my health would play a major role in the years between 1960-61, when our five-straight Stanley Cup reign ended, and 1970-71, the final season of my playing career.

Even today, the occasional older fan will remind me of a story that circulated at that time. I was supposed to be a "Cadillac with a Volkswagen engine," hampered by a heart that wasn't big enough or strong enough for my body size and my demanding sport.

The story is true, but while the Cadillac remained a constant, the smaller vehicle used for comparison purposes tended to change model every now and then.

The story originated in 1953. When I signed my first contract with the Canadiens, team management thought it prudent to secure insurance on me, considering the $100,000-plus contract we had agreed to. This way, the team would be protected if my playing days came to an abrupt end, through accident or misadventure. Naturally, I underwent a stringent physical, during which doctors noted a "cardiac anomaly" – one or two steps down from an "abnormality." Nonetheless, Frank Selke was shocked to hear that the insurance company would not issue the policy. The examining physician had written in the file: "He has an Austin's motor in a Cadillac's chassis." (The Austin was a tiny British car, the most underpowered vehicle the doctor could think of on the spur of the moment. I don't remember whether the Volkswagen Beetle was on the scene at that time.)

No one suggested that this condition was at all life-threatening. Still, there were problems. My "pump" could not move enough blood throughout my system when I was physically stressed. Symptoms of this anomaly included fatigue, nausea, temporary loss of sight, a shortness of breath that sometimes felt like suffocation, and chest pains so sharp that I felt my heart was ready to burst.

Plainly, I should have looked for other work. Instead, I went out and helped the Canadiens win five straight Stanley Cups.

After the 1961-62 season, however, things started to catch up with me. By now chronically fatigued, I decided to visit the Leahy Clinic in Boston, where I underwent a full regimen of stress tests. I ran on a treadmill and blew up balloons, and when I'd finished, they wheeled out the electrocardiogram machine. This "scientific approach to physical fitness" is common in any health club today, but back then it was brand new and faintly mysterious, at least to me. My first two minutes on the treadmill were tough and I ran rapidly out of breath. Then my system slowly adjusted, and by the end of six minutes, when the doctors called a halt, my engine was humming and I felt I could have continued for several minutes more.

Still, the doctors were amazed that I could function as a professional athlete. According to them, I sorely lacked the necessary physical gifts. At the same time, they concluded that I wasn't at risk if I kept on playing. There might be a degree of discomfort, but nothing to worry about. My body, it seems, had adapted to this condition many years before, setting a pace that I could live with. That pace, as the treadmill test showed, meant that I was a slow starter, but became stronger as I went along. And while I haven't checked my statistics over the years, I wouldn't be surprised to find that I scored more often in the second and third periods than in the first.

Despite this physical anomaly, I managed to play eighteen years in professional sport. Some athletes aren't so fortunate. You can imagine my reaction when I heard about the tragic deaths of the basketball players Hank Gathers and Reggie Lewis, both of whom lost their lives on the court because of similar deficiencies. It amazes me to think that someone with a fine-tuned athlete's body can have something so utterly wrong with his or her system – an ever-present danger about which nothing can be done, that can strike without any warning. I considered myself very lucky to be able to "manage" my condition, and worked hard at keeping negative factors at bay.

The physical "anomalies" I couldn't control were the injuries I suffered in action. Some were worse than others. During the 1960s, I began to feel jinxed as far as these injuries were concerned, especially since an alarming number were suffered when we played Chicago.

The worst setback occurred during the third game of the 1961-62 playoffs. I was in the corner, scuffling for the puck with my former teammate Dollard St. Laurent, when suddenly the lights went out. I didn't know it at the time, but while Dollard and I were scrambling around, the other Chicago defenceman, big Jack Evans, left his post in front of the net and charged me into the boards, catching me in the head with his stick, then driving my head into the glass. Even though I dressed for the remaining games, I was finished for the playoffs. With Henri Richard out with a broken arm, we were down two centres, and the Hawks won the series in six.

I suffered what was diagnosed as a "mild concussion" in the Evans incident, but no concussion, mild or otherwise, ever stayed with someone longer than this one did. All that summer and during September's training camp, I continued to feel its effects. Convinced that my skull had been fractured, I underwent several more examinations, but everything looked fine. It didn't feel fine, however. My game was off, well into the following season.

Two other injuries which seriously affected my play also were sustained while we were facing the Black Hawks. On December 17, 1966, we tied them 4–4 in a game at the Forum. Yvan Cournoyer, Bobby Rousseau, and I were pressing deep in the Chicago zone. I came over the blueline with the puck and moved toward Glenn Hall in the Chicago net, as defencemen Doug Jarrett and Ed Van Impe waited to check me. Just as Jarrett was moving toward me, I suddenly felt an excruciating pain. Stan Mikita was checking me from behind, and his stick had moved up my arm and clipped me right on the eye.

This was my introduction to the "banana blade," the almost absurdly curved stick favoured by both Mikita and Bobby Hull. While the blade may have terrorized goaltenders, it also was capable of inflicting grievous harm on other players, and was later outlawed. If Mikita's blade had been straight, it might have clipped my eyebrow or caught me beneath the eye. Instead, its sharp curve allowed it to get past the orbital bone that encircles and protects the eye socket, and nick me directly on the eyeball. A year earlier, the Detroit defenceman Doug Barkley had a promising career snuffed out due to the loss of an eye, as had Claude Ruel in junior. These thoughts were not far from my mind as I writhed on the Forum ice. The pain eased, and my eye mended, but it cost me seventeen games.

The press seized upon this as proof yet again that I'd become accident-prone. According to media wisdom, I grew "brittle" in the early 1960s. I was "often injured" and "never quite able to turn in a full season." But this simply wasn't true. Admittedly, my injuries tended to get a lot more attention than other players', but the numbers speak for themselves. In 1960-61, I missed a single game due to injury. The next season, by contrast, wasn't so hot: I sat out twenty-seven games. In 1962-63 and 1963-64, I missed a grand total of three games. I was absent for twelve games in 1964-65, but only three in 1965-66. I lost, as mentioned, seventeen games in 1966-67 because of the eye injury, and eleven games in

1967–68 through thumb and chest injuries. In 1968–69, I missed one game, in 1969–70, seven. In my final year, playing as a brittle basket case, I somehow managed to make an appearance in all seventy regular-season games.

In other words, in four of my eleven seasons from 1960–61 to 1970–71, I sat out ten games or more. In six of eleven, I missed three games or fewer. My absenteeism rate was, in fact, about average, at slightly less than ten per cent.

None of which seemed to matter. By 1962–63, my relationship with the media had taken a puzzling turn. Not only were the "Will He Retire?" stories rearing their heads each time I turned around, I was continually being analyzed by the press pundits, who didn't like what they saw, or made up what they wanted to. My mental stability was called into question. Was I strong enough to handle all this adversity? There were two basic themes to this. One was: Jean Béliveau is profoundly wounded by the accusations that he no longer contributes, or cannot play up to his standards of the 1950s. The other: Jean Béliveau has always been a "gentle giant" and, like most gentle people, has never had a strong psyche or well-developed fighting instincts.

These instant analyses were folded up, tucked under countless arms, and carried into the Forum. On some nights in 1962–63, I heard the heretofore unfamiliar sound of boos and catcalls directed at me, which, in turn, set off another round of "Béliveau the Wounded Giant" stories, with attackers and defenders filling up yards of newsprint.

Perhaps I can show you what I mean by quoting a number of headlines that appeared in newspapers and pictorial magazines. Most date from 1962, when we were struggling to find ourselves as a team; the last few come from 1966, around the time of my eye injury.

• "If I score 30 goals during the season, I think the fans should be pleased with my performance"

- "Could Béliveau abandon the Canadiens in the middle of winter?"
- "A hot rumour circulating that Béliveau is suffering from a serious illness"
- "Béliveau responds to the boos: 'We are not bums!'"
- "Even during practice, Béliveau is hitting the posts"
- "Will Béliveau ever receive the homage he merits?"
- "Béliveau has become a completely different man!"
- "Jean Béliveau is not dying: Father Aquin confirms it"
- "Jean Béliveau: the best was never enough"
- "At 35 years of age, is it time for Jean Béliveau to retire?"
- "Jean Béliveau is mortally worried: should he retire?"

I could go on, but you get the picture – a miserable slump that never seemed to end. I felt at times as if I were reliving my Quebec City days, but with the circumstances reversed. Then, the media couldn't wait for me to come to Montreal. Now, it seemed, they couldn't wait to show me the door.

Fans, of course, can be as fickle as the media. I remember one night, Terry Harper, a defenceman whom I'll talk about later, took the puck from behind our net. He hadn't been playing too well, so he was booed. Then he crossed the opposition blueline, got behind the net, and just as he was hammered by two defenders, passed the puck to a free John Ferguson, who scored. The crowd wasn't booing any more.

Truthfully, I wasn't booed for eighteen solid years, not really booed. There were isolated incidents, of course. The booing always came from a small proportion of the crowd. One guy was after me all the time. He must have weighed three hundred pounds. One time I said to him, "How can you boo me? You can't even bend down to tie your shoes." Fan reaction is always blown out of proportion. The press hears four or five guys boo and it's a headline.

The headlines are to be expected, of course. There's always been tough competition among the Montreal media. If anything, it's even more intense today, and it has contributed to the loss of two Canadiens coaches in the past decade – Jacques Lemaire and Pat Burns (both of whom, as I write these words, are leading their teams into their respective conference finals). Journalists have a job to do, which is to sell newspapers and magazines, or to ensure that people listen to radio and watch television stations. The louder and more sensational the cover story, the more attention it will attract as potential customers walk quickly past the newsstand. That's obvious, but in Montreal, it's sometimes taken to extremes. When I used to see a relatively minor sports story boldly featured on the front page, I asked myself if there weren't more important things happening in the world.

There were two consolations at the time that these headlines appeared. First, I wasn't being singled out. Boom-Boom Geof- frion had troubles of his own, particulary during the 1961-62 season, the season after the one in which he'd scored fifty goals. In 1961-62 he slumped, his goal-getting dropping to only twenty- three, with the inevitable result that everybody said he was fin- ished. Second, a number of journalists, thankfully, took the time to think about what was happening to Boomer and me. Paul Émile Prince, in *La Presse*, for one, raised one or two interesting points: "The marked players, like Béliveau and others, labour con- stantly under pressure ... The fans who recognize their success want to see them do better still ... they are not forgiven a slump, a bad night, a bad period. There are many things that can affect perfor- mance during a game or a series of games, with the main one being an injury. These are the things that the public often doesn't know about, or forgets, but that have to be overcome. Therefore, the role of star is not as easy as is believed."

Besides injuries and media speculation, one other factor disturbed me and my game during the early 1960s. It should have been a happy and positive development, but it soon took on its very own negative spin. This was my selection as team captain, a position that fell vacant when Frank Selke sent Doug Harvey to the New York Rangers in the summer of 1961.

My selection came as a huge surprise to me, because my name wasn't even on the ballot. Strictly speaking, there wasn't a ballot at all. We'd troop into the dressing room, write down the name of the player we wanted to vote for, and the winner was announced when all the slips were counted. But as far as I was concerned, there were only three guys in serious contention: Tom Johnson, Dickie Moore, and Bernie Geoffrion.

I was not at my best the day the vote took place. That fall, we'd trained in Victoria, B.C., and enjoyed unusually luxurious accommodations at the Empress Hotel. Our plan was to barnstorm back across the country, playing exhibition games against Western Hockey League clubs, just to keep our edge. The first of these games took place in Trail, B.C., against the Smoke Eaters, a highly rated team who'd won that year's world amateur championship. I was terribly sick the day of the game, running a high fever and sweating a lot.

Naturally, Toe came to me around five o'clock. "Jean, the people here expect and want to see you. Just make an appearance."

I could hardly stand up to get dressed for the game, and my legs were wobbly in the warmup skate. On the second shift, I tried to go around one of the Trail defencemen, but I was so weak and my legs so rubbery I couldn't get my speed up. He leaned into me, we both fell, and I tore half the ligaments in my knee. The team continued on its cross-country tour, while I returned to Montreal for treatment and to convalesce. I would play only forty-three games with the Canadiens in the '61-62 season – a high price to pay for a token appearance in an exhibition match.

On October 11, the Friday before our season opener, Toe called me to the Forum for the vote on the captaincy. My leg was in a full cast, and one of my friends, a car dealer in Longueuil, had loaned me a four-door car to enable me to sit sideways in the back seat while Élise drove me downtown.

I voted for Dickie Moore that Friday. I loved Boom-Boom like a brother, but I felt that he didn't convey enough seriousness to be captain. As his roomie for eleven years, I knew that he had a serious side, and that he was as tough and as committed a competitor as any of his teammates. Perhaps the others hadn't had the chance to get to know him as well as I did, hadn't seen and heard his concern for the team's well-being. If they had, perhaps he would have won the vote.

Dickie's knees were a consideration to some of us. Every time he put his equipment on we held our collective breath, willing those shaky pins to carry this consummate pro through one more game. Few players believed that Dickie would be around for the long run, which coloured their voting. Similar concerns affected Tommy Johnson's candidacy. He was thirty-three, and, as it turned out, a year or so away from being traded to Boston. I also didn't think Tommy had the temperament for it. He was very quiet and wouldn't have enjoyed a Montreal captain's many public duties.

But who can say why the individual players voted the way they did that day? When the slips of paper were counted, my name led the list. I was stunned by the result. Unfortunately, so was Boom, who took it badly. He never said anything to me directly, but it was no secret that he was deeply disappointed.

Several weeks into the season, I went to Toe Blake and volunteered to give up the "C" I was wearing on my jersey. Toe was aware of Boom's displeasure, and knew that I would be honoured to wear the "A" (for alternate) instead, if it contributed to team unity. As a coach, he wanted all of his superstars happy and productive, so he took me upstairs to meet with Frank Selke.

The boss, however, would have none of it, and spoke sharply to us. "There is no question of doing that. The players voted for

Jean, and to name Geoffrion, I would have to throw out their vote. I will never do that. Mr. Geoffrion will have to learn to accept his teammates' ballot."

As mentioned, there was never an open disagreement between Boom and me. How could there be? With one look, sometimes one word, he'd have me laughing like a fool. Then he'd join in, and everything would be right with the world. But the other teams tuned in to his displeasure and tried to exploit it. Boston coach Milt Schmidt went so far as to make a public offer for Boom: "He'll be captain of the Bruins if Mr. Selke will trade him," he said. For the second time, Frank Selke said, "No question."

There was, of course, a solid statistical reason why Schmidt wanted to get Geoffrion away from Béliveau: we were one–two in the points-per-game average. I led with 1.16, but Boom was right behind me at 1.02, followed by Andy Bathgate at .993, Gordie Howe at .977, and Bobby Hull at .924. Splitting up our dynamic duo would be a terrific boon to the other five NHL teams.

In 1960-61, Bernie had scored fifty goals and we had finished one–two in the league scoring, with Dickie Moore and Henri Richard joining us in the top ten. The following season, both of us fell far back. In fact, Montreal's top four forwards missed a total of sixty-four games in 1961-62 — twenty-seven games for me, sixteen for Henri Richard, thirteen for Dickie, and eight for Boom. It was a measure of the Canadiens' extraordinary strength that we were still the highest-scoring team in the league, and finished first, thirteen points ahead of Toronto, even though the big guns had been in a tailspin. Ralph Backstrom and Claude Provost took up some of the slack, but the year marked the first time since the 1942–43 season that a Montreal forward had failed to make either the First or Second All-Star team, although Jacques Plante and Jean-Guy Talbot were First-Team choices, along with Doug Harvey (who by that time was in a New York Ranger uniform).

None of which did us the least bit of good at playoff time. We got pushed around in the 1961-62 finals, and much the same thing happened all over again in 1962-63, when the Maple Leafs put the icing on the playoff cake by defeating us 5–0 in the fifth game of our semi-final.

By this time, Frank Selke had decided that drastic measures were called for. We'd picked up New York tough guy Lou Fontinato when Harvey moved to the Rangers in the summer of 1961, but lost him on March 9, 1963, in a scary accident at the Forum. Lou tried to throw a check on rookie Ranger forward Vic Hadfield behind our net, but missed, and was off-balance when Hadfield turned to body him head-first into the boards. Lou lay motionless for the longest time, and was finally removed on a stretcher, his head and neck immobilized. He had a crushed cervical vertebra and was paralyzed for quite a while. He eventually made a complete recovery, but he never played in the NHL again.

Lou was replaced by rookie defenceman Jacques Laperrière for the rest of the season. Earlier that year, another newcomer, Terry Harper, had joined the team when Tom Johnson was hurt. These additions were part and parcel of Frank Selke's ongoing makeover, as he continued to ease out the team of the 1950s and put in place the team of the 1960s.

Indeed, the changes on the blueline that began in 1961 all but made our blueline unrecognizable from that of the 1950s. Harvey and Bob Turner exited in 1961, then Fontinato and Tom Johnson went in 1963. J.C. Tremblay was still in place, having joined us in the 1959-60 season. But when the 1963-64 season began, Jean-Guy Talbot was the only defensive holdover from our five-straight Stanley Cup run. In the meantime, we'd also witnessed the departure of Dickie Moore, whose rickety knees had finally defeated the strongest heart in the game.

By the time the 1963-64 season rolled around Frank Selke had assembled a vastly different and far tougher Canadiens team than had previously existed – the toughest in the entire league, as I'll describe in a moment. Still, I would never in a million years have anticipated Selke's most daring step, which some observers at the time felt was akin to curing the disease by killing off the patient. To hasten the club's rejuvenation, Selke decided to trade Jacques Plante and talented centres Don Marshall and Phil Goyette to the New York Rangers for Lorne (Gump) Worsley and solid wingers Dave Balon and Leon Rochefort.

Jacques Plante had been the Canadiens' goalie throughout my first ten seasons, backed up by the able and steady Charlie Hodge. From 1955-56 through 1961-62, he was a First or Second Team All-Star every year but one, and won six of seven Vezina trophies as the league's top netminder.

I rate him and Terry Sawchuk as the best goalies I've ever seen, with Ken Dryden, Glenn Hall, Bernie Parent, and Patrick Roy on the next rung down. (Patrick is a late addition, who has finally convinced me with his excellent play over nine seasons. I have a hard time with Roy and many other goalies today because I am not a great fan of the butterfly style, having always favoured stand-up, angles goalies. I will admit, however, that I am finally coming to realize that few goals today are scored by shots to the upper part of the net, and that perhaps seventy per cent of all shots will be stopped by means of the butterfly technique, especially since referees have a tendency to allow interference and open assaults on goalies in their creases.)

Many things we teach young goalies today are the result of Jacques's innovative spirit. Everyone knows that he was the first goalie to regularly wear a mask in NHL action. Jacques had used a mask in practice, but Toe refused to let him wear it in games until he got hit in the nose by an Andy Bathgate slapshot in New York on November 1, 1959. Andy, a classy player, had one of the hardest and most accurate shots in the league, and he got everything into this one. Streaming blood, Jacques was taken to the Madison Square Garden's clinic where a doctor sewed him up and managed to get the nose back into place. However, when Jacques came back into the room, he told Toe: "I'm ready to go back out there, but I'm wearing the mask."

Toe and Jacques had a stormy relationship in the many years they were together. Both were strong personalities unafraid to speak their minds. That night, something in Jacques's voice must have conveyed a unequivocal message. He went out with the mask on, and, in short order, it never came off. Before long, every goalie had facial protection, thanks to Jacques Plante's good sense. You should have seen the stitches holding his nose in place. They formed a big, ugly C – but this time, it stood for Courage. I couldn't believe he was able to return to the game in that condition, mask or not.

Nobody approached the position of goaltender with as much precision and science as Jacques Plante. His extreme mobility revolutionized the game: he was the first goalie to routinely go behind his net to intercept a pass around the boards. He would rush out to challenge forwards who chased long passes into his zone, or go into the corner to get iced pucks. Other goaltenders attempted to do these things, but they as a rule were clumsy skaters and often had difficulty getting back in place.

Jacques's speed and agility enabled him to develop a deadly poke check; he could hold back deep in his net and then strike like a serpent at a breaking forward – hence his nickname, "Jake the Snake." Add to that a very quick glove hand and fast feet, and you had pretty much the ideal netminder.

Here is just one example of Jacques's uncanny precision. One night we were playing in Chicago, and during the first period, he complained vociferously that the crossbar on his net was at least one-sixteenth of an inch lower than any other net in the league. Naturally, we thought he might simply be crouching differently.

"No," he insisted, "when I take my position in nets, I do it the same way in every rink. I haven't changed, this net has, and it's probably out by a sixteenth of an inch, maybe even an eighth of an inch." The issue was left at that, although Jacques continued to belabour it after the game. The next time we played in Chicago, we asked our trainers to measure the net. It was exactly one-sixteenth of an inch out of alignment.

Like many goalies, Jacques was pretty much a solitary sort, and could be abrasive at times. That doesn't mean that he wasn't a team man. He was, but he had his own way about him.

Jacques received a lot of media attention for his habit of knitting in the dressing room and on trains when we travelled around the league. His needles clicked away, knitting and purling and turning out socks, toques, underwear, and camisoles. There were two theories about why he did it. Perhaps the concentration of manual busywork had a calming effect on his mind, especially before important games. I personally think he did it to economize. A lot of goalies are tight when it comes to money. Ken Dryden used to leave his car way past Greene Avenue in Westmount, just to save a few dollars on parking at the Forum.

Needless to say, some of the jokers on the team were tempted to bug Jacques about his pastime, but I tried to head them off. I knew full well that his temper was nothing to be trifled with. "Leave him alone; it's not our business. If he's happy like that, he'll probably be better off after his hockey career than most of us." Which turned out to be true.

As you might imagine, after the trade to New York, it was a shock for me at first to look back at our net, and not see Jacques Plante standing there. Moving to New York proved to be a shock to him as well. After a year and a half of rubber "therapy" with a fifth-place team, he returned to Quebec, and took a job as a sales representative with a brewery.

Jacques was too young to retire, and soon the temptation to put the pads back on became overwhelming. In 1965, he, Noël Picard, and several other Quebec Aces joined the Junior Canadiens to defeat the touring Soviet national team 2–1 at the Forum. Jacques was so spectacular that the full house gave him a standing ovation that Forum regulars said rivalled those for the Rocket in his heyday. Jacques continued to play in Quebec for a couple of seasons, until the St. Louis Blues came for him in 1968. At first he was reticent, but they dangled a $35,000 contract in front of him and off he went to share the netminding duties with Glenn Hall for two seasons. The two veterans shared the Vezina Trophy in 1969. Later, Jacques moved to Toronto for three seasons, then joined Boston in March 1973 for the Cup playoffs. He still had a few more games in him, though, and surfaced with the Edmonton Oilers of the World Hockey Association (WHA) in 1975. That was his final season. In all, he played 300 games in the NHL and WHA after his original retirement.

In my mind, he will always be Mr. Goalie.

As I intimated earlier, we became the toughest team in the league in 1963-64, which dismayed the opposition. Terry Harper and Jacques Laperrière added size to our defence, aided by the even heavier-duty Ted Harris. Later, big Noël Picard did his part in our 1965 Cup win. In the meantime, Dave Balon, Léon Rochefort, Bryan Watson, Claude Larose, and Jim Roberts added a good solid two-way work ethic up front.

But the club's new toughness was best personified by the most formidable player of the decade, if not the club's history – John Bowie Ferguson. Fergie was the best fighter I've ever seen in the NHL, but he wasn't a brute enforcer. He could beat you, variously, with his fists, his play in the corners, or his scoring ability. He had huge hands, and no one wanted to be on the receiving end when they were clenched into fists. But for us Fergie's greatest contribution was his spirit; he was the consummate team man and probably succeeded in intimidating more of us in the dressing room than he did our opponents on the ice. You would not dare to give less than your best if you wore the same shirt as John Ferguson.

As for his "countless" penalties, let's count them. Fergie never topped 185 minutes in penalties in any of his eight seasons. Over the years, he totalled 1,214. *The NHL Official Guide & Record Book* doesn't even bother to list players who clocked fewer than 1,500 career minutes in their Top Sixty penalty leaders, which includes former Canadiens Chris Nilan, Bryan Watson, Carol Vadnais, Doug Risebrough, and Chris Chelios. I'm not in the upper echelon, either. I only managed 1,029 – less than 200 fewer than Fergie. The point is that Fergie wasn't, and didn't have to be, a non-stop brawler. His hard-earned reputation preceded him, and he could keep the opposition in line without spending all night in the penalty box.

Besides, Fergie wasn't quite so intimidating when we first met at training camp that September. The guy with the big nose wasn't the greatest skater to come out of the AHL, where he had played with the Cleveland Barons. He knew his limitations, and was ill at ease. He came up to me one morning, worry written all over his face. "Jean," he said, "if you only knew how much I want to stay with this team . . ."

"Fergie, I've been watching you. Don't worry . . . just keep on doing what you're doing."

Fergie had been, in essence, a free agent, very rare in those days, and Toronto, New York, Boston, and Montreal had all tried to land his services. The Canadiens won out, and considered themselves lucky, but Fergie didn't seem to understand that we were impressed by his work ethic, and felt that he deserved his place with us. If he laboured as a skater, his more talented teammates would learn to help him along.

Toe put Fergie with Boomer and me right from the start, perhaps remembering how well Bert Olmstead had done with us during my first few years. My regular winger, Gilles Tremblay, moved over with Henri Richard for a while, while Fergie broke in with us. He broke in quickly: twelve seconds into our season opener with the Bruins, he had the unlucky Ted Green in his clutches. That first night, Fergie received two majors for fighting and scored two goals, in a 4–4 tie. It didn't take long for the word to spread up and down the league.

How intimidating was Fergie? In 1968, the brash, new Boston Bruins were full of cockiness and swagger as they prepared to meet us in the playoffs. They had Phil Esposito, Johnny Bucyk, Johnny McKenzie, Wayne Cashman, Ken Hodge, Bobby Orr, Derek Sanderson, and Ted Green. We had Fergie.

Early in the first period, the sparks flew again between Ferguson and Green. Ferguson grabbed Green, got his sweater over his head, and pummelled him for several minutes. The Bruins exited in four straight games.

I'm getting a bit ahead of myself here. Back in 1964, the "new" Canadiens made a strong showing throughout the regular season, and once again finished first, but fell to the Leafs in a seven-game semi-final. I suffered a knee injury after game four, and tried to return for the seventh contest, but we were out. The series is remembered for the brawling that erupted in games one and four, especially Eddie Shack's famous "coco-bonk" head butt that sent Henri Richard off for stitches. You had only to look at Fergie's eyes after the game to know that we wouldn't be repeating that scene very often in the future. You also knew that Shack would be on his best behaviour whenever he saw the *bleu-blanc-rouge*.

In retrospect, we didn't have much of a chance that year – partially because of Punch Imlach's canny late-season acquisition of Andy Bathgate and Don McKenney from the New York Rangers in exchange for Dick Duff, Bob Nevin, and three minor leaguers (including Rod Seiling, who was then playing for the Canadian National Team). This gave the Leafs the edge they needed against us, and they went on to win the Cup.

With the completion of the 1963-64 season, Boom-Boom Geoffrion decided to retire, at age thirty-three, and go to Quebec City to coach the Aces.

Boom's retirement meant that only six regulars remained from teams that had won any or all of our five straight Cups: Henri Richard, Claude Provost, Bill Hicke, Jean-Guy Talbot, Ralph Backstrom, and myself. Three of us were starting centres, so the team was still in good shape up the middle, despite the transition we were going through. I've already mentioned the physical players who made a difference on the team, but we had a group of talented goal scorers as well. Bobby Rousseau, Gilles Tremblay, André Boudrias, and Yvan Cournoyer all made an appearance in 1964, and Serge Savard, Jacques Lemaire, Carol Vadnais, Jude Drouin, and Christian Bordeleau were just around the corner.

Still, Henri, Claude, and Ralph, by virtue of their seniority, were absolutely vital to the 1960s Canadiens. They were there every night, year-in and year-out, leading us to victory after victory, Cup after Cup, and yet remaining low-key about our extraordinary success.

Claude Provost was the typical front-line soldier, a good guy, usually quiet, but capable of laughter, too. NHL play during the 1960s was dominated by Bobby Hull, except when the Hawks came up against the Canadiens, and the reason why we prevailed against them can be summed up in two words: Claude Provost.

Claude's job when we played Chicago was to shadow the Golden Jet, and he carried out that task in an honest way – no hooking, tripping, or slashing behind the play, just clean hockey. He used this speed and close checking to frustrate the great Chicago left-winger, but also found time to contribute to our offence. In 1964–65 he was the First Team All-Star right-winger, ahead of Gordie Howe.

Hull was the first to admit that Claude was the best defensive winger of his day. While others would use questionable means against him, his response was, "They can't check me like Claude Provost."

Ralph Backstrom would have been a big star on any other team in the NHL, especially during his first seven or eight seasons. He had won the Calder Trophy winner as rookie of the year in 1959. As it turned out, he became our third-string centre, playing behind Henri and myself, thereby not getting a lot of time on the power play, and having to take on a more defensive role, even though he had been a high-scoring junior player.

If John Ferguson brought respect to the 1960s Canadiens, Henri Richard provided the character. I had plenty of admiration for Henri from his earliest days, not only for what he did on the ice, but off. When you're the younger brother of a hockey legend, it will take people a while to recognize you for what you are. Maurice had been retired for several years before fans began to notice that Henri was a star in his own right. All through his long career, everywhere we went, the first question anybody ever asked him was, "How's Maurice?" Each time, he was remarkably patient. "Maurice is fine."

He was a very productive hockey player (1,046 points in 1,256 games), and very tough. He was also a great team player, and a great captain after I retired. It is not by chance that Henri Richard holds the all-time record of eleven Stanley Cup wins.

In my first year with the Quebec Aces, my left-winger was Ludger Tremblay, the oldest in a family of eleven children from Montmorency Falls, just outside Quebec City. He had returned from a career in the AHL with the Cleveland Barons to be close to family and roots. Playing with the Aces and working for Anglo-Canadian Paper allowed him to accomplish this. A decade later, a taller version of Ludger Tremblay appeared on my left wing – his kid brother Gilles, fifteen years or so his junior.

Gilles' career with us would last only nine short seasons, abbreviated by an asthmatic condition that robbed the league of one of its most exciting players. Like Ludger, Gilles was blessed with upper-body strength and fantastic speed. He had great natural talent, and was second only to Bobby Hull at his position. Gilles could forecheck and backcheck with the best defensive players in the league. At the same time, when the situation required, he was most dangerous offensively. Toe once was quoted as saying he would not trade Gilles straight up for Frank Mahovlich.

Gilles and I worked a break-in play to perfection. Whenever the slightest opening would arise, I'd throw the puck up the left side and let him take it in full-stride. Once he got a step ahead of a defender, Gilles would leave all but the fastest players in his wake.

While Claude Provost often played Bobby Hull to a standstill, Gilles Tremblay did the same with Gordie Howe. Unfortunately, Gilles was snakebitten. He lost half of one season with a broken leg, and a large chunk of another with a viral infection.

I got more than my share of assists in those days, with Gilles on my left wing, and Yvan Cournoyer, perhaps the only guy in the league who could out-skate him, playing right. I sometimes felt like the Alouettes' Sam Etcheverry, laying out long bombs to Hal Patterson and other fleet receivers. Defensive backs had to lay off them, and defenders had to treat our forwards with respect. If they came up too close, Yvan and Gilles could give them a move and blow by them. If they tried to press me, I could use my size and reach to flip up a pass to the speedsters on either side of me. Even when we played against explosive teams like Chicago and Boston, they had to be wary of our counter-attack.

Terry Harper and Jacques Laperrière quickly established themselves on our defence. Both were tall and lanky; if they stood shoulder to shoulder, you'd swear that their long tentacles could reach out and cover the boards on either side of the ice. Jacques had a booming slapshot, which enabled him to set a scoring record for defencemen in the Ontario Hockey Association Junior A that stood until Bobby Orr came along, whereas Terry's shot couldn't break a pane of glass, as his fourteen goals in ten seasons with us would prove. But the lanky Regina native was a gamer who never stopped working to improve himself and emerged as one of the NHL's premier defencemen.

In Montreal, a lot of fans were displeased by Terry's awkward style, arguing that he could never be a Flying Frenchman or bring honour to the *bleu-blanc-rouge*. Terry has five Stanley Cup rings to prove them wrong, but his decade with us was spent with boos and accusations ringing in his ears. This unfair treatment upset his teammates, and we would occasionally vent our frustration in our comments to the press.

The fans never saw Terry's work ethic, the long hours he and other players, like John Ferguson, put in during and after practice to improve their play. I mentioned earlier that Fergie's skating was a liability at first, but midway through his time with us, he was getting the jump on veteran defenders. In much the same way, Terry practised until he'd become the strongest backward skater in the league.

Teammates weren't Terry's only supporters. Bobby Hull, for one, complained that he "could never get around or by that Harper in Montreal." And in his first-ever televised interview on *Hockey Night in Canada*, Bobby Orr told Ward Cornell that he liked to pattern his play on two NHL blueliners: Tim Horton and Terry Harper.

Terry failed to improve in one respect only, namely pugilism, and earned a reputation as perhaps the worst fighter in the league. He'd never retreat when the going got rough, and only challenged the tough guys, which accounted for his 1–40 record (his sole victory came on points over Toronto's Bob Pulford). We admired his grit. He was a real needler on the ice, and his thin-lipped sneer often would drive opponents to distraction and into the penalty box.

Terry played 1,066 games in nineteen seasons in the league, and earned every penny he was paid. But the most remarkable chapter of his story had been written long before he arrived in the NHL. As a twelve-year-old boy in Saskatchewan, he received severe burns on his legs. For several months, his doctors were convinced he would never walk again. We saw evidence of his fortitude in the dressing room; the livid scars were frightening to look at. They also helped to explain Terry Harper's tremendous force of character.

Jacques Laperrière was a reticent man, who anchored our blue-line for a decade. He won the Norris Trophy as the league's top defenceman in 1966, just prior to the arrival of Orr. Ted Harris was a quiet, physical Manitoban who was a top heavyweight in the league. His battles with Orland Kurtenbach of the Rangers and Leafs were legendary.

Lest I give the impression that I'm simply going down the roster and saying nice things about all my teammates, let me reiterate the point of this chapter: the Montreal Canadiens of 1964-65 to 1970-71 are probably the least-respected dynasty in NHL history, given the five Cups we won in seven seasons.

You've certainly heard about the Wayne Gretzky-Jari Kurri-Mark Messier-Kevin Lowe-Glenn Anderson-Grant Fuhr Oilers who accomplished the same feat in the 1980s. Edmonton was bursting with superstars back then. We had our share, but we were at heart a collection of team players whose dedication to hard work equalled or surpassed that of the 1950s edition. Claude Provost, Gilles Tremblay, John Ferguson, Ted Harris, and Terry Harper were card-carrying members of what Don Cherry calls the Lunchpail Hall of Fame. They always showed up to play, and gave their best. We won, and kept on winning, because Frank Selke and later Sam Pollock knew how to surround us with players who would later be inducted into the NHL Hall of Fame.

And so while the decade had begun on a sombre note, things were definitely sunnier by 1964 – a momentous year for the team which saw Frank Selke retired as general manager, over his objections, and replaced by his protegé Sam Pollock.

One of Sam's first moves was to swap Billy Hicke to the Rangers for veteran winger Dick Duff, a trade that paid off throughout the remainder of the season and into the playoffs. A smallish forward, Dick was deadly around the net, with a heads-up style that nicely complemented his centreman. He could score, or return a pass on a give-and-go that would lead to many wide-open nets. He joined me and Cournoyer, while Fergie moved over to the checking line with Ralph Backstrom. Duff had a move that would drive defenders to distraction. He would come in quick and low, kick the puck into his skates and through the defenceman's, and pick it up again behind the opponent. In effect, he was passing to himself, and it worked much of the time. He'd make that move while driving toward the net or crossing the ice out at the blue line, opening up miles of room for Yvan and myself.

Detroit bumped us out of first place by four points at the end of the 1964-65 season, led by centres Norm Ullman and Alex Delvecchio. However, we'd been held back by injuries, as had the Hawks, whom we considered to be our major opposition. In fact, Stan Mikita, Bobby Hull, Pierre Pilote, and Glenn Hall took the Hawks past the Red Wings in a tense seven-game semi-final, while we downed fourth-place Toronto in six games.

Who would win the final was anybody's guess. Home-ice advantage proved to be the difference. We won our first three home games, and so did the Hawks, forcing a seventh game at the Forum on May 1. Both teams had seen stars come and go: Chicago defencemen Pierre Pilote and Ken Wharram missed the first two games, which we won 3–2 and 2–0, but returned for 3–1 and 5–1 wins in Chicago. Gump Worsley was replaced by Charlie Hodge for the fourth game, and although we lost it, Charlie turned around and blanked the Hawks 6–0 at the Forum in game five, as we scored four power-play goals and a short-handed one by J.C. Tremblay.

We returned to Chicago, eager to end matters, but Glenn Hall was having none of it. Ralph Backstrom gave us the lead early in the second period, but goals by Wharram and Mohns early in the third meant we would go down to a sudden-death seventh contest.

Game six had been a rough affair, with referee Frank Udvari sending Terry Harper and Stan Mikita off together with seventeen minutes each on a minor, major, and misconduct. Sam Pollock made a lot of noise after the game to the effect that the crowd had influenced the official's penalty calls.

We were determined to take game seven out of the referee's hands, and to deal with Glenn Hall in the process. After all, we had shut out the Hawks in the last two games at the Forum. Toe Blake, always looking for an edge, surprised many observers by returning Worsley to the net.

Serious hockey fans realize that home-ice advantage in a seventh game often isn't all it's cracked up to be. When one bounce of the puck can make all the difference, where you're playing doesn't matter that much. Chicago had proved that in the semifinal against Detroit. Both teams had traded home victories down to the seventh and final game, which the Hawks won 4–2 in Detroit. As it turned out, that would be one of only two games won by a visiting team in the 1965 playoffs (our sixth-game triumph in Toronto was the other).

When we took to the ice for the final game against Chicago, the Forum fans were Cup-starved, and showed their desire to end our four-year "drought" with a huge ovation that pumped us from the first drop of the puck. Fourteen seconds into the game, Dick Duff fed me a beautiful pass and we led 1–0. By the end of the first period, we were up 4–0 on additional goals by Duff, Richard, and Cournoyer. That score (our third-straight home shut-out) held up. Shortly after 10 p.m. that night, I hoisted my first Stanley Cup as captain of the Canadiens.

A year later, after beating Toronto, we went into the final against the Detroit Red Wings, and did something we had never done, at least in my memory: we lost the first two games at home. Those games were televised by an American network, and special lighting had been installed for the April 24 opener. We must have been dazzled by the lights, because we slunk out of town and into Detroit, our tails between our legs after 3–2 and 5–3 setbacks.

We normally stayed in downtown Detroit at the Sheraton-Cadillac, but this time, emergency measures were in order. Toe was determined to isolate us from all the usual distractions, so he'd booked us into the peace and tranquility of the suburbs, in Dearborn. Unfortunately, he failed to notice that our hotel was the headquarters for a convention of barbershop quartets. As a result, harmony-heavy renditions of "Sweet Adeline" and "By the Light of the Silvery Moon" could be heard at all hours of the day and night. I remember Toe, running up and down the halls in his pyjamas, trying to get the conventioneers to shut up. "My guys have a big game tomorrow night. Knock it off," he'd yell, until he was drowned out by the next chorus.

I can't recall if Sam Pollock joined Toe on the anti-noise crusade, but Sam was there, all right. A Detroit or Chicago playoff series could represent a bit of a nightmare for him, because these were the two most remote NHL outposts. Sam wouldn't fly, and the trains took too long when games were played every second day. His chauffeur Brian Travers would put in thousands of miles of driving in a three-week period. Sam sat in the back of the car, propped up on pillows, with all his files spread in front of him. We finally convinced him to take the plane home with us after we won the Cup in St. Louis in 1968, and Brian had to drive all the way back from Missouri by himself.

When we arrived in Dearborn, Sam was in a mood for positive reinforcement. He handed me $500 and said: "Jean, find a good restaurant and take the boys out tonight. If you need any more, pay it and I'll reimburse you." Sam was very conscious of the fact that we needed to take some of the pressure off. And it worked. We won the next four consecutive games, three of them in Detroit.

The following spring, we were supposed to win again, and deliver a present to Montreal Mayor Jean Drapeau during Expo

'67 and Canada's centennial year celebrations. However, somebody forgot to tell Terry Sawchuk, Johnny Bower, and the rest of the Over-The-Hill Gang in Toronto. They sent us down in six games, taking the Stanley Cup on May 2.

The 1966-67 season was the last hurrah for the so-called Original Six teams. Our training camp that summer was unbelievable – 110 players from our affiliates all over the hockey globe gathered in Montreal to be classified with a view to the coming expansion. Afterward, they scattered to outposts such as Cleveland, Houston, Quebec City, and points north, south, east, and west.

When the expansion draft took place the following spring, we were allowed to keep only one goalie and eleven skaters. But Sam's foresight paid off. While we provided the six new teams with a large number of quality prospects, we lost no core players ourselves. This allowed us to make it back to two more Cup finals, both against the St. Louis Blues.

As I mentioned earlier, our four-game semi-final sweep of the Bruins in 1967-68 was keyed by Fergie's battles with Ted Green. He won, and so did we, going on to meet and beat the Blues. A year later, Boston posed a more difficult challenge, having finished the season in second place, with 100 points to our 103, and took us to six games in the East Division final.

Fergie had shocked the hockey world in 1968-69 with a twenty-nine goal season, playing alongside Cournoyer and me. Injuries had ravaged the team, and both Rogie Vachon and Gump were having problems in the nets, to such an extent that rookie Tony Esposito ended up starting eleven games. We struggled until February, then turned it on in the homestretch to finish first.

However, the Bruins would not be intimidated. We won the first two games at home in overtime, by identical 3–2 scores, and warily returned to Boston to face a supremely confident team.

Boston was doing all the talking that year. "We won't lose another game in this series," Harry Sinden told the Boston papers.

Two of his young Turks, Derek Sanderson and Bobby Orr, agreed with him. Buoyed by that spirit, the Bruins chewed us up and spit us out 5–0 and 3–2 to even the series. We took game five by another 3–2 score, but it was by the skin of our teeth again. Having gone up 3–0 in the second period, we hung on desperately as the Bruins bombarded Vachon with twenty-six shots.

We returned to Boston for game six on Friday night, with both teams expecting to face a seventh-game showdown in Montreal on Sunday. Phil Esposito set up Ron Murphy at 2:29 of the first and the Garden went crazy. That goal was scored at about quarter past eight o'clock, and very few fans among the capacity crowd expected that they'd still be rivetted to their seats in the small hours of the following morning – but they were.

Early in the third, I won a face-off to Gerry Cheevers' left and drew it back to Serge Savard at the right point. Both lines came together in a milling scrum, and Cheevers never saw the Savard shot that went along the ice and into the far corner to tie the game.

We went into overtime, and survived a scare in the first twenty-minute supplemental period when Fergie took a penalty and the Bruins almost scored. Our coach, Claude Ruel, was nervously chewing gum behind our bench midway through the fifth period, when a move he'd made earlier in the game paid off. During the regular season and much of the playoffs, I had been up against Derek Sanderson, a talented but cocky centre who was very good on the draw. Fergie, Cournoyer, and I had our successes against him, but by game six, Harry Sinden was double-shifting Phil Esposito's line. Claude had reasoned that, unless I played against Esposito head-to-head, our top scoring line would be sitting on the bench for lengthy periods of time.

He moved Claude Provost to the right wing, and I was out with him and Fergie when the game finally was brought to an end early that Saturday morning. We lined up against Esposito, Ken Hodge, and Murphy, just past the eleven-minute mark of the fifth period,

Jean Beliveau

What NHL player in the 1950s would not have loved to have
Boom-Boom Geoffrion on his right and Rocket Richard on his left?

In April 1956 I played on my first Stanley Cup–winning Canadiens team. Here I am savouring the moment with Rocket Richard.

Above: Deking Lorne "Gump" Worsley of the New York Rangers during a game in the mid-1950s. Gump would later be a Vezina Trophy-winning netminder with the Canadiens. (*Jacques Doyon*)
Below: Playing in the ninth All-Star Game against the Detroit Red Wings in October 1955. Glenn Hall was in goal for the Wings. My All-Star teammate is Sid Smith of the Toronto Maple Leafs.

Our Stanley Cup win of 1965 was extra-special for me as I was named the first winner of the Conn Smythe Trophy, awarded to the most valuable player for his team in the playoffs.

With Toe Blake, celebrating our Stanley Cup victory of May 1, 1965, over Chicago.

Above: In December 1968 my daughter Hélène surprised me with a specially made Forum usherette's uniform. (*Gilles Corbeil*/Le Petit Journal) *Below:* Receiving the first cheque for the Jean Béliveau Fund (later Foundation) on March 24, 1971. (*David Bier Photo Inc.*)

Above: Here I am (centre) in the heat of action against the Toronto Maple Leafs, circa November 1955. That's Jacques Plante in goal, and behind him are Bert Olmstead and Rocket Richard. The Leafs are (from left): Brian Cullen, unidentified, Rudy Migay, Tim Horton. (*David Bier Photo Inc.*) *Below:* Hitting the ice in 1966 after being clipped by the "banana blade" of Chicago Black Hawk forward Stan Mikita. Looking on are (from left): Doug Jarrett, Mikita, Pierre Pilote, and Glenn Hall.

In 1963, for the fourth time in his career, Gordie Howe (right) won both the Art Ross and the Hart Trophies. Here I am with the previous season's Ross and Hart winner, Bobby Hull (centre), giving Gordie his awards.

In February 1971 I scored my five hundredth goal, completing a hat-trick against the Minnesota North Stars. Celebrating the occasion later were (from left) my stepmother Mida, my wife Élise, my daughter Hélène, and my father Arthur. (*David Bier Photo Inc.*)

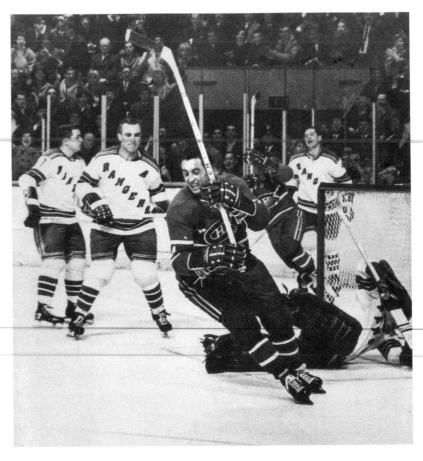

Scoring against New York Rangers goalie Ed Giacomin sometime
in the 1966–67 season. The disgruntled Rangers are (from left):
Rod Gilbert, Harry Howell, and Arnie Brown. (*Aussie Whiting/
The Gazette*)

the ninety-first minute of the game (and believe me, we were counting). I won the draw and we chased the puck into the Bruins' zone. Fergie was in the corner, forcing the defenceman to hurry his clearing pass. Don Awrey, the other defenceman, tried to tame a skittering puck near the blueline, but it bounced free. I saw Provost heading for it and knew that he'd get there first, so I turned and moved toward the net, on the opposite side of Cheevers.

In a flash, the puck was on my stick, and off again, into the top corner of the net. We had won the series, and I had the only over-time playoff goal of my career. Having bested the Bruins, we went on to handily beat the West Division Blues in four straight games.

We failed to make the playoffs the following year, and Boston's fine young team was able at last to win the Cup. I had originally intended to retire after the 1969-70 season, but Sam Pollock asked me to stay for one more. It turned out well for all concerned. A year later we were back, armed with fresh new weapons.

Our playoff success in 1970-71 hinged on the acquisition of Frank Mahovlich from the Detroit Red Wings, as well as the arrival of several talented players from within the Montreal organization: Peter Mahovlich, Guy Lapointe, Pierre Bouchard, and, especially, Ken Dryden. Frank stepped into our style of play without missing a beat. His presence also improved the performance of his talented younger brother – but I'd be lying if I said we went into the playoffs brimming with confidence that April.

Our third-place finish in the East Division meant that we would be up against the first-place Bruins in the opening playoff round, and (once again) not too many observers gave us much of a chance.

As in the playoffs of 1969, our success in 1971 hinged on a tremendous goaltending performance and one key game. Phil Esposito, Johnny Bucyk, Jim Pappin, and Dennis Hull can all attest to Kenny Dryden's powers that year. The six-foot, four-inch McGill law student had come to us from the Montreal Voyageurs with about six games remaining in the regular season, and proved his worth at once. The key game in the quarter-final was the second, in the steamy confines of the Boston Garden, and to this day they still talk about it.

We'd played a strong game to lead off the series but the Bruins were better, beating us 3–1. For some reason, Harry Sinden decided to change goalies in the second game, substituting Eddie Johnston for Gerry Cheevers. Still, it didn't seem that his move would affect the outcome, as the Bruins roared to a seemingly insurmountable 5–1 lead midway through the second period.

Then, with about four minutes remaining in the period, Henri Richard stripped the puck off an embarrassed Bobby Orr and beat Johnston to give us a glimmer of hope at 5–2. Early in the third, I banged in a Fergie rebound. Two shifts later, I got another tally on passes from Fergie and Cournoyer, to make it 5–4. Then Jacques Lemaire stripped the puck off a Bruin to tie the game with half a period to go.

Now we were the ones feeling young and cocky, and the Bruins were feeling their age. At 15:23 of the third, I thanked Fergie for his two assists by slipping him the puck from behind the Boston net. He beat Johnston and we went ahead. Big Frank iced it with an insurance goal three minutes later, and the series returned to Montreal tied 1–1.

The Bruins never recaptured their momentum after that and we went on to win the series in seven. After outlasting a determined Minnesota team in a six-game semi-final, we beat Chicago in seven to win the Cup – my fifth as captain and tenth as a Canadien.

That 3–2 win on May 18, 1971, in Chicago sounded the Last Post for our team of the 1960s. It was time for a new generation to take over, and we all knew it. I clearly remember the plane trip home from O'Hare. I sat with Fergie, sharing a few beers, contemplating the future. The toughest player I'd ever seen had tears in his eyes.

"Jean, I can't do it any more," he said, resignedly. "Reggie

Houle carried me all through these playoffs." (Réjean, another Sam Pollock discovery, could skate like the wind.) "I can't do it; I think I'm going to retire with you."

His heart was heavy, but John Bowie Ferguson could leave with his head high, as could Claude Provost, Ralph Backstrom, Bobby Rousseau, Gilles and J.C. Tremblay, Terry Harper, Jimmy Roberts, Claude Larose, Jacques Laperrière, Gump Worsley, and Rogie Vachon. They were the heroes of the Canadiens' "forgotten decade."

As I spoke with Fergie, my mind drifted back to another conversation that had taken place nine long years before. In 1962, when I felt that my personal fortunes were at their lowest ebb, I went to see Senator Hartland Molson, the Canadiens' owner. I wasn't experiencing a burnout, as they call it nowadays, but I think I might have been headed in that direction. I felt a great deal of pressure to perform on the ice, and I was working very hard outside the game as well. Perhaps too hard. It was difficult for me to gain perspective on this. I was internalizing everything, unable to share my stress with anyone else.

"Senator," I said. "I'm starting to doubt that I'm ever going to play the same way as I did before."

Hartland de Montarville Molson was, and remains, a rock. He has always been there for me in so many different ways. I spoke with him again just the other week, at his offices. He's an amazing man, bright and chipper at age eighty-seven, and still a ferocious hockey fan. It's heartwarming to think that I've had him by my side ever since I arrived in Montreal, forty-one years ago. Each time I was sick or injured, he'd be one of the first persons on the telephone. He's been a friend, a mentor, a second father to me.

Back in 1962, he glanced at my face, and knew that I was in need of comfort and advice. "Jean," he said, "over the course of a long career, there will be ups and downs, especially for someone of your temperament. You take everything so seriously. When you're not performing up to your very high standards, it will get you down.

"Any doubts you are having now will pass with time. You have the talent and the strength of character it takes to come back. The public might not realize it, but you have even higher standards than they do."

I was cheered by his words – and, as you know, I took them to heart. After two years of struggle, my teammates and I went on to win five Cups. In 1964, I was awarded the Hart Trophy (for the league's most valuable player), and followed that, in 1965, with the Conn Smythe Trophy (most valuable player in the playoffs). I did come back – but the pressure never for an instant went away.

From my vantage point today, I can say without fear of contradiction that it made me a better player. I was forced to perform, night after night. I was, for better or worse, a star – and stars, especially those identified as goal scorers, must live with the constant scrutiny of their offensive statistics. I used to think that the fans and the media were more up to date on my statistics than I was. The same holds true for goalies. Their performance, like a goal scorer's, is measured in the simplest terms: goals scored, saves made. It's easy to keep track of – not as complicated as plus-minus statistics for a defensive player. Some people have a hard time with intangibles.

This is where one's temperament comes into play. How will a player react to and deal with the pressure? I've always been too much of a perfectionist. I wanted everything to be first-class all the way. Seventy wins, no losses, would have been fine with me. I was there every night to do my very best.

Pressure is part of any professional athlete's life; it comes with the territory. The expectations of others will force you to improve, to perform at a higher level. In Montreal, winning is not only expected, it's demanded.

The team of the 1960s knew this, and did their part.

7

✦

THE PLAYERS

My career in professional sport spanned the crossroads of the "old game" and the "old league" in the NHL, and the modern game we know today. Later, I'll explain how I feel the game has changed, and who I think was responsible. Now, however, I wish to talk about some of the more important players both old and new.

The game's mathematics were very different in the first part of my career. I played in the six-team league for fourteen of my eighteen seasons; in a twelve-team league for three seasons; and in a fourteen-team league the season I retired from active competition.

Just look at this chart to see what a difference thirty years can make:

	1964	1994
Games	70	84
Playoffs	2	4
Travel	Train	Airplane
Teams	6	26

Nationality	All-Canadian*	Multinational
Bench	Max. 20 players	Min. 24 players
Coaches/team	1	3
Size/player	5' 10", 180 pounds	6' 1", 205 pounds

* Tommy Williams of the Boston Bruins was the NHL's lone American in 1964.

In 1966, we were still six years away from the first Soviet-Canada hockey summit, although international hockey techniques and training systems were starting to make inroads. Canada's "senior teams" had suffered several embarrassing defeats abroad, and the National Team program, spearheaded by Father David Bauer, was born.

Players from European countries and the former USSR, many of whom would eventually graduate to the NHL, played much the same game we did, but prepared for it in ways that seemed totally alien to us. As it turned out, we trained wrong and we ate wrong, and the man to tell us so was Lloyd Percival, the exercise guru, who would later help Soviet coach Anatoli Tarasov devise new and better training programs.

Percival, a founder of the Fitness Institute and the Coaching Association of Canada, launched his strongest attacks the year before the first league expansion took place. The NHL's training methods were archaic and absurd, he charged. The basic drill hadn't evolved in forty years. Players who arrived at the September training camps were subjected to intensive regimens without adequate preparation. That, he said, was why many of them were running on empty by mid-season and became prone to slumps and injuries. (In the days of the six-team league, we had plenty of time to get out of shape. The playoffs were over by April 15, which guaranteed five idle months. In 1993, the Montreal Canadiens won the Stanley Cup on June 9, and reported to camp three months and four days later. Those extra eight weeks make a tremendous difference in a player's conditioning and healing processes.)

Percival, who wrote his first book on hockey in 1951, said that any self-respecting NHL club should more carefully monitor the health of its athletes by submitting them to regular tests, always with a view to the physical and mental limitations of each individual, and that each team should include in its professional entourage a physiologist, a psychologist, and a dietitian.

"Race horses are more humanely treated and trained by horsemen than hockey players are by their team management," he wrote. "In recent years, training techniques have evolved in all major sports around the world. Only the NHL has done nothing to allow its athletes to benefit from the results of [that] research."

Toe Blake took great exception to this, saying that forty-year-old training methods had shown positive results over those forty years. Moreover, players weren't thrown into the cauldron too quickly, he retorted, because they took care to show up for training camp in ninety-five or 100 per cent playing shape, having spent the summer playing golf, tennis, or softball. Toe said that he never forced his players to perform gruelling stops and starts – a Percival criticism – until two weeks into the camp, and that those players with ankle, knee, or groin injuries were excused.

"You will never convince me to have my players running to stay in shape; no more than I could convince Mr. Percival to have his runners skate. The same muscles are not used by athletes in the different sports."

Pretty soon, somebody thought to interview Butch Bouchard. He defended hockey's training methods as reasonably effective, but went on to suggest   something that was, for the time, way out: "Hockey should probably be like football, with a coach for the defence, one for the offence and maybe one more for the goalies."

In the meantime, Hervé Lalonde, a Quebecer who was coaching in Switzerland at the time, Jacques Saint-Jean, the physical education director of a Montreal-area school, and Dr. Guy Charest, professor in biokinetics at the University of Montreal, were agreeing with most of Percival's contentions.

Saint-Jean had observed the Soviet, Czechoslovakian, and Swedish hockey programs first-hand, and reported that, while the Europeans recognized the talents of our players, they were disappointed by our training methods. "In Europe, hockey players play more scientifically. They analyze their play. In Canada, when a team loses, the coach says: 'The puck didn't roll for us tonight,' or 'Our players were a bit off on their shots.' Often, he doesn't even know why his team lost."

This is the only argument I can ever remember Toe Blake losing, even though his point ("we use what works for us") is more or less valid. If you're weak on face-offs, you won't improve by jogging at the Y. It took the Soviet-Canada summit of 1972 to convince us that we didn't know how to run a training camp, especially for all-stars. Fortunately, our system of playing ourselves into shape, as well as our less regimented on-ice strategies, allowed us to overcome the Soviets' machine-like precision, but just barely.

You may recall that Percival startled many in the NHL establishment with his prediction that the Summit Series would not be the high-scoring romp expected by most fans. Since then, however, we've gone on to implement nearly all of Percival's suggestions, including the physiologist, psychologist, and dietitian. Every team dressing room features a state-of-the-art gym with weight machines, exercise bikes, treadmills and measuring devices, and players are monitored at regular intervals throughout the season.

The Canadiens used to hold their team meeting at eleven o'clock on game day morning, but we didn't go on the ice. Toe wanted us up and alert, which meant not keeping late-night hours. That was his primary reason for getting us together. These days, players convene at the rink at ten or eleven for a light skate to get limbered up, although I've seen some teams conduct what appears to be a regular practice – something, I'm sure, of little, if any, value.

What has value, of course, is the new approach to diet. Nobody, but nobody, sits down to a pre-game steak in the afternoon before an 8:00 p.m. start. Today it's all complex carbohydrates (pasta, pasta, and more pasta) and carefully monitored food intake throughout the season. When I first came up in the 1950s, I would eat around three o'clock. When I got a little older, this became two-thirty. When I edged into my thirties, the meal edged back to two o'clock. My body was telling me something, even though I didn't know what it was. Instinctively, however, I was trying to remedy the situation.

By 1976, the Canada Cup team had included jogging in its pre-tournament training regimen, along with calisthenics and off-ice training, nutrition counselling, and close monitoring of each player's oxygen intake and stamina – exactly what Doctor Percival had ordered a decade earlier. Within two years, every NHL team was adopting and adapting "European" training methods, although land training never really caught on, except for the weight machines, treadmills, and exercise bicycles.

In the early 1960s it was all much simpler. We would return from the off-season, be outfitted with white or red Canadiens sweaters, then start to prepare for the coming season with some intra-club scrimmaging. Twenty years later, I'd wander into the dressing room after a regular-season game and see players who'd just come off the ice climbing onto the exercise bikes for a half-hour, before they went to the showers or the whirlpool.

Over the years I noticed a major difference in the treatment of injuries, as well. For example, if we suffered a knee injury in the 1950s and 1960s, immobilization and rest were the orders of the day, mainly because large and heavy casts prevented us from doing much of anything. In the 1980s, a player who emerged from surgery would be up and around as soon as possible, working within a week or ten days with trainer Gaëtan Lefebvre on a recovery regimen that included leg curls and extensions on the exercise machines, lots of bicycling in the training room, and special massage. That player rarely wore a cast, but was fitted instead with a succession of knee braces which allowed progressively greater movement without sacrificing support during his recovery period.

Today's player tends to take this sophisticated medical support for granted. And when you know that the finest medical care and the most advanced rehabilitation programs are available, you may tend to be more reckless on the ice. The players of the 1950s and 1960s feared injuries. We knew there were ten or one hundred players ready to take our places in a six-team league. We knew an injury almost invariably meant a long layoff, often with an extended hospital stay. We knew, too, that our equipment was, by today's standards, flimsy and primitive – a bit of felt, some leather, and plastic shoulder cups – intended only to guard against damage caused by the occasional errant puck or stick. As a result, we tended to show more respect for an opponent, even if he was the dirtiest SOB in the league.

As you know, we also didn't wear helmets and face shields back then, so our sticks were carried at ice-level most of the time. Despite what happened to me on a couple of occasions, we rarely charged opposition players into the boards from behind. Today's player wears as much body armour as an NFL lineman, and opponents armed with aluminum sticks aren't averse to delivering vicious two-handers across the forearm or the leg, figuring that the recipient's equipment will protect him – or, if it doesn't, that he won't see that player or his team for the next several months, whereupon tempers will have cooled.

As for today's season being fourteen games (a full month) longer – twenty per cent longer than in the six-team league – it takes advanced training methods for players to go so long and so hard. In 1959-60, we won our fifth straight Stanley Cup by sweeping the playoffs in eight straight games, for a total of seventy-eight games that season. Our Cup-clinching game took place on April 14. In 1994, the playoffs didn't even begin until April 16. Today, a

Stanley Cup winner will play at least 100 games from start to finish.

The conclusion is inescapable. Because the game has changed so radically, today's players have been forced to change right along with it.

This chapter is all about those players who have impressed me on both sides of hockey's transition period. I'll talk first about the old-game days, and concentrate on the opposition. I think you've heard enough about my teammates, in both Quebec City and Montreal.

It goes without saying that Gordie Howe was the special player of my generation. Witness his twenty-one nominations to the First or Second All-Star Team, at a time when Maurice Richard, Boom-Boom Geoffrion, and Andy Bathgate were his competition on right wing. Because of our size and temperament, especially off the ice, Gordie and I were compared almost as often as he was to Maurice during our playing days.

He was every bit as tough as everybody says but his toughness was exceeded by his hockey smarts. Many observers, however, couldn't get past Gordie's famous elbows and seemed to underestimate his on-ice intelligence. Gordie was a master of positioning, whether or not he was in possession of the puck. Even in his fifties, he was often the most savvy player out there.

I have seen many players who stood taller than Gordie's six foot, one inch, and outweighed his 205 pounds. I don't know if I've ever seen anyone stronger, with the possible exceptions of Bobby Hull and Tim Horton. Gordie didn't have the big, square shoulders of a Kevin Hatcher or a Larry Robinson. His shoulders were thick and rounded, and sloped into a huge chest that was all knotted muscle. He could come up behind you, gently slip his stick under your armpit, and effortlessly lift you right up off the ice. Trying to muscle Gordie off the puck in a corner was akin to wrestling with a telephone pole.

Even today, I'm often asked: "How could Gordie play in the NHL in his fifties?" The answer is easy: incredible strength, high on-ice IQ, and a low-key personality with a streak of meanness when the situation demanded it – the definition, in short, of a formidable player. Don't forget that even in the 1950s Lloyd Percival was predicting a long career for Gordie.

Bobby Hull, on the other hand, was muscle concentrated into fantastic speed, the hardest shot the sport has ever seen, and pure power rooted down into the ice. Asked to compare the Golden Jet with his son Brett, I'd reply that Bobby was a couple of inches shorter, half again as strong, and twice as fast on his feet. He had an even better shot and release. Having started his career as a centre, he was also an expert playmaker, apt to put a beautiful pass on a linemate's stick at the very moment when an opposition winger and two defencemen converged on him. Bobby scored 610 goals and added 560 assists in sixteen NHL seasons, most of them obtained before moving to the WHA at the peak of his talent. I'm convinced that he would have challenged Gordie's 801 goals long before Wayne Gretzky did, had he remained in the NHL.

I remember that goalies like Terry Sawchuk spoke about my shot with some awe in my early years in the league. When Bobby Hull came along, my shot was forgotten.

Bobby was the first player to have multiple fifty-goal seasons (five in all) in an era when only two other players, Rocket Richard and Boom-Boom Geoffrion, had been able to accomplish the feat once. And only once in those five times did it take him more than seventy games to do it.

Bobby's arrival with the Black Hawks somewhat overshadowed the debut of another beautiful hockey player, but not quite. That man was Frank Mahovlich, who played with Toronto and Detroit before moving to the Canadiens as my linemate in 1971. Frank and Toronto had a love-hate relationship. While he was a major contributor to four Stanley Cup victories in his twelve seasons there, Frank and his classic skating were often denigrated by both the fans and Punch Imlach. At six-feet, two inches, and a solid 200 pounds, the Big M was supposed to throw his weight around, flattening opposition forwards against the boards. This wasn't his style, however, yet no one wanted to credit him for his type of game. The knock on him was that he was lazy. As well, Frank had a fragile psyche, which led to a minor burnout in Toronto before he was traded to Detroit.

Once while in Toronto, during a delay before a face-off, I told Frank that his style would fit in beautifully with the Canadiens. Frank never forgot that little compliment. He still mentions it whenever we get together. In fact, he brought it up in January 1971, when he joined our team on the road in Minnesota. We'd sent Mickey Redmond, Guy Charron, and Bill Collins to the Wings in order to get him.

"Jean, you remember that night in Toronto, when you said I would fit in well with the Canadiens?" he asked.

"I said 'fit in beautifully,' Frank, and we'll start proving that tonight." A month later, he set up my 500th NHL goal, and my statement proved true over the years, with Frank contributing to two Stanley Cup wins.

But there's something more to that story. One of his teammates on the Leafs must have reported my original comment to Punch Imlach when he got back to the Toronto bench. When I was going through Mahovlich-like problems of my own with the Montreal fans a couple of years later, Punch was only too happy to inform the world that "Béliveau should be playing for us in Toronto, where he would be much better off."

One September after his team lost an exhibition game to a minor-league team, Punch fumed at the abilities of a couple of what he described as his "so-called superstars." But to no avail; it was always difficult to kick-start NHL stars when the competition was AHL, WHL, or lower. On the other hand, the AHL and WHL players were ready to run through the boards to prove their worth, and sometimes scored upset victories. You couldn't take anything or anybody for granted.

Anyhow, on this September night, Punch was heard to loudly proclaim: "If only I could get the player I really want. Jean Béliveau played for me when I coached the Quebec Aces, and I probably know him better than anyone else does. In my opinion, he would do better with the Toronto Maple Leafs, and I've always hoped that he would finish out his career in a Leafs' uniform."

Punch knew better than to question Toe Blake's handling of me, but he wasn't shy about taking the Canadiens' fans to task. "Montreal fans have never understood Jean Béliveau's style. He's a classic player, and you don't have to be a big expert to know that. Imagine Béliveau, being booed at the Forum. He doesn't deserve such treatment."

This was quintessential Punch. In one swoop, he circumvented the league's tampering rules by couching his comments as a concern for my feelings, antagonized his archrival, Toe Blake, and subtly let me know he didn't appreciate my sweet-talking his star winger – a "classic player" he hadn't stood up for when Frank was having problems with the home-town crowds.

It obviously comes as no surprise that I write about Howe, Hull, and Mahovlich. All three were automatic Hall of Fame inductees when their careers ended. But there are other Hall of Famers who may have slipped the memories of today's fans and deserve homage.

Four of my era's outstanding centres were Stan Mikita, Norm Ullman, Dave Keon, and Alex Delvecchio. I knew them intimately because we played each other fourteen times a year in the course of the six-team league's seventy-game season, and lines were often matched up for an entire season, or several seasons in a row.

It's a mistake to assume that the players of the 1950s and 1960s were somehow lacking because they couldn't sit around analyzing videotape. We didn't *need* video; there were probably no more than seventy-five other guys in the entire league, and we saw them first-hand every other week. When we played Boston in the late-1960s, I knew they'd put Derek Sanderson on me, along with Johnny McKenzie and Don Marcotte. In Chicago in the early 1960s, I faced the Mikita line, and Henri Richard had the Red Hay, Bobby Hull, and Murray Balfour line. In Toronto, I was up against Dave Keon's line most of the time, and in Detroit, Norm Ullman would be out there.

Was the prospect of seeing a limited number of familiar faces boring for players or fans? Certainly not for me. I enjoyed it. When the Bruins played us in Montreal on a Saturday night, and we went at it again in Boston on the Sunday, it seemed like a single, six-period game. This happened almost every weekend. Yes, there were a limited number of players, but they were the finest hundred-odd players in the world. How could that possibly be boring, on the ice or in the stands?

Today, on the other hand, teams might not see each other in an entire calendar year. Let's look at the Montreal-Detroit schedule over the past three seasons:

October 10, 1991	Montreal at Detroit
February 1, 1992	Detroit at Montreal
March 8, 1992	Detroit at Montreal
November 4, 1992	Montreal at Detroit
November 7, 1992	Detroit at Montreal
December 18, 1993	Detroit at Montreal
April 13, 1994	Montreal at Detroit

In calendar year 1993, the Canadiens didn't play a single regular-season game in Detroit. And, when they finally did play that year, in Montreal, it was just two weeks before the start of 1994. To fans in both cities who would like to see Steve Yzerman, Sergei Fedorov, and Dino Ciccarelli take the ice against Patrick

Roy, Kirk Muller, and Vincent Damphousse, it must feel sometimes as if these two clubs are in separate leagues, like the Montreal Expos and the Detroit Tigers.

Let me go back for a second to my customary opposition –
Ullman, Keon, Delvecchio, and Mikita. All four centres are in the
Hall of Fame along with me. Now, let's compare this with hockey
in the 1990s. How often do the fans get to see Wayne Gretzky
face off against a future Hall of Famer? He might play only two
games a year against Buffalo's Pat LaFontaine or Dale Hawerchuk.
In his own division, he's more apt to play five, six, or seven games
of a total eighty-four against Calgary's Joel Otto, a defensive specialist who probably won't make the Hall.

The game is different today in that offensive and defensive
responsibilities are clear-cut and largely separate. In my day Mikita,
Delvecchio, Ullman, and Keon had to both shut down me and
my linemates, and score the occasional goal themselves, while we
attempted to return the favour. Match-ups of this nature are simply
not done today.

How outstanding was my competition at the time? As of the
1993-94 season, Mikita stood as the fifth-highest scorer in NHL history with 1,467 points; Delvecchio was tenth with 1,281; Ullman
was thirteenth with 1,229; and Keon was fortieth with 986. Quite
a few of those goals, I can assure you, were scored against the Montreal Canadiens.

Stan Mikita was the first prominent European-born player to
achieve NHL stardom. He came into the league in 1958-59, and a
year later was teamed up with former Canadien Ab McDonald and
Kenny Wharram on the Scooter Line. Stan started as a chippy player
who wouldn't hesitate to use his stick on an opponent, and he had
the penalty minutes to prove it. In 1966-67, however, he changed
his tune, and won the Art Ross, Hart, and Lady Byng trophies in
that one season. He had excellent vision and was very smooth on
the ice. He and his teammate Bobby Hull were jointly responsible

for the "banana blade," which Bobby used to unload howitzers at cringing goalies. But Stan presented a more varied threat, because he could not only blow the puck past a goalie, he knew how to pick a corner neatly, unleash a beautiful backhand shot, or make an equally beautiful backhand pass to Wharram or McDonald.

Ab McDonald was a good, workmanlike left-winger, while Wharram was a fast right-winger with excellent hands. If an opponent fell asleep for even a second, Mikita (a right-hand shot) would hit Kenny on the tape in full stride, and he'd be on top of the goalie in a blink. A couple of years later, Doug Mohns replaced McDonald, and the second-generation Scooter Line took off.

Dave Keon was a smallish centre, an effortless skater who seemed to be in perpetual motion. Punch Imlach sent him out against me for several years. In 1963 and 1964, he starred in the games in which the Leafs eliminated us in the playoffs. My skating style demanded lots of room, and I always looked for openings for myself and my wingman to make the puck work for us. Keon was the perfect centre to put opposite me because his mobility would take away that open ice. Even when we'd worked our way down the ice for a chance on net, he was quick enough to recover and impede us all over again.

Dave was tough to beat, a centre who could play off the wing himself, but to do that, he needed linemates who could swing him wide passes off the left wing. Another winger/centre like Mike Walton or Bob Pulford could combine with Keon to switch positions on the fly, causing problems for our wingers when we tried to match up against them. Later on, Toronto put Norm Ullman's line against me, and Norm and I would usually take the opening face-off.

Norm didn't have Dave Keon's speed and breakaway potential, but he was an excellent player nonetheless. He was steady and smart, magical when it came to working with his wingers, and difficult to check because he was always on the move, skating in circles, then changing direction and going the other way. He was very skilled at moving the puck from behind the net or out of the corners, and at maintaining possession while he looked to make the play. Experienced wingers like Floyd Smith and Paul Henderson, who played with Norm in Detroit and Toronto, had the speed to find the openings, and often had simple tip-ins after Norm got the puck to one of them behind the defence.

Ullman often would leave me gasping for air. As a result, Toe Blake loved to put Henri Richard against him. If Dave Keon was a perpetual-motion machine who could switch from defence to offence at will, the Pocket Rocket was the prototype. If Ullman wore me out, Henri wore him out, skating with him effortlessly, bumping him off the puck in the corners or in open ice, sticking to him mercilessly, hampering his playmaking ability.

I think you get the point. Punch Imlach would put his future Hall of Famer on me. Then Toe Blake would shuffle lines, and put another of our future Hall of Famers on him. Now throw people like Bob Pulford, Ron Ellis, Red Kelly, and George Armstrong into the mix, add Boom-Boom Geoffrion, Dickie Moore, Yvan Cournoyer, and the Richards (Hall of Famers all), and you'll begin to appreciate the level of competition. I haven't even mentioned the Toronto defencemen – Tim Horton, Allan Stanley, and Marcel Pronovost – or our Tom Johnson, Doug Harvey, Jacques Laperrière, and Serge Savard (again, Hall of Famers all). And then, if we'd managed to survive thus far, we'd have to stare down a whole raft of Hall of Fame goaltenders, like Terry Sawchuk and Johnny Bower (together in Toronto in the mid-sixties), Glenn Hall in Chicago, Gerry Cheevers in Boston, and Gump Worsley and Eddie Giacomin in New York.

Johnny Bower was the hardest goalie to deke in the entire league. He would simply refuse to go for a move. As a result, he was difficult to score against on a breakaway. He positioned himself in such a way that he drew you toward him almost as if you were moving down a funnel. I remember sending John Ferguson in on him several times. Fergie didn't have the greatest moves in close, so quite often he'd just keep on going, and run right over Bower. Allan Stanley, Carl Brewer, Kent Douglas, and Tim Horton would come steaming to their goaltender's rescue, but Johnny would get up, shake himself off, and mumble, "It's part of the game, guys." They were happy to hear that, because nobody was anxious to "correct" John Ferguson's behaviour.

Terry Sawchuk was different. He was an angles goalie who wanted you to shoot. But, if you preferred to put a move on him, he was happy to oblige. Both he and Bower were pushing forty in 1967, when we lined up against the Leafs in the league final, and both came up with great performances. Sawchuk was amazing, especially during a 3–0 shutout in the second game, April 22, in Montreal, after we had taken the series lead with a 6–2 win in the opener. Later in the series, I walked in on him in Toronto, and how he caught that puck I'll never know.

When I started out, most opposition centres were much smaller than I was, and that remained the case until the second half of my career. George Armstrong and Alex Delvecchio had good size, as did Eddie Litzenberger, but the rest were built like Ullman, Mikita, Keon, and Henri Richard – maybe five feet, nine inches tall, and between 170 and 180 pounds. Then along came Phil Esposito, Garry Unger, Walt Tkaczuk, Red Berenson, Ivan Boldirev, Peter Mahovlich, and Darryl Sittler, who raised the height and weight ante to record levels.

I don't like to hear myself saying, 'In our time, we did it this way' – the implication being that it was better. Perhaps you feel it was better, but you can't always use what's gone before as your basic reference point. Not surprisingly, I hope my future life won't be a constant revisiting, or reworking, of the past. Today's players are as different as the game they play – but I've always maintained that our best would hold their own now, and that their best would have done well in the six-team league. Of course, as a former centre, I cannot help but be impressed by Wayne Gretzky and Mario Lemieux, two very talented but very different players.

The first thing I noted about Gretzky was that he had adapted his game and size to the kind of hockey being played today. If he'd played in our time, he would have been checked very closely – and probably by someone more talented than he'll find today. He would have been relieved to see less stickwork in the six-team league, but you can check a player like Gretzky in other ways. I don't think he would have had 200-point seasons in our day. Very few of our games were lopsided 10–2 blowouts; 3–2 or 3–1 scores were far more common. Still, he'd probably have won the scoring title in our day, especially if he'd played with a solid supporting cast.

The same holds true, by the way, in other sports. I remember watching the Boston Celtics in their NBA prime, and the scores were along the lines of 85–80 or 90–87. Now they're 120–118 or 125–124, and 140-pointers are fairly commonplace. You get so many 10–9, 9–2, or 12–4 games in post-expansion major league baseball because good arms are scarce; the pitching hasn't kept up.

Fans are always asking about Gretzky and Lemieux, and some people want to hear something negative about today's superstars. Mention the Great One, and they're bound to ask, "Is there anything you don't like about him?"

Not really. He makes that beautiful soft pass right on the stick. I used to tell my wingers, "When you see I'm not free, keep skating. I'll push it up ahead of you. Find the opening and we'll make a play." Gretzky makes that play, unlike too many centres who force the play and put the puck into the winger's skates, or make him slow down to take the pass. There's nothing wrong with anticipation; but if you're not good at it, you're going to look silly. I've seen players trying to anticipate and making the wrong move. Gretzky has great vision on the ice, and if someone is going to get open, he'll find him, a lot like Norm Ullman used to do.

What I like most about Gretzky is that he's not selfish. It used to be said that I passed the puck far too much, and I'm willing to bet that Gretzky hears the same thing. But he's a centreman; it's his job to make those passes.

I like what I see of Gretzky away from the rink, as well. We've met on a few occasions at NHL events, but we're not as close as he and Gordie Howe seem to be. He's a gentleman and lives his life responsibly, although he's a bit more flashy than I was. But that's life today and he's in tune with his generation. I have a lot of admiration for his longstanding efforts to sell the game across North America.

Mario has never really done anything in this area, but his courageous battle against back injuries and cancer prove that he's made of stern stuff. Mario Lemieux is probably the player closest to me in style, and I'm delighted that people have compared us, because he's a fantastic talent. I concentrated on taking advantage of my long reach to make plays all over the ice, along the boards and in the corners. I would come down the right side and keep the puck away from my opponent with my reach, and I've seen Mario do the same thing on the opposite side (he's a right-hand shot; I shot left-handed).

Some people have complained that Mario doesn't pass enough, but that's ludicrous. Just ask his wingers Kevin Stevens (fifty-five goals and fifty-six assists in 1992-93) and Rick Tocchet (forty-eight goals and sixty-one assists that same season) if Mario passed enough for their liking, even while missing twenty-four games due to injury.

The Canadiens tried to get hold of Mario in 1984, when he was with Laval National of the Quebec Major Junior Hockey League. The trade of Pierre Larouche to the Hartford Whalers in December 1981 was the first step toward this end. The Whalers were near the bottom of the NHL heap, and the Canadiens gained their first-round pick for the "Lemieux draft," as it was starting to become known. But the Whalers rose in the standings, finishing fifth from the bottom, and the Penguins claimed his services.

Perhaps this was just as well. If Mario had become a Canadien, he would have had to suffer through a year or two of Jean Béliveau comparisons, with Richard–Howe comparisons thrown in for good measure. Moreover, the Montreal fans would have made huge demands on his off-ice time, and he has proved reluctant to do this sort of thing in Pittsburgh.

Besides, Mario has a temper. Late in the 1993–94 season, he was sent to the penalty box by referee Kerry Fraser. After brooding about it for a while, he jumped out of the box and made an aggressive gesture toward the official. He was immediately thrown out of the game, and subsequently fined $500 – a pittance that would lead to charges of favouritism.

I don't think Mario realizes that he dodged the bullet here. He threatened to withdraw his efforts to promote the league – but, as we know, these efforts have been few and far between. Still, he's a supreme talent and a beautiful player to watch, the only player in Wayne Gretzky's class.

There are several other big and powerful centres today who cannot avoid comparison with me. The most obvious is Eric Lindros, whom Maurice Richard once called a "mean" Jean Béliveau. While I always hesitate to differ with Rocket, I don't think our styles are similar at all. Eric looks and plays like a tank. He's not all that smooth when it comes to face-offs and playmaking. He plays a much more physical game than I did, and has had the injuries to prove it. He's got to be careful not to see his career end at an early age with a bad knee, as Bobby Orr's did.

Part of Eric's problem is his supporting cast on the Philadelphia Flyers. I get the impression that he feels he has to overachieve, because the team hasn't made the playoffs since his arrival. And, of course, he wants to justify his salary.

Philadelphia will have to get a few more top talents to play with him to ensure that Eric doesn't feel compelled to force himself the way he does. It's nice to see a centreman making plays, but if there's nobody there to finish them off, a lot of talent goes to waste. There's no doubt that he's an excellent hockey player, but how long will he last?

You've got to respect his decision not to join the Nordiques, and sit out a season before going to the Flyers. He took a calculated risk – and compounded the risk by choosing to play with Team Canada. You also have to respect the talent: even in two injury-shortened seasons, he still managed to score eighty-five goals and total 172 points.

There are plenty more highly skilled centres in the game today, and they are a pleasure to watch. High among them is Ottawa native Steve Yzerman, a very fluid and intelligent player. He's a beautiful skater and a great playmaker, with very quick hands, not only around the net, but for making a play. He lays a good pass out there for his wingers; when there's open ice, he'll find the player who has shed his checker.

I'll be interested to see how Yzerman will develop in Detroit, now that Sergei Fedorov has moved into the top ranks of the league. Fedorov is similar to Yzerman in many ways, but he's even more of a defensive talent, which makes him a very valuable commodity in today's NHL. The Yzerman–Fedorov combination is probably the best one–two centre pairing since Wayne Gretzky and Mark Messier during the Oilers' glory years, and recalls the time when most teams had two or three stars in the middle.

Can the Wings afford to have both of them on their payroll? I saw Fedorov go around a defenceman during a recent telecast. It was a beautiful rush. While many players can make spectacular plays out in the middle of the ice, most can't follow through to score. Fedorov can. He has excellent hands in close, and he should be a superstar in this league for many years to come, as should his former linemates on the Soviet junior team, Pavel Bure and Alexander Mogilny.

A trio of American-born centres regularly show me how much the game has developed south of the border: Chicago's Jeremy Roenick, Buffalo's Pat LaFontaine, and Mike Modano of Minnesota/Dallas. Roenick is a fine, dedicated player. He's not afraid of the traffic. If you get lazy and try to check him with the end of your stick, or if you give him too much open ice, he'll burn you. He skates well and has a very quick release on his shot.

LaFontaine and Modano went in opposite directions in 1993–94. LaFontaine was plagued by injuries, while Modano had the season of his career. Modano is big and strong, a hard worker, and has the good fortune to be coached by Bob Gainey. The fruits of his learning experience are starting to show. Each year he becomes a better and better two-way player, but not at the expense of his offensive game.

I'm sure that when LaFontaine came out of the Quebec junior league, a lot of people wondered if he would succeed in the NHL. Nobody questioned his talent as a junior, but he looked too small to make it with the Sabres. But he's shown an ability to avoid most of the hard bodychecks, move deftly with the puck, and thwart opponents in close with his quickness.

The one player in the NHL who amazes me the most is Doug Gilmour of the Toronto Maple Leafs. He may not be as physically gifted as the others, but he more than makes up for this in heart and brains. If you see him in street clothes, he seems pale and wan. You think he might fall down any second. You'd never figure him for a gamer, but he's always there, putting in lots of time. He also has to be made of rubber. He seems to bounce off people and keep on going.

The Rangers' Mark Messier baffles me. Is he a good team player? Is he well-liked by his teammates? I don't really know, but I get the feeling sometimes that he isn't. He was among the Oilers' leaders during his Edmonton years, especially in 1990, when they won the Cup after Gretzky had been traded to Los Angeles. He's very strong, a powerful skater, a physical presence on the ice in the manner of Eric Lindros, especially when riled. When he's on his game, he's a beautiful player to watch. Unfortunately, he see-saws. He has really good games, and really bad ones.

Joe Sakic is the quiet superstar of the Nordiques. He doesn't have a flashy style, but plays the same solid game every night. If you bring somebody to a hockey game for the first time, and he doesn't know any of the players, he'll notice a Bobby Orr right away, but Sakic might take him a while to catch on to. He's been a very effective player since his arrival in 1988, although lately I've noticed that he looks less enthusiastic than he used to.

Was it a mistake to make him captain? It depends on how he does his job. Does he enjoy all the responsibilities? He doesn't speak French, which must make things difficult. Moreover, I don't think it's in his nature to be a captain. At the same time, you can't deny he's a very effective player, and he proved it with the Canadian team that won the World Championship in April 1994.

Another player I should mention, especially because of the various roles he has adopted in recent years, is Ron Francis of Pittsburgh. When he played with Hartford between 1982 and 1991, he was that team's offensive star. Some observers, in fact, argued that he cared mostly for his statistics but when he moved to Pittsburgh, he showed his true character. He took on a defensive role, behind Mario Lemieux, and became an important member of a team that won two Stanley Cups.

I remember when the Penguins were trying to avoid elimination by the Islanders in the seventh game of the 1993 playoffs. Francis kept rallying the team, tying the game in the final moments of regulation time, before the Isles prevailed in overtime. He seemed to take that loss harder than any of his teammates. You need players like that to win championships. He gets his share of goals, but he's more important than that to the overall effort.

Boston's Adam Oates doesn't seem to be as talented as some of the players I've mentioned, but he has produced at a tremendous rate everywhere he's gone (Detroit, St. Louis), and quickly adapts himself to a new team's style. Mention here should also be made of Joe Nieuwendyk of the Flames, Vancouver's Trevor Linden, Pierre Turgeon of the Islanders, Michal Pivonka and Joe Juneau of Washington, and Kirk Muller and Vincent Damphousse in Montreal. Each of them is doing well, just a short step down from superstar status. Another European player who impresses me is Jaromir Jagr – a skilful stickhandler who'd do even better if the game got rid of the stickwork. As for the goalies, what new adjectives can be coined for Patrick Roy, Félix Potvin, Mike Richter, Domenic Hasek, Martin Brodeur, Kirk McLean, Ed Belfour, and Arturs Irbe? I'll talk about today's defencemen later on, when we come to the legacy of Bobby Orr.

French-speaking hockey stars who find themselves playing in Quebec have a particular cross to bear. The expectations of an entire province often go with them, and the pressure exerts itself in unusual ways.

Maurice Richard had been the first real Montreal superstar since Newsy Lalonde, who played in the 1920s. The Rocket wore the mantle well – in part, because of his spectacular performance. He had his critics, but no one could question his greatness over time. Off the ice, his natural humility and blameless family life meant that the media were hard pressed to find a bad word to say.

After Richard, other French stars came and went – J.C. Tremblay, Yvan Cournoyer, Jacques Lemaire, Guy Lapointe, Serge Savard – but none stirred the emotions as did Guy Lafleur, who followed me down the highway from Quebec City. We both discovered that when you garner more than your share of publicity during your junior days, the fans have dramatically heightened expectations right from the start. In my first few seasons, if I scored two goals in a game, I'd hear "He should have had three." When I scored three, this became "He could have had four," and so on. The temptation to bang my head against the dressing-room wall was sometimes overwhelming.

When Guy arrived in 1971, he wanted to wear my number four, just as he had done in junior. I was flattered by this, because I'd worn Maurice Richard's number (nine) in both junior and senior hockey. Rocket, however, still wore his number when I joined the Canadiens, so I had to settle on another one for myself.

I remember warning Guy that the number four might weigh heavily on his shoulders, intensifying the inevitable comparisons. I counselled him to make a fresh start: "Find your own number, and make every boy in Quebec want to wear it." Which he very wisely did.

Other francophone stars who might have stirred Lafleur-like passions – Gilbert Perreault, Denis Savard, Mario Lemieux, and Pierre Turgeon – all fell victim to the vagaries of expansion, and wound up elsewhere. Denis received the most attention because he was the only one of the four who was actually available to Montreal when he graduated from junior. However, the team selected Doug Wickenheiser, and watched as Savard became a superstar with the Chicago Black Hawks.

Ten seasons later, in 1990, when Denis was traded to the Canadiens, he'd lost a step or two, but still had enough entertainment value to keep the Forum crowds enthralled. As well, he was a sympathetic person, well-liked by all his teammates, so even when it appeared that he could not contribute as he used to, the media and the fans accommodated him. Had he started his career with the *bleu-blanc-rouge* in 1980, there is no doubt in my mind that Savard would have been a spectacular addition to the team.

Gilbert Perreault was indeed a superstar in Montreal – but for the Junior Canadiens. He then was drafted by, and spent his entire career with, the Buffalo Sabres. He too would have made an enormous impact, had he been able to stay in Montreal. Pierre Turgeon, for his part, was also drafted by Buffalo, then moved to the Islanders, where he has done extremely well. I've already spoken about Mario, earlier in this chapter.

Three francophone stars of more recent vintage, all of whom had to leave Montreal to further their careers, are Stéphane Richer, Claude Lemieux, and Pierre Larouche. (As this was being written, Claude scored the tying goal, and Stéphane the winner, in double overtime, to lead Jacques Lemaire's New Jersey Devils to a 4–3 victory over the New York Rangers in the opening game of the East Conference Stanley Cup final.)

As Canadiens, however, each of these three players ran afoul of their coach, or of team management. When a coach isn't sure how someone will react in a certain situation, he is not disposed to keep that player on board. Stéphane Richer, for example, could not adjust to the media spotlight, which led to several unfortunate incidents.

Claude Lemieux was an abrasive guy unafraid to shoot from the lip. He became embroiled in a war with coach Pat Burns, but could not garner support among his teammates. I gather that the same problems have arisen in New Jersey. To give Claude his due, he was one of the major architects of the Canadiens' twenty-third Cup victory in 1986, when he helped eliminate Hartford in the seventh game of the semi-final, then scored the only goal in a 1–0 win over Calgary in the fourth and final game. Pierre Larouche experienced difficulties with maturity throughout his hockey career and could not last in Montreal. All three players saw the writing on the wall and eventually requested trades.

Is there anything I don't like about the modern game? My main criticism is the non-stop stickwork – the slashing, the hooking, the cross-checking, the tripping – and the inadequate response of the officials. When I was playing, Bill Friday, John Ashley, Frank Udvari, and the other referees didn't seem to alter their calls to suit the time clock. If you tripped someone in the first minute of play, or late in the third period, or halfway through overtime in a play-off game, it didn't matter: you were going off for two minutes, and that was that. Today, the officials let the players get away with far too much, and it detracts from the game. Using the stick to check is the lazy player's crutch, because it's very easy to do. When an opponent makes a play on you, all you have to do is turn around and hook him. Chances are you won't get penalized anyway.

The only way to check a player properly is to keep skating. If players were coached to remain in motion, the game would get back to good, clean bodychecking, hip-checking and shoulder-checking. It would be so beautiful to watch. You could really appreciate the star talents, who could then accomplish so much more.

But don't misunderstand me – I don't advocate letting stars run free. We certainly weren't free to do what we wanted in the 1950s and 1960s. Maurice and I always had someone on us, but there were ways around this. When I had a checker all over me in the opponent's end, I'd latch on to some other guy, one of their defencemen. If the checker had orders to follow me at any cost, so much the better. I'd be tying up two players instead of one, which left somebody else on our team in the clear.

Interestingly, in my third season with the Canadiens, I decided to use my weight a little more. In fact, I was the team's most penalized player that season, with 143 minutes. But then I also won the 1955-56 Hart Trophy as most valuable player and the Art Ross Trophy as top scorer. Perhaps in previous seasons the opposition was taking advantage. Perhaps I wasn't responding as physically as I should have. It's funny, but until John Ferguson joined us, I was consistently the most penalized player. But really, playing a very physical game wasn't in my temperament. My game was making plays, scoring goals, not thumping the other guy, and in all my days as a professional player I was never directly advised to change my style.

What impresses me most about today's game is the amazing supply of talent that's come on stream. The league has been able to more than quadruple in a single generation, and still find enough young players to make the teams competitive and put people in the seats. The doom-sayers have been proved wrong. The NHL hasn't spread itself too thin. Instead, interest in hockey is growing and its importance rising correspondingly, because the sport remains what it's always been – the most exciting game played on two feet.

When I began to make notes on some of the athletes who had impressed me during my era, as well as those who have played well in today's NHL, I found my thoughts drifting to figures outside the hockey arena. I had the opportunity to meet many other sports figures throughout my career. In the early 1950s, professional wrestling in Montreal and Quebec was almost as popular as it is today, and Whipper Billy Watson, Killer Kowalski, Jean Rougeau, Larry Moquin, and Yvon Robert would perform to capacity crowds. There was, in turn, a crossover between the contact sports of boxing and wrestling, and frequently big-name boxing stars would be brought in as draws to warm up the audiences. I met both Jack Dempsey and Joe Louis when they made guest appearances to promote the Monday wrestling programs at the Tour de Québec.

Later, after I'd moved to Montreal, I got to know Whitey Ford, Billy Martin, Mickey Mantle, and other Yankees stars who would show up at the same sports banquets as me and my teammates. Of course, harking back to the John Nault days in Victoriaville, I favoured the Red Sox and was a great admirer of the incomparable Ted Williams.

For some reason, the Canadiens always seemed to have an affinity for Boston teams. Whenever we could, we would check out

Celtics basketball games on Sunday afternoons at the Garden, before preparing for our contest that same night against the Bruins. If we arrived in Boston during the baseball season, off we'd go to Fenway to take in a game. Once, Ted Williams invited me into the clubhouse, and we spoke privately for twenty minutes or so.

When I came out, the local reporters clustered round me, wanting to know what we'd been talking about. Apparently I'd been more favoured than I knew; Ted never gave them anything more than a couple of sentences. In fact, he and I started off talking about baseball and hockey, then graduated to the Splendid Splinter's great passion, fishing. Williams often travelled into the wilds of Quebec on fly-fishing expeditions. My friend Jacques Côté had a wonderful trout stream, and I knew it was his dream to have Williams join one of our fishing parties.

Several years after I retired as a player, Élise and I were driving to Cape Cod, Massachusetts, through Maine when I read in the paper that the Yankees were in Beantown for their traditional September showdown with the Red Sox. The three-game set would start the following night. I turned to Élise, and announced a change in plan: "Let's go to Boston tomorrow."

The following evening, I took her for a walk around the perimeter of Fenway Park, just to give her a taste of the atmosphere surrounding a big-league stadium. I had no intention of going in. We'd assumed that there were no tickets available for such a classic contest, and were simply killing time before a meal. As we passed by a ticket window, a man called me over. "Jean! What are you doing here?" He knew me by sight, because he also worked at the Boston Garden. "Going to the game?"

"No, just showing my wife the sights."

"Wanna go?"

"Sure."

He returned in a moment with two tickets, which, as Élise and I soon found out, placed us right beside George Steinbrenner, the

Yankees' owner. It was really quite special to sit there, unrecognized, to watch the Yankee stars put on their show, with George in the stands and Reggie Jackson and friends down on the field. Our seats were right behind the Yankees on-deck circle, and we watched Reggie Jackson take his big warm-up swings, as the Boston fans heaped abuse on him all the while. Halfway through the game, he hammered a homer over the fence in right centrefield, about 420 feet away, and he had this little smile on his face as he looked at his tormentors in the stands on the way to his dugout.

In 1971, when I retired, the Expos had a night for me at Jarry Park, and I had my picture taken with Willie Mays, then in the latter stages of his career as a member of the San Francisco Giants.

My best baseball memory, however, dates from earlier that year, and it doesn't have very much to do with a ballpark.

On the night I scored the hat trick that gave me my 500th goal, Élise and I had planned to go out to dinner with my business manager Gerry Patterson and his wife. We got together late that night, because the interviews dragged on and on. I felt bad. I figured there wouldn't be anything special open at that hour, but Gerry reassured me.

"Don't worry, Jean," he said. "We're going somewhere very special, very hard to get into – it's a new place in Westmount Square."

We crossed Atwater and walked half a block west, entered an apartment building, and rode the elevator to one of the higher floors. On an apartment door we saw a big hand-printed sign that read: "Only 500-Goal Scorers Allowed."

Inside, we met a Montreal Expo player with a talent for fine cuisine that serves him well to this day, and feasted into the early morning hours on oysters Rockefeller and Dover sole. Rusty Staub had been at the Forum that night, and had left to prepare the meal the second I'd scored my big goal. Since then, of course, we've often visited his two Manhattan restaurants, both named for their owner. Rusty Staub was a fine ball player and a talented amateur cook, who turned professional (as it were) when he retired. He's a great guy, a hard worker, and I've always taken most of the credit for launching his second career.

Throughout the years, I have continued to meet many stars of many different sports – baseball's Tom Seaver and Pete Rose; pro basketball greats Bill Russell, Bob Cousy, John Havlicek and Wilt Chamberlain, and Hall of Fame jockeys Willie Shoemaker and Eddie Arcaro. I occasionally followed the vibrant local boxing scene in Montreal, and made the acquaintance of Robert Cléroux, Yvon Durelle, Archie Moore, and George Chuvalo, as well as two tough competitors in the lightweight class, Armand Savoie and Dave Castilloux, who recently passed away.

My most exciting crossover into another sport occurred in the late 1960s, when I was filming a commercial for American Motors at the Mont Tremblant race track. Al Unser was featured in the commercial as well. When we broke for lunch, Al invited me to play his game for a couple of laps – using a normal North American compact car.

"Come on, Big Jean, ah'll take you for a little spin," he drawled. Here was this race track, here were these cars (admittedly, not the cars that Al was accustomed to), and here he was with some free time and a new friend to scare the wits out of.

Al Unser took me around that track at about 150 miles an hour. Or so it seemed. I refused to open my eyes to look at the speedometer.

"That's it, Al," I said. "You've just proved that car racing will never be a serious second-career option." That was it for lunch, too. I was afraid to go anywhere near food, my stomach was still circling the track.

Al went on to win four Indy 500s, but, unlike Rusty, I've never taken any of the credit for inspiring him.

8

✦

THE COACHES

In July 1969, I was hired to do a series of television commercials for Purepak containers, and was pleased to learn that one of the commercials would be filmed in Los Angeles. A patch of temporary ice was installed at the Forum (now the Great Western Forum), and filming went on for about a day and a half.

We had just wrapped up when a Purepak executive asked if I would be interested in attending a session of the pre-season training camp of the National Football League L.A. Rams.

We drove south from Los Angeles, to California State College in Fullerton, that afternoon. There I got my first close-up look at a professional footballer's pre-season training regimen. It was an education to me. What struck me most was the sight of 300-pound linemen sweating out a scrimmage in 102-degree-Fahrenheit temperatures, then putting in another hour or two under the hot sun as the defence, offence, and special teams split off to continue work on their particular drills.

I was marvelling at the players' stamina and athleticism when I was spotted by head coach George Allen. We'd met only once before, at a sports dinner, but he greeted me with surprising familiarity. I was even more surprised when he invited me to dinner with the team that evening.

The daily agenda at the Rams training camp was fairly standard throughout the NFL. The players reported at seven in the morning for taping and calisthenics, followed by breakfast, playbook study, and a "mid-morning" workout at nine-thirty. After lunch and a short rest period came more playbook study, followed by a return to the practice field for a scrimmage and other drills at three o'clock. At six, the team would reunite for a meal. Then the various squads retreated to their corners of the meeting hall for a final round of playbook study, broke off at nine, and trooped, exhausted, to bed for lights-out at ten.

In the 1960s hockey players went through their own version of Hell Week in September, but we were spared the hot California sun in mid-summer, the hours and hours of playbook study, and the endless repetition of what seemed to me to be rather basic drills.

I sat at George Allen's table with his coaching staff and we spent an amicable hour discussing professional sports in general, asking questions about football and answering others about hockey.

Toward the end of the meal, George surprised me once again: "Jean, could you say a few words to the players during our team meeting? Just talk about the success you and the Canadiens have had over the years."

At least I had something to talk about. Two months earlier, we had won our second Stanley Cup in a row – our fourth in five years, and my ninth overall. But I doubted that these experiences would be of interest or use to a roomful of tackles and guards. "I wouldn't mind talking to your players," I told him, "but what can I possibly say? I don't think many of them know who I am; they don't know hockey."

"You'd be surprised, Jean. A lot of the players live here in the off-season and go to the Kings' games. Don't worry – they'll have heard of you. Tell them how you and the Canadiens approach each season. We have an older team, a veteran team, and I'm trying to get them to think championship. You're a champion, and I'd really appreciate it if you could communicate that to them."

When he introduced me to his players, George Allen stressed two factors: my age – thirty-seven at the time – and my long career in a demanding sport. "He's a guy who plays a tough game in a tough league, as tough as the one you play in. He's been with his team for sixteen seasons, going on seventeen. Does anybody here hope to do the same? Can anybody name a football team that's won four Super Bowls in five years? Jean Béliveau proves that age is not a negative if you stay in shape."

George Allen gained another fan that day – both for his gracious comments, and for the way he demonstrated that he was always thinking about his sport, about his team. He would take advantage of any opportunity to motivate his players, to give them an edge that would go a long way during the demanding season.

In other words, George Allen was a coach.

For sixteen seasons, between 1952 and 1968, three men held primary responsibility for directing my daily hockey fortunes. All three joined me in the Hall of Fame. Punch Imlach is the only one who was inducted strictly by virtue of his coaching prowess, and appears in the Builders category. Both Dick Irvin and Toe Blake entered the Hall as all-star players in their own right, but I think that each would agree that his contributions behind the bench overshadowed the successes of their individual playing days.

I've already mentioned that the man who started it all was Roland Hébert, my first coach in affiliated hockey, during my initial season with the Victoriaville Tigers of 1948. Roland understood the most basic tenet of coaching at the junior level: the most promising players need lots of ice time. He made sure I got it. Often, he'd put me out there forty minutes a game.

When I arrived in Quebec, Pete Martin of the Citadels provided more of the same, and the pattern of my progress toward the NHL was firmly established. Each year I improved as I was matched up with better and better teammates and faced off against stronger and stronger opposition. My two years with the Citadels were important character-builders. The Quebec City media often complained about Pete Martin's leadership, and the team added former NHL player Kilby Macdonald as a "special adviser," but I can honestly say that I personally had no complaints about Pete's handling of me.

I will admit, however, that George "Punch" Imlach introduced me to a game that was played and coached at an entirely different and considerably higher level.

Punch Imlach played for Frank Selke's Toronto Marlboros in the late 1930s, but moved to Cornwall, Ontario, in 1941, after he and Selke had a blowup over salary. This dispute would continue to colour their dealings through the years.

After playing a season in Cornwall, Punch enlisted in the army, and served three years in a "hockey company" which happened to include such names as Jack Riley, Tommy Ivan, Jimmy Conacher, and Buzz Bastien. Punch obtained the rank of lieutenant, was demobilized, and promptly attended the Detroit Red Wings' training camp. But he had lost ground, and fell short in his attempt to play in the NHL. Fortunately, Punch was a realist; he was in his late twenties, at a time when few players continued past their early thirties. He needed the promise of a secure future, and got it when coach Lex Cook offered him a job with the Quebec Aces. Punch accepted, but held out for an off-ice job as well, with Anglo-Canadian's accounting department. Two years later, he became a playing coach when Cook went off to Dallas.

When I arrived in Quebec City, and began to play with the Citadels, Punch was a fixture behind the Aces' bench and a respected member of the hockey community. Two years later, he would become my coach.

I think the most important point to make to today's hockey fans, especially to the younger generation, is that there was a lot less emphasis on coaching "style," or schools of coaching, back in the 1950s. Very little differentiated Imlach, Irvin, and Blake. All three were veteran hockey men who had played the game. All three had been well-schooled in the basics. The words "strategist," "tactician," and "bench general" were unfamiliar terms.

All three men were successful because they understood the demands and responsibilities of leadership. A coach cannot put his game plan into effect if he's unable to convince his team to play for him. To do so, he must have their respect. To have that, he must have discovered what it takes to earn respect from a group of individuals.

The Quebec Senior Hockey League was a relatively small pond, and Punch Imlach was hockey's best-kept secret in 1957 when he was hired as general manager of the Springfield Indians, a team owned by the legendary Eddie Shore, but operated by Boston. The previous spring, Imlach's Aces had won the Edinburgh Cup, the Canadian minor professional hockey championship. By that time, they'd become literally Imlach's team. When attendance dwindled in the mid-1950s, Punch and two other investors purchased the Aces from Anglo-Canadian, hoping to move them into the American Hockey League. Punch had a twenty-five per cent interest in the Aces, but not enough money to convince the AHL to expand to Quebec City. When Springfield came calling, he accepted the offer on the spot.

When he arrived in Springfield, Punch was dismayed to learn that he was expected to coach the Indians as well as manage them. A season-long feud developed between Shore (who contested every move Punch made, and was on the telephone to Boston demanding his dismissal at regular intervals) and Punch, who took the Indians to the league final, something no one had expected.

Nonetheless, Shore wasted no time ending the agreement with Boston in the off-season, and Imlach was offered a position akin to today's director of player development, heading the Bruins' minor league teams. Then, Toronto's Conn Smythe came calling. When the 1958-59 NHL season began, Punch was Toronto's assistant general manager. The Leafs got off to a dreadful start under Billy Reay's coaching that year, and were in last place with a 5–20 record in late November. It was obvious to Punch and everyone else that the Leafs were not playing for Reay. When Punch convinced the Maple Leafs hierarchy to promote him to general manager, he fired Reay and took over the coaching duties as well.

His first actions as coach were to cancel a team practice, parade his players one by one into a room with him, and secure promises from each that he would follow his lead. Punch put his stamp on the team right away, signing Johnny Bower and trading for the defenceman Allan Stanley and forwards Larry Regan and Gerry Ehman, character players all. On the final night of the season, we beat the Rangers 4–2 at Madison Square Garden while the Leafs overcame the Red Wings 6–4 at the Olympia, to make the playoffs. They went on to eliminate the Bruins in seven semi-final games, before we beat them in five.

Punch was new to the NHL, but he'd spent more than a decade in the minors, and knew exactly what he wanted. His plan for Toronto involved a slightly older, well-balanced team, with good, young forwards up front for speed, supported by experienced guys on defence and a pair of veteran goaltenders – exactly the kind of team that had flourished in the QSHL during the post-war years. For most of his first tenure, from 1958 to 1968-69, the Toronto Maple Leafs looked and played remarkably like the Aces.

Punch insisted on mutual trust, and he gained the trust of his players by treating them as individuals. When I started with the Aces, Punch told me he didn't want to make any major changes in my game, but had me work on little things that would improve my performance.

"After a couple of steps, you have big strides and you can really move," he told me. "But you have to improve your quick starts." After each practice, he'd place me on the red button of the face-off circle, with one of the quicker forwards out on the circle itself. The forward would chase me to and fro, then we'd switch places, and I would chase him for a while. This went on for weeks, until Punch was satisfied that I was quicker off the mark.

A lot of things have been said and written about Punch Imlach, especially about his move to Buffalo in 1970 and his subsequent second mandate with the Leafs. Some of these comments may have left the impression of a man well past his prime, out of touch with the modern game. That's not the Punch Imlach I knew. When the Leafs were going through their rollercoaster ride in the Harold Ballard years, I took the anti-Punch brigade's remarks with several grains of salt.

Punch had a saying: "About ten per cent of players can motivate themselves. The other ninety per cent you drive hard, and some of them might even thank you later on when they realize what you've done for them. A coach's most important job is to motivate his players."

At the time Punch was struggling with the Ballard Leafs, both Dick Irvin and Toe Blake would have been away from coaching for more than a decade. Had they been active in the 1970s, they might have shared Punch's fate, despite the fact that they were Hall of Famers. A profound change had taken place in the player-coach relationship, with players often second-guessing or questioning the coach's most basic decisions. Neither Dick, Toe, or Punch had been raised to tolerate this sort of insubordination. In the "old days" a coach could occasionally act like an army sergeant – "We do things my way. Period." – because there always was a line of hopeful talents in the minors ready to take our places.

Players of my generation were bothered, too, when we saw what was happening. We realized that the youngsters of the 1970s had come from a society that had changed a great deal. By this time, I was part of the Canadiens' management team, and we tried our best to instill team values in young men who had grown up amid a climate of rampant individualism and decreased personal responsibility. Suddenly, it had become a bother for players to wear a jacket-and-tie on game day and to dress well on the road.

Emerging as we did from the Second World War, our generation responded to lines of authority fashioned after the military model. By the late 1970s, however, this approach had little mainstream appeal. Younger players seemed unable to relate to it, and senior management seemed unable, or unwilling, to compromise.

But times always change, and a balance sometimes is restored. In 1993, I was invited to speak to a convention of wholesalers in Montreal. I told them that hockey had taught me many things – among them, determination, pride, teamwork, respect, and discipline – and that I had simply applied these values throughout my playing and post-playing careers. Perhaps that message is coming into vogue again: I received a very nice letter from the convention's sponsors, stating that my short address had been the highlight of the evening.

While Punch Imlach, Dick Irvin, and Toe Blake were all disciplinarians, this didn't mean that they were exactly alike. We didn't have sports psychologists back then, and there weren't two or three assistant coaches stacked up behind every bench. There was just the coach, and twenty-odd sometimes unruly players. Since the coach had to be all things to all of them, Punch's style naturally differed in its particulars from that of Toe and Dick.

Dick Irvin, for example, had an acid tongue. He could sting you long-distance. During my four-year courtship by the Canadiens,

Frank Selke had taken a *laissez-faire* attitude, confident that I would show up when I was good and ready. But Dick was not averse to sending messages across the province. I was in my first season with the Aces when a story came down the wire from Montreal: "'Boom-Boom' Geoffrion Greatest Rookie To Enter NHL, Says Dick."

"That kid is a better player right now than Rocket was in his first season," Irvin was quoted as saying. At the same time, he took care to add that, when I showed up in the NHL, he would put me at centre between Boomer and Dickie Moore.

Irvin was toughest on what he perceived as shirking, or signs of physical weakness. This sometimes led him to confuse an injury with malingering, or to the premature decision that a particular player wasn't suited to the wear and tear of the NHL. And there were injuries aplenty. Maurice Richard, Gordie Howe, and I almost saw our careers end before they started, because of rookie-season injuries. Rocket had seemed particularly snakebitten, ever since he had suffered a severely broken ankle in his first season of senior hockey. The next season, he broke his wrist, and followed that up with another ankle break in his first season with the Canadiens.

"Richard may be too brittle to play in the National Hockey League," said Irvin. This was not what Maurice wanted to hear. Dick was oil to Rocket's flame, and the two of them became a dangerous combination – one of the reasons why, in the wake of the Richard Riot, Frank Selke advised Irvin that he wouldn't be coaching the Canadiens any more.

My first season was curtailed by injury, and the least sympathetic person in this circumstance was Dick Irvin. I cracked my ankle in a road game, but I didn't know it was fractured. Nor did Dick, who considered the whole thing a minor incident. I'll never forget the night we got back to Montreal, and the walk along the platform from the train through Windsor Station. By the time I made it outside, the entire team was gone and everything was locked up tight.

That's how long it had taken me to hobble the two hundred yards or so. The next day, X-rays revealed the crack, and I was in a cast, feeling both bad and relatively lucky: Gordie Howe, after all, had suffered a fractured skull and severe concussion in his freshman year. I always wondered if Dick would have thought he was exaggerating.

Having said all this, let me offer some observations in Dick's defence. Joe Blake, who would become my best coach ever, was his greatest student. Indeed, many older veterans were convinced that Toe was the "second coming" of Dick Irvin.

Irvin and Frank Selke were friends, and when Frank informed Irvin that he would not be coaching the 1955-56 Canadiens, Dick was offered a position in the team's front office. Dick refused, and moved behind the bench in Chicago. A little more than a year later, he died of bone cancer. Nobody knew that he was ill when he was still with Montreal, but he must have been suffering the painful effects of that debilitating disease for most of the two years he was my coach. In short, he was tough, and he expected us to be tough as well.

Toe Blake would be my coach for the next thirteen years, and lead the team to eight Stanley Cups. It's astonishing now to recall that Kenny Reardon had to lay his job on the line to ensure that Toe would be hired in the first place. It helped that Kenny was both Montreal's assistant general manager and the son-in-law of Senator Donat Raymond, the team's owner. With Dick's departure, Raymond and others were leaning toward Billy Reay as a replacement. Frank Selke wanted one of his former Toronto players, Joe Primeau. The newspapers held up veteran Quebec hockey coach Roger Leger as an ideal candidate. In Selke's defence, he had just let go a coach whom he felt could not channel the Rocket's desire to win into positive results. He might have believed that Toe was simply too much like Dick Irvin.

As for Roger Leger, the French-language media had begun to lobby for a greater French-Canadian presence on the team, both in management and on the ice. Dick Irvin was often assailed for his indifference to that need, and for what some saw as a bias in favour of big, tough players from western Canada. Selke was sensitive to these charges, and had done his best to improve the on-ice French-English ratio by pouring time and money into the Quebec minor leagues. And the French players had come – Plante, Geoffrion, St. Laurent, Talbot, Henri Richard, Provost, Goyette, Pronovost, Bonin, and Béliveau.

But when it came to coaching, Ken Reardon, himself a westerner who'd made good with the team, knew that the best candidate by far was Toe Blake. Toe had seen his own playing days end during the 1947-48 season after breaking his leg. Sent to our affiliate in Houston, and coaching on crutches, Toe led his team to the league championship. The following September, the Canadiens assigned him to Buffalo, but he had a run-in with the owner there, and left to coach the Valleyfield Braves in the QSHL. He was successful, and might have been an automatic choice for the Canadiens, except for the fact that he'd antagonized Frank Selke during his years with the Braves.

Eventually, Reardon prevailed, and Toe rejoined a team he'd left six years before. However, only two of his former teammates remained – Rocket and Butch Bouchard. Butch, although still captain, would only play sporadically that year, and on several occasions went to Toe and suggested retirement. Toe wanted him to stay because, like Imlach, he wanted a full quota of veterans on his team. On the last night of our Stanley Cup final against Detroit, a 3–1 win which gave us the championship in five games, Butch was there in uniform to receive the Cup.

As for Toe, the man Frank Selke had been reluctant to hire went on to win five straight Cups. Toe's greatest quality was his knack for getting a team of superstars to work together as a unit. This is perhaps the most important element in a victory. In the spring of 1993, the Canadiens surprised a lot of people by winning their twenty-fourth Cup. Quebec and Pittsburgh, two teams with superior talent, were eliminated in the playoffs. Both had great players but neither squad was playing as a team – the Nordiques because they were unaccustomed to success, the Penguins because they had stopped listening to their coach. You can't win the Cup if your superstars put themselves ahead of the team's well-being.

Toe Blake drilled that lesson into us time and time again. I learned it, and later, as captain, was expected to pass it on – nothing is won by a single effort, especially not the Stanley Cup, which is now decided over four rounds of play. You need a contribution from every player – soldiers and superstars – and Toe treated everyone equally, from the Rocket to the youngest rookie. More importantly, he had us totally convinced that his egalitarian approach was the only one that would work.

Toe believed that hockey was a simple game, and that the most successful teams were those who stuck to the basics. Our pre-game preparations reflected his philosophy. Game plans went on the blackboard, but we seldom needed them. "Hockey is very easy," Toe used to say. "It is played in two V's – one moving out away from our net, and the other moving toward theirs." He would hold his arms up in a V to demonstrate the point.

As a centre, I was expected to do my job in both ends, to key the transition game when we got the puck by joining our defencemen, and putting myself in position to start or support the next play. Toe believed that constant movement of players and the puck was the key to success – you'd give the puck to someone, and then hustle so that he could give it back to you. We were expected to play with our heads up, fully functioning, finding the open ice and our teammates, getting into the flow. Today, wingers camp out "high" along the boards near their own blueline, waiting for a breakout pass from a defenceman down "low" in front of the net or along the back boards. As I mentioned earlier, we didn't do this very often, because it drove Doug Harvey nuts, and he simply refused to pass to us unless we were on the fly.

Nowadays, of course, this style of play is known as the "Russian" or "European" game. When the so-called hockey experts of the 1970s and 1980s kept dumping on the North American game and lauding the Europeans as innovators, I had to laugh. The Montreal Canadiens played that style in the 1950s, with puck control in all three zones. Toe insisted on this. He wouldn't tolerate lazy play or poor basics: "How can you catch a pass? You've been skating with your stick up around your waist. If you want the pass, keep the stick on the ice."

The major difference between the 1950s and today, which I'll talk about when we come to Bobby Orr, is that 1990s defencemen play a much more mobile game. They can pull it off – but when I see them passing the puck in front of their net, I can almost hear Toe yelling, "Away! Get it away!"

We followed Toe's game plan, game in, game out, and no one dreamed of questioning Toe Blake's leadership. That's not to say we didn't have our quirks and idiosyncrasies. Punch, Dick, and Toe knew this, and made allowances for it, but not too many.

For example, Doug Harvey loved to control the play. Sometimes he'd hold onto the puck for what seemed like forever and dare the world to take it away from him. One night in Detroit he was stickhandling happily a bit too close to our net, while Toe fumed behind the bench. The fedora halfway off his head, he announced that "the way Harvey's playing around, he'll get a penalty in the next thirty seconds." Sure enough, Doug kept up his stickhandling display, until somebody poked the puck away and he had to hook the guy. Doug went off for two minutes, and Toe's blood pressure went up into the rafters.

Toe wouldn't stand for anything less than 100 per cent effort that night, or any other night. His hat pushed back on his head, he would pace back and forth behind the bench and talk to the clock – but you knew his comments were directed at you. The only people in the rink who heard what was really going on were those of us on the bench, and maybe the fans in the first two rows of seats, which is just as well. But Toe never reamed us out in public, never went face-to-face with his players the way, say, Quebec coach Pierre Pagé did with Mats Sundin and Martin Rucinsky the night the Canadiens eliminated the Nordiques in the 1993 playoffs.

Toe trusted his players, and we trusted him, because he always treated us like men. He'd go to the wall for players he believed in, even if the fans or the media were on their case – I think particularly of Jimmy Roberts, Claude Provost, André Pronovost, and Terry Harper. Montreal fans have always loved spectacular players, and scorned the "plumbers," but plumbing is nothing to be ashamed of. It takes skilled tradesmen to win Stanley Cups – a lesson some fans and media commentators are hesitant to learn.

A classic illustration of this for the 1990s concerns forward Mike Keane. When Pat Burns was coach, I read many articles questioning Keane's continued presence on the team and Burns's "unreasonable" devotion to him. Then Jacques Demers took over as coach, and made a lot of trades – but the one guy he was determined to keep was Keane.

Keane, like Jimmy Roberts, has more heart than talent, but he's made a huge contribution to the team. Every time a coach sends him – or someone like him – onto the ice, you'll see an honest worker doing his best. Toe knew this. He was an astute judge of talent, who'd never ask more of a player than he could give. But, if someone was mired in a slump, Toe would be the first to back him up, and help him pull out of it as soon as possible.

Our team didn't change much during Toe's first five years. There wasn't any need. We were winning everything in sight. In the early 1960s, however, change seemed to sweep through the team. After the Maple Leafs had manhandled us in both the 1963 and 1964 playoffs, Frank Selke and Toe moved quickly to build a bigger and much stronger team, adding players like Terry Harper, Jacques Laperrière, Ted Harris, Claude Larose, and John Ferguson. We weren't the Flying Frenchmen any more. We were deluxe plumbers, according to many, but we won four Cups in five years, and Toe was there for three of them.

Coaching was a lonely profession in the 1960s. There were no assistants behind the bench with you during games, and the only people you could socialize with to some degree on the road were the training staff and the journalists, who weren't nearly as numerous as they are today. A classic example of the workload Toe carried came during a trip to Chicago. We played home-and-home series back then, which meant that we'd play at the Forum Saturday night, hop on the midnight train, and ride all night and the next day to Chicago, usually arriving about an hour before game time at a suburban station. There we'd climb on a bus, and rush downtown with a police escort. Because our schedules were so tight, the team's assistant equipment manager, Eddie Palchak, would go ahead of us on Saturday morning, taking a second set of equipment with him, so that it would be there waiting when we arrived. The only things we'd bring with us were our skates.

In those days, Toe was both coach and road secretary. He carried our train tickets and meal money and other incidentals in his briefcase. One night it was snowing heavily when we finally arrived in Chicago at 6:35 p.m. The game was scheduled to start at 7:30. Our police escort was waiting – but there wasn't any bus.

Toe came to me: "Jean, I forgot to reserve the bus. What are we going to do?"

"Let's ask the cop to radio and see if there are other cops available with their cars, or if they can call taxis to take us to the Stadium." Of course, with a storm on, it was useless to even try to get a cab. Thankfully, an enterprising constable called for a paddy wagon. As it happened, Sam Pollock had decided to come along with us on the trip. I rode in the police car with three other players, and everybody else – including Sam – piled into the paddy wagon. Away we went, with the lights flashing and the sirens wailing.

In the meantime, they'd announced that the game would be delayed. When we pulled up with a flourish in front of Chicago Stadium, there were a lot of people milling around outside. The doors to the squad car and the paddy wagon opened, and a flood of athletic young men in suits and overcoats emerged, toting skates and looking jet-lagged before anyone knew what that term meant.

One guy yelled out: "Here comes the *famous* Montreal Canadiens organization!" as we trooped into the building. I never found out whether or not those cops received complimentary tickets to the game, but they certainly deserved them.

While Toe was not as acerbic or abrasive as Dick Irvin, he had a temper and was the fiercest behind-the-bench competitor I'd ever seen, which probably led to his leaving the game when he did.

Our five-straight Cup string ended in Chicago in 1961. We had finished seventeen points ahead of the third-place Hawks during the regular season, the one in which Boomer scored his fifty goals, but Boomer was sidelined with a serious knee injury when we faced off March 26 for game three with the series tied at one. The late Danny Gallivan described that game as the best he ever broadcast. The crowd was in shirtsleeves because the night was so incredibly hot, and it got hotter as the evening wore on. The teams were tied 1–1 after the regulation three periods, and we had two goals called back in overtime by referee Dalton McArthur, who had been feuding with Toe throughout the game.

A little more than halfway through the third overtime, Dickie Moore was sent off for tripping and Murray Balfour, who'd started out with the Montreal organization in the late 1950s, scored his second goal of the game in the ensuing power play. Toe, his face redder than the light behind our goal, made a beeline for McArthur and took a punch at him, for which Clarence

Campbell immediately fined him $2,000, a fortune in those days. We bounced back to take the fourth game in Chicago 5–2, but Glenn Hall shut us out 3–0 in both the fifth and sixth games. The league final proceeded without us. With Chicago battling Detroit for the Cup, we were on the outside looking in for the first time in years.

We wouldn't win a Stanley Cup or even appear in the finals for the next three years, but we were competitive each season, and made it back to the Cup in 1965. In the meantime, evidence was mounting that Toe was having a tougher time coping with the pressures of his job. When he'd started out behind the bench, television was not much of a factor in sports. By the mid-1960s, however, we were televised at least twice a week. This prompted even more print coverage, which led to higher expectations and a more critical attitude on the part of fans.

It's nothing compared with the situation today, of course. In May 1994, immediately after the Canadiens had been eliminated by Boston in the seventh game of the divisional quarterfinal, Guy Carbonneau, Patrick Roy, and Vincent Damphousse decided to unwind on the golf course. The morning was cool and wet. They weren't even playing, just taking a stroll to decompress, when they were confronted – some might say ambushed – by an enterprising newspaper photographer. Guy was not in the mood for this, and gave the journalist what we call in French "the finger of honour" – a gesture which was duly enshrined on the front page of the *Journal de Montréal*. Two days later, the furor had died down. In the 1950s and 1960s, it would have continued for weeks.

In any case, the occasional media bashing and fan booing really got to Toe, especially when we brought up the highly touted and very exciting Yvan Cournoyer in 1963-64. Toe relegated the Roadrunner exclusively to power-play duty, and the fans were on his case. One night, we had to grab him during the first intermission because he was on his way into the stands to chastise a non-stop boobird.

On another occasion, Toe ran afoul of a somewhat exalted member of the audience. For years, the first two seats in the second row behind the right-hand end of our bench had belonged to the Canadian National Railway. One was usually occupied by a distinguished gentleman who wore a three-piece suit, and mumbled throughout the game. I never heard precisely what he had to say, but Toe could obviously pick up stuff as he walked up and down behind the bench.

On this particular night, after the siren had signalled the end of the first period, I was walking toward the dressing room when Toe pulled me aside, into the coach's cubicle.

"Jean, who's this guy on the right-hand side of the bench who's always mumbling?"

"Second row, old brown hat, blue suit, and round glasses?"

"That's him."

"That's Donald Gordon. President of the CNR."

I understated the case. Donald Gordon was not simply the president and chairman of the CNR, he was a Canadian business icon. During the Second World War he had served as chairman of the Wartime Prices and Trade Board, and had held several executive management positions with the Bank of Canada before joining the CNR in 1950.

It was his task to modernize the railway, a process which included the integration of more French Canadians into senior management. Queried one time about his rate of progress in this regard, Gordon had flippantly responded that he was "doing his best with what he had to work with," a remark that launched a media storm in Quebec. He was burned in effigy on Dorchester Boulevard in front of the CNR headquarters. Political scientists later identified this incident as one of the first public stirrings of *indépendantiste* sentiment among students of the time.

"Are you sure of that?" asked Toe.

"Yes, I'm sure; I've met him at the Beaver Club, at the Queen Elizabeth Hotel. Why do you want to know?"

"Well, just before we came in here, I told him to go to hell."

Toe looked worried, already playing over in his mind the next day's conversation between Senator Hartland Molson and Donald Gordon, two captains of Canadian industry. Toe's head, as it were, might well be on the platter.

I did my best to set his mind at ease. "Relax, Toe, you probably made his day. He'll be on the phone with his friends all over the country, bragging that the famous Toe Blake told him where to get off."

Toe reached the end of his rope in April 1968. We usually sequestered the team in the Laurentians during the playoffs, and we were camped out that year at La Sapinière in Val David, about an hour's drive from Montreal. We would come downtown for games or a late-morning practice, and at about two o'clock the bus would take us back up north. Toe liked to sit in the last row on the left side, and my usual seat was right in front of his. Just before the bus pulled into the hotel parking lot, he tapped me on the shoulder. "Jean, come and see me in ten minutes," he said.

When I entered his room, I found him pacing back and forth like a caged bear.

"Jean, I don't know what's wrong with me. Something is going to snap here." He clutched his head with both hands, and repeated, "Something's going to snap."

I realized that I was probably the only person he could talk to about this, apart from his wife Betty. Thirteen years of performance pressure must finally have overwhelmed him. We sat and talked for a couple of hours, until he finally calmed down.

For years, Toe had been the man most responsible for our Stanley Cup successes. Outsiders had speculated that the most influential person on the team was named, variously, Plante, Harvey, Richard, Geoffrion, Moore, or Béliveau. The players, however, knew better. Hector "Toe" Blake was the real cornerstone of the Canadiens' dynasty, and we simply followed his lead.

On Saturday, May 11, we defeated the St. Louis Blues to win the Stanley Cup final in four straight games, taking each game by a one-goal margin. It was our last game in the "old" Forum as well, as demolition crews were scheduled to show up Monday morning to begin extensive renovations that would raise the roof, remove the pillars that obstructed sightlines within the building, and deliver a "new" Forum to Montreal hockey fans when it re-opened six months later.

Late that Saturday night, long after the party had ended in the stands, the veteran sports photographer Denis Brodeur waited in the Forum. Something, he knew, was up. His intuition did not go unrewarded, as just before midnight Toe emerged from his office, uncharacteristically hatless, overcoat over his left arm and a large suitcase in his right hand. Denis waited until Toe, walking slowly, head down, reached the exit in the northwest corner of the Forum before clicking the shutter. The next day, this photograph would appear in newspapers all across North America, with the announcement that Toe Blake had resigned as coach of the Montreal Canadiens. We had had two coaches in twenty-eight years.

One month later, Sam Pollock appointed Claude Ruel as Toe's replacement. "Piton," as he was known, was the consummate company man, well liked by everyone, and a superior judge of hockey talent. He had coached at other levels of the Montreal organization, but was best known as an instructor of young talent rather than a take-charge coach.

Claude was positively lost in the huge shadow cast by Toe Blake, although you'd never have known it by his early results. With Claude at the helm, we finished first in the East Division that year, and went on to win the Stanley Cup for the fourth time in five years after a second straight sweep over St. Louis in the final.

Claude's biggest problem was communication. We were a veteran team, and realized that he knew the game – but sometimes he'd go to the blackboard, and it just wouldn't come across. It took a while for us to realize that Claude was hurting, that he understood these shortcomings, and wanted to do something about them.

In the early hours of a January morning, the phone rang at my house. It was Jacques Beauchamp of *Le Journal.* "Jean, are you going to be at the Forum early tomorrow morning?"

He knew very well I would be. Our practice time was ten o'clock, no matter how late a game or a road trip had kept us up the night before. I'd fallen into the habit of arriving even earlier than that, to have a coffee in the cafeteria at around eight-thirty. I reminded Jacques of this, and asked why he was calling me at two-thirty in the morning.

"Because Claude Ruel will hand in his resignation to Sam Pollock this morning, that's why." Piton usually arrived at the Forum only fifteen minutes or so before practice. When I saw him coming through the door shortly before nine o'clock, I knew that Beauchamp was right.

I was upbeat and smiling when I greeted him. "Boy, Claude, you're sure early this morning. What's up?" For a second he looked as if he was debating what to tell me. Claude Ruel has big brown eyes, and when he was down, he could look sadder than a bassett hound.

I immediately became his Father Confessor.

"Jean, I can't take it any more. I want to go back to my scouting. That's where I'm happy," he began.

When he had signed on, Claude was aware that he was in for increased attention from the media, but probably hadn't realized that his appointment was bigger than just a coaching job – at least as far as many people were concerned.

"Claude, you're the first French Canadian to coach this team in I don't know how long. You can't quit. A lot of people are depending on you. Don't worry. I'll get the other senior guys on the team, and we'll support you. Stay with me on this."

To tell the truth, I don't think Claude was sold, but he reluctantly agreed to try it my way. Right after practice I got Henri, Jacques Laperrière, J.C. and Gilles Tremblay, and Claude Provost together, and made them aware of the situation.

"We've got to pull for this guy. We've got to keep him there until spring. Let him resign in the spring. He's the first French Canadian that we've had behind the bench in our lifetime. We can't let him go in the middle of the season." It didn't take a big sales pitch on my part, because everybody loved him.

But Claude detested the social or media aspects of his job. In Los Angeles, when the *Times* asked for an interview with the coach of the Montreal Canadiens, Claude went into a panic.

"Jean, you have to come with me. I can't do this by myself."

"Claude, you're the coach. They want to talk with you. Maybe they don't want to see a player there; they might want to ask you questions about your opinions of certain players." Still, I ended up attending the interview with him.

We saw another sign of Claude's growing anguish one night in Minnesota. There were about three or four minutes to go in a close game, when I returned to the bench after completing a shift. Claude was nowhere to be seen.

Yvan Cournoyer called me over.

"Where's Claude?" I asked.

"Jean, Claude said you're to finish the game for him." Which I did, making line changes both from the bench and on the ice.

The following season, 1969-1970, we failed to make the playoffs – something that hadn't happened since 1947-48, the year Toe Blake broke his leg. Claude took the defeat personally, even though we had finished tied for fourth with the New York Rangers in the East at ninety-two points, seven behind the Bruins and the Hawks, who tied for first. (New York got the nod for playoff action because its goals for/goals against statistics were better than ours. St. Louis won the West Division that year with six fewer points than we had. The West's fourth-place Oakland Seals had thirty-four fewer points than us, but nonetheless made the playoffs.)

Claude tried to resign once more, but Sam Pollock absolved him of all responsibility and convinced him to stay. He also hired Al MacNeil as assistant coach to take some of the pressure off for the 1970-71 season.

Sam also had another sales job to do, and this one involved yours truly. I didn't feel that my contribution had been up to par, and I'd decided to retire. After all, I'd had only 19 goals and 30 assists in 63 games.

Sam, however, wanted me to stay another year. "Jean, the team is changing," he said. "We're in a transition period. Please play one more year. Don't worry about the points. I'm not worried about them. I'll feel more at ease if you're in the room. It's hard to go through a full season without a slump. We have a lot of young-sters, and I want you there to make it easier for them." I didn't know that he'd already spoken with Claude Ruel, and wanted a veteran captain in place in case Claude couldn't last out the upcoming season.

I relented. "Okay, but I'll leave after next season. I'll be forty next year. That's definitely the end." We shook hands on it.

As it turned out, 1970-71 was a season to remember, for many reasons – my 500th goal, the trade for Frank Mahovlich, the late-season call-up of Ken Dryden, our Stanley Cup win, and Claude Ruel's mid-season resignation. When Piton went to Pollock for the last time, Sam Pollock took the merciful way out, and returned him to a lower-profile position elsewhere in the organization.

Al MacNeil took over and did a great job, before he ran into the same media buzzsaw that had nicked Claude. Al led us to third place in our division with ninety-seven points, but that was far behind the Bruins' 121. Still, we managed to upset Esposito, Orr, and company in a seven-game quarter-final, and then held off a tough Minnesota team in six to come up against Chicago in the final. We were aided by young players including Phil Roberto, Marc Tardif, Chuck Lefley, Pete Mahovlich, and Réjean Houle, but the going was rough, and would get rougher still.

I remember John Ferguson exploding in frustration after a game against the hard-fighting North Stars. Fergie stayed in a bad mood for the rest of the playoffs – a mood that wasn't improved when the final's fifth game resulted in a 2–0 loss on Chicago ice, giving the Hawks a 3–2 series lead. Henri Richard warmed the bench for almost the entire sixty minutes, and he was livid when the media gathered in the dressing room. He blew up, calling MacNeil the worst coach he'd ever played for. I was in the shower when I heard the commotion, and emerged to find Henri surrounded by eager journalists and talking in a very loud voice. I immediately dragged him into the showers, and kept him there until the reporters had gone, but the damage had been done.

The media monster's bite was soon forthcoming. Back in Montreal the next day, we picked up the French newspapers and discovered that our team had a language controversy. Nobody felt worse about this sort of coverage than Henri, a man with his share of the famous Richard temper, who hated to lose as much as his elder brother. But Henri could not take a benching in stride. Try as he might, he couldn't defuse the situation, although he won the Stanley Cup for Al MacNeil with two goals in our 3–2 seventh-game victory in Chicago, after we had trailed 2–0.

A native Maritimer, Al MacNeil was "promoted" to coach and general manager of the Halifax Voyageurs the following season, and Scotty Bowman, who had taken the expansion St. Louis Blues to three straight Cup finals, was our new coach.

Even greater changes were to come. Scotty remained behind the bench for eight years, winning five Cups of his own, until he too went his way in 1978. It had been a shock when Toe Blake left ten years earlier, considering that he and Dick Irvin had combined to coach the team for almost three decades. But it was just as shocking in 1978, when Sam Pollock took his leave, appointing Irving Grundman as his successor and ending thirty-two years of Selke-Pollock stewardship in the front office. Still, as was the case when Toe departed, we managed a Stanley Cup win the following season. That was Scotty's last, however, and he joined the Buffalo Sabres as their general manager, a week before the NHL meetings and entry draft.

For some reason, Irving Grundman took his time appointing Scotty's replacement, and for the first time, no coach sat at the Canadiens' table during the annual draft.

That July, I reminded Irving that we were coachless, and that we needed to hire someone soon. He said something about taking care of it. Time went by, and in August we spoke again.

"Irving, you've got to have someone in place, to give him a chance to acclimatize himself to the Canadiens' organization and prepare for the new season." We talked for a while, and Irving finally confessed that he had Bernie Geoffrion in mind.

Boom had retired from the Canadiens in 1964, after struggling for two years with a pair of bad knee injuries and drastically lowered production. Frank Selke asked him what he wanted to do.

"I want to coach the Canadiens," he replied with typical flair. Papa Frank drily reminded him that the position wasn't vacant, thanks to the presence of a certain Hector Blake. Boom's salvation lay in the fact that Floyd Curry (who had been coaching the Quebec Aces, now a Montreal farm club) could not speak French, and it was decided that Boom would replace him. Boom later said publicly that he felt he had been promised a shot at coaching the Canadiens when the opportunity arose. He went to Quebec City, coached the Aces to a pair of first-place finishes, but was fired.

"I came back to Montreal, and David Molson told me that I could have the Junior Canadiens if I wanted, but I wasn't going to take a step backwards. I told him I was going to un-retire, and that I would return to the Forum and beat his ass." And so forth. Boom was busily negotiating a deal to play with the Ballard Leafs, which would have been something to see. But the league intervened, and the last-place Rangers claimed his playing rights. He signed with them – and, in his first game back at the Forum, he scored two goals against us.

Boom later went on to coach the Rangers and the expansion Atlanta Flames, but left both jobs for health reasons. Now, Irving Grundman wanted to bring him back to Montreal as head coach, and right onto the firing line.

At another late summer meeting when the subject came up again, I told him: "Irving, I don't think Boom can do the job, for three reasons. First, I don't think he can follow in Scotty's shoes. Second, in New York and Atlanta, he got ulcers from coaching and had to quit. Third, don't forget that his son Danny is on the team. It's always difficult for a coach to have a son or brother out there; he's got enough to worry about as is. [Danny would play only three seasons in the NHL, retiring from the Winnipeg Jets in 1982.]

"The final decision is yours, Irving, you're the general manager. I've told you my opinion but you'll have to decide for yourself."

On September 4, ten days before the start of training camp, the media convened in the Forum's Mise au Jeu lounge for a press conference. I was sitting with Toe Blake in the back row when Irving entered the room with Boom.

My former roommate wore an Armani suit and dark glasses. His hair was in a perm, a popular style at the time. Toe and I just looked at each other and said nothing.

Boom made his first official statement, and he never should have made it, officially or otherwise.

"Me, pressure?" he said. "I'm used to it; it doesn't bother me." Conscious of his history in New York and Atlanta, he might have thought it was good strategy to pre-empt the obvious question.

About six weeks went by. One November morning before practice, he came to see me. The team was playing like the Keystone Cops; they couldn't seem to do anything right that month. And when the Canadiens are playing like that, you hear about it everywhere you go. You cannot escape a bad performance in Montreal.

"Jean, I can't do it any more. The stress is killing me," he moaned.

"Boom," I said, "it's always bad for a coach to quit in the middle of the year. It depends on what you have in mind for your future. If you quit after a month and a half, you can say goodbye to coaching in this league forever. The organization and I will support you a hundred per cent in whatever you do, but try to go to the end of the year."

Two weeks later he was back.

"That's it, Jean. I'm going to see Irving."

Boom resigned on December 12, 1979 – the hundredth day of his mandate as Montreal coach. It was probably the longest hundred days of his life.

When I was speaking with Boom, I couldn't help remembering a similar conversation I'd had in early 1969 with Claude Ruel, who had finally resigned on December 3, 1970.

Nine years and nine days later, Irving Grundman introduced the Canadiens' new head coach. His name? Claude Ruel.

Since then, the Canadiens have been coached by Bob Berry, Jacques Lemaire, Jean Perron, Pat Burns, and Jacques Demers. Of that group, only Perron and Demers have said they were comfortable with the pressures of coaching in Montreal and dealing with the Montreal media every day.

When I retired in 1971, I did so very publicly – during the NHL meetings in Montreal. I told all of the hockey writers what my plans were – and weren't. "There are two jobs I don't ever want in hockey: coach and general manager." Everyone must have believed me, because I never received a serious offer to coach. Mind you, I wasn't completely inexperienced in the coaching game. In the 1968 season, the team was playing in Boston. Since I had suffered a minor knee problem in New York the night before, I was sitting this game out in the press box.

At intermission, however, one of the trainers waved at me from the bench.

I went downstairs, and Larry Aubut said, "Toe just got kicked out of the game. You're coaching." We were down 1–0 at that point, and the Bruins added another early in the second, before they took a penalty.

I'd always wondered why Toe never put Jacques Lemaire on the point. The rookie had the best slapshot on the team – hard, heavy, and accurate.

"Here's my chance to try out my theory," I thought. I sent him out on the point – and he promptly scored. For the rest of the game, Jacques was on the point for every power play. We finally won 5–2 or 5–3.

After the game, Toe was sitting in his usual seat at the back of the bus. When I got on, all the players spread it on very thick: "Coach, where do you want to sit? Up front, middle, at the back – you name it, Coach." "Can we get you a drink, Coach?" They hammered it up for the longest time, making sure that Toe heard each and every word.

So why would I ever want to coach again?

I'm batting 1.000 – one game, one win – and it's always wise to quit while you're ahead.

9

✦

THE LEGACIES
OF BOBBY ORR

One spring night in 1964, we gathered a collection of hockey veterans in Oshawa, Ontario, to honour two of hockey's finest skaters.

One was the fabulous Jo-Jo Graboski, a legend in senior amateur ranks who had played with the Quebec Aces well before my time. Jo-Jo was venerable even in the early 1950s, but Punch Imlach would ask him on occasion to act as our skating instructor, because he had much to teach. He took me aside one day, and impressed on me the importance of his skill. "Jean," he said, "skating is going to become the major factor in this game. You just mark my words."

Now, after more than a decade had passed, as we swapped some Aces and Imlach yarns before the banquet started, Jo-Jo asked me if I remembered his prophecy.

"Absolutely," I said. "The Canadiens' game has always been built on skating."

Jo-Jo nodded in satisfaction, then nodded again in the direction of another head-table guest – a rather bashful and very youthful all-Canadian kid with close-cropped blond hair.

"Ah," he said, "but that's the guy who will really make my words come true."

I can't for the life of me recall who else attended the banquet, but I'll never forget either Jo-Jo's words, or my first introduction to Robert Gordon Orr. That night, the past and future of brilliant skating had come together on the same dais, and I felt privileged to witness the event.

Time passes quickly in hockey, and memories are short. Therefore, let me say, for the benefit of the Lindros generation, that Bobby Orr was an equal, if not a greater, phenomenon. The stories of his exploits in the junior ranks of the Ontario Hockey League began to circulate when he was just fourteen and competing with players four and five years his senior. Unlike Lindros, however, Orr did not enjoy the advantage of size. He stood about five feet, eight inches, and weighed perhaps 140 pounds – much smaller than the opposition. But he starred in every game he played, and everybody, from stickboys to scouts, believed that he had a one-way ticket to the NHL.

Those of us who'd taken our own one-way ride were impressed, but cautious. We'd heard of prodigies before, and decided to wait and see.

The Boston Bruins stumbled on Orr by accident in 1960, at the Ontario Minor Hockey Association bantam championships in Gananoque, Ontario. He was then two inches shorter and thirty pounds lighter, but had so dominated the peewee ranks in his native city of Parry Sound, Ontario, that he'd been moved up a notch, into the older age category.

Lynn Patrick, the Bruins' general manager, and Wren Blair, then coach and general manager of the Kingston Frontenacs of the Eastern Canada Professional League, attended the bantam playdowns to scout two local defencemen, Rick Eaton and Doug Higgins, who were up against Parry Sound in the first game of the tournament.

Nobody knows what Eaton and Higgins accomplished that day, because the total attention of the Bruins' braintrust was captured by a miniature dynamo who wouldn't let anyone else come near the puck. After a "Who is he?" – "I don't know, I'll find out" exchange with his boss, Blair came back with a name.

Then came the next most important question of that hockey era: "Is he sponsored?" Prior to the arrival of the universal draft, NHL teams had territories and sponsorships, which were literally all over the map. Sometimes they overlapped. For example, when the Montreal Royals faced off against the Regina Pats in the 1949 Memorial Cup final, both teams were affiliated with the Montreal Canadiens. When the Citadels played against the Barrie Flyers two years later, we were up against five or six future Boston Bruins.

At any rate, Blair scurried off to find out the second answer. To his relief, it came back negative. On that day, unbeknownst to the Orr family and the rest of the hockey community, Boston began a low-key though determined campaign to acquire the talented youngster, and to secure his signature on a Junior A card. They started off with some goodwill gestures. Funding was provided for the Parry Sound Minor Hockey Association. Blair's Kingston team "dropped in" to the city for exhibition games. Blair made regular visits to the Orr family home, and established a relationship with Bobby's parents, Doug and Arva.

The secret couldn't, and didn't, last long. A Canadiens scout had attended the bantam championships, and reported back to Frank Selke. While Bobby continued his stellar play the next two seasons, Scotty Bowman was sent to check him out, and both Detroit and Chicago made overtures by telephone. Ironically, it was the Toronto Maple Leafs who paid the least attention to the gold mine in their own back yard.

In August 1962, Blair's persistence bore fruit. He convinced the Orrs to allow their fourteen-year-old son to attend a junior tryout camp, sponsored by the Bruins in Niagara Falls. Despite his agreement, Doug Orr worried about how his son might fare against the bigger boys. Bobby, however, was the revelation of the camp, even though some of the older players had obviously targeted him for special attention. After a summer of anxiety and suspense, the Bruins finally signed him to the coveted Junior A card and assigned him to the Oshawa Generals of the Ontario Hockey League.

In his first year, he scored thirteen goals and earned a spot on the OHL's second All-Star team. A year later, he scored thirty, breaking the record held by Jacques Laperrière, and became sports-headline news all across Canada. Barely sixteen, he also became a story in the United States, where the Bruins were floundering dismally. In 1959-60, they wound up in fifth place, miles out of the play-offs, and followed that with five straight last-place finishes. In 1965 Lynn Patrick was replaced as general manager by Hap Emms, and the pressure was on to sign the youthful saviour as soon as possible.

The Boston organization was convinced that Orr had the talent to make the jump to the NHL, even at age sixteen. The theory was that his talents would be better utilized, and would develop more rapidly, at a level where everyone played his kind of game. He was clearly too good for his minor-league competition, and might start to stagnate or coast along if no one pushed him on to greater heights. It was the same kind of reasoning I had always followed in my career: when possible, move up and play with better players. Once you're the best, you tend to stop growing. There's nowhere else to go.

As an aside to this, let me note that while many players make excellent juniors, some can't make the adjustment to the NHL, where speed, especially in the post-Orr era, is everything. At the same time, I've seen good NHLers who could have been great NHLers. Among the superstars, in fact. But they were lazy. They were content to fall back on their natural ability. If they'd worked, they would have gone so much further – and had so much more satisfaction.

Bobby's parents rightly resisted placing Bobby in the NHL, claiming, astutely, that sixteen was much too young to take on the strongest hockey players in the world, none of whom appeared to be playing for Boston. The Bruins, meanwhile, finished second-last in 1966, prompting their restive fans to look northward to a far-off Canadian city for salvation. In the meantime, Bobby certainly wasn't coasting along in Oshawa. In his final two seasons, he would score seventy-one goals and 119 assists. Although injured, he led the Generals to the Memorial Cup final against Edmonton, where they came close to winning, but finally lost in six games.

Bobby's first legacy to the NHL was a gift to every player – the result of his father's determination, like mine, that his son would have money, respect, and freedom of choice. In the spring of 1966, Hap Emms seemed to do everything he could to alienate the Orrs. He ordered Bobby not to play in the Memorial Cup final against Edmonton because of a groin injury, even though Bobby was determined to appear, and, in fact, did so. Emms also submitted an insultingly low contract offer for his future star.

In Bobby's final season with Oshawa, the media routinely talked about the Bruins' "Million-Dollar" superstar-in-waiting. Thus, when Doug and Bobby met with Emms to first discuss contract, they were flabbergasted by his offer of $8,000 in salary and a $5,000 signing bonus. Emms further antagonized them by pointing out rather loftily that Gilles Marotte, another prospect from Quebec who had been discovered by my friend Roland Mercier, had let the Bruins decide what a fair salary was, and that Bobby should do likewise until he proved himself with the team.

The Orrs walked out, and returned with Alan Eagleson in tow. The Toronto lawyer had begun to make a reputation for himself by representing Maple Leafs such as Carl Brewer, Mike Walton, and Bob Pulford. When Emms discovered that all future negotiations would involve Eagleson, he balked, and most of the summer went by with no further contact.

Eagleson, no stranger to the theory and practice of well-planted publicity, let it be known that he was negotiating with Father David Bauer's Canadian National Team for Orr's services. (This was within the realm of possibility. When Punch Imlach and Carl Brewer became embroiled in yet another contract dispute that same fall, Brewer would leave the Leafs for "amateur" hockey.) When Boston papers picked up on the story, Emms was caught in a tornado of adverse comment, as Eagleson had intended.

On Labour Day weekend in 1966, Emms sailed into Parry Sound harbour, and after an all-night negotiation session chaired by the sea-going Eagleson, Bobby Orr joined the Boston Bruins. He did a little better than he might have had he accepted Emms' original $13,000 offer. Instead, Orr signed a two-year deal for approximately $70,000, bonuses and incentive clauses included. That contract resulted in many league stars getting salary increases in the next two years, myself included. The deal also launched Alan Eagleson – who later that year began to lay the foundation of what would become the NHL Players' Association.

Bobby was all of eighteen years old when he started with Boston, but I can honestly say that I have never seen a player of that age with his maturity and hockey sense. He scored his first career goal in the NHL against us, in his second-ever game. It came on a slapshot from the blueline that raised both everyone's eyebrows and the roof at the Boston Gardens. The game was played on a slow night – a Thursday in early October – but the Gardens erupted in a long and drawn out standing ovation that had Toe Blake saying, "I ain't ever seen anything like it."

Toe was describing the crowd's response, but his words might just as well have applied to Bobby, who went on to win the 1967

Calder Trophy as the league's top rookie that season. Of course, he could not salvage the Bruins single-handed, and they once again finished in the league basement. But the following season was a different story, as Boston finished third in the East. Three years later, we were fighting Boston for our playoff lives. They had, meanwhile, gone out and found Phil Esposito, Ken Hodge, Wayne Cashman, Johnny McKenzie, Dallas Smith, Gerry Cheevers, and Don Awrey to support their superstar defenceman.

Like any player, Bobby had his ups and downs. He was the finest player of his era, but he would suffer mistakes and bad games for the simple reason that the people he made mistakes against were the best, and were capable of capitalizing quickly. All that did was prove that he was human. In his early days, too many opponents, both on the ice and in the stands, were looking for feet of clay. He took too many chances, they said. He got caught up ice. He was weak inside his own zone. He held on to the puck too much. All of these criticisms were trotted out and repeated as Gospel truth.

Watching him play, and playing against him, I knew right away that he was something very special. Also, having experienced the same big-build-up, big-criticism rollercoaster in my early years in the league, I knew what he was going through, and sympathized.

I said earlier in this book, and I still firmly believe, that Doug Harvey was the best all-round defenceman I've ever seen, able to dictate the terms of any game in which he played. Orr was good defensively, but not that good. (In fact, in Boston there's another name in the running, Eddie Shore.)

Simply put, however, Bobby Orr had the greatest impact of any player to come along in my lifetime. He earned his place in hockey history by single-handedly changing the game from the style played in my day to the one we see today.

In my mind, there can be no greater legacy. What is most remarkable is that he accomplished this in fewer than ten full seasons, before being "betrayed" by knees that, while braced by six operations, finally collapsed under the relentless stress and strain. Bobby's premature retirement at the age of thirty is one of the saddest episodes in the modern NHL.

How did Bobby Orr change hockey?

He redefined the defenceman's role, bringing him into a new, more aggressive offensive strategy, and opening the door for all-out attacks off quick transitions. His rushing exploits made it difficult (if not impossible) for defensive teams to zero in on Boston forwards. Bobby could race ahead of the play, immediately putting pressure on our defencemen while catching forwards off guard. Or he could come from behind a screen of teammates, cut left or right at speed, thereby drawing two or three defenders to him, before laying off a pass to someone in the clear.

Prior to his arrival in the league, defencemen rarely "jumped up" into the play. Rearguards were supposed to "head-man" the puck, getting it quickly up to quick-breaking forwards, while following – not leading – the play up the ice.

The greatest change in the game in the last quarter-century is this vastly increased mobility of defencemen. Before Orr, defencemen generally were big, stocky guys – heavy hitters who, for the most part, tended to move slowly and awkwardly. Naturally, if a defenceman was a lumbering skater, he wouldn't be able to join in the offensive flow. He'd be constantly backing up or standing still, because he was unable to come up to and challenge an attacking forward. Slow skaters are always at a disadvantage, no matter what their position. If you slow down at the opponent's blueline, your pass, your shot, and your deke will all be slow. But if you're skating like Orr did, all your moves are running at the same speed – carrying the puck, stickhandling, and releasing the shot. Thus Orr dictated the pace not only of a given game, but of all future games, by cranking the speed limits up to previously unknown levels.

Not only did Orr play the game at high speed, he was good in all departments. Harry Sinden offered perhaps the best comparison of Orr, Gordie Howe, and Bobby Hull: Howe could do everything, but he couldn't do it quickly. Hull had great speed but couldn't do everything. Orr, however, could do everything at high speed, which changed the rules forever.

Orr presented problems that opposing teams had never had to solve before. For example, when the face-off was in your end, the right- or left-winger (depending on where the face-off took place) would go directly to the point. With Orr on the ice, wingers would have to be in motion sooner. This disrupted their strategy, and brought pressure on their teams that the fans could not appreciate at first. When the Bruins faced off in our zone, it didn't matter who they had up front – Esposito, Hodge, Cashman, Bucyk, or McKenzie. How we lined up was dictated by one factor – the position of Bobby Orr. When the puck was dropped, everyone's attention was divided, with nervous glances in Orr's direction predominating.

Don Cherry tells a funny story about what players thought of Bobby: "We were playing the Washington Caps, and Bobby was out for a face-off. The Caps' centre was lining up his players around the face-off circle, and motioned to a rookie defenceman to stand over to the right. At that moment the rookie looked at Bobby, but Bobby shook his head and told him to go back over to his left – and the guy did it. I couldn't believe it. The kid thought so much of Bobby that he knew Bobby wouldn't lie to him. And Bobby wasn't lying – the puck went to the kid."

Bobby's talent led to other changes as well. For many years, the strategic standby was man-to-man or man-on-man defence. This meant that you would pick up your man or assignment as he came out of his zone and into yours. It was difficult to cover defencemen, however, because they'd normally be so far behind the play. Quite often, the plan was to get back to our blueline quickly, and "stand up" the attackers there. If the other team managed to set up inside our blueline, our wingers would generally cover the point men.

According to orthodox thinking, when we were forechecking, attacking forwards or defencemen in their defensive zone, we might put one or two forwards in deep to press, with the third stationed out high near the blueline to cut off break-out passes. When defencemen were slow, this scheme worked well. When Orr arrived, it went right out the window. Orr would often easily sidestep one or two forecheckers and lead a four-on-three or other odd-man rush. Toe Blake always counselled us to "not let him get wound up in his own end," because that's where the ball started rolling, due to his speed. If he got going and the play ended up in our end, the wingman would have to favour him, which would occasionally provide an opening for one of the Boston forwards. Orr was closely watched – but you couldn't watch him in the same way as, say, Claude Provost did when he was shadowing Bobby Hull all over the ice, for the simple reason that Orr was a defenceman. If you went in too deep after him, he had the talent to pull back a little bit, feed a perfect pass to a winger, and trap the forechecker. Bobby was a beautiful playmaker for a defenceman. That puck would be on his teammate's blade, not in his skates or too far in front of him.

Killing penalties against Boston was difficult as well. In a regular power-play defence, the forwards place themselves between the point men and the wingers on their side. If Orr was out there, you'd naturally lean toward him more, which would open up ice from the middle to the deep end of your zone. Even if we got outnumbered "down low" in the process and the Bruins scored, we wouldn't change that game plan. I'd certainly have coached someone to favour Orr rather than a winger, no matter how good the forward was, because Orr was capable of getting off a large number of shots.

In the 1969 semi-final, we were tied after four games, and returned to Montreal for game five. We were on our way to our retreat at La Sapinière when I began to read the game summaries, and noticed that Orr was getting a great number of shots from the point.

"We've got to pay more attention to Orr at the point," I said, and I didn't get much of an argument. Orr had scored the winning goal in game four to tie the series, after Gerry Cheevers had somehow managed to get his glove on the puck after a hard shot by Yvan Cournoyer. Bobby took the rebound, raced up the ice, and put the game away.

"The winger should favour him more," I said. "He's getting seven, eight, and nine shots a game." Bobby was all of twenty years old that season, and most of our game plan involved neutralizing him. For the next few games, that's exactly what we did, and we cut down on his offence from the point. But don't get me wrong, he was good all over the ice.

Despite these woes, we had plenty of success against the Bruins. The Orr–Esposito editions never beat us in the playoffs, although they did win the Cup in 1970 and 1972 when we weren't there to face them. I always thought that, man for man, we had the edge in skating. With players like Cournoyer, Jacques Lemaire, Frank Mahovlich, Claude Provost, Henri Richard, Ralph Backstrom, Mickey Redmond, Chuck Lefley, Bobby Rousseau, Réjean Houle, and Marc Tardif up front, and Guy Lapointe, Serge Savard, Terry Harper, and Jacques Laperrière on the backline, we could play the game at Bobby's pace. Our strategy was to play a tight, careful first period. If we could stay within one goal of the Bruins, we'd get our legs back in the second and third periods, and surge ahead.

Journalists loved (and still love) to sucker NHL players into critiques of our opponents, with questions like: "What are Orr's weaknesses? What do the Canadiens see in his game that you can exploit?" I steadfastly refused to bite on that particular hook.

I knew from observation that Bobby Orr could be his own toughest critic. Sometimes after making a mistake on the ice he would go back to his bench and rage at himself. But I also noticed that he did something only the greatest players do: he corrected his mistakes and didn't repeat them. Orr knew better than most that there was no such thing as a perfect hockey player, but he came as close to it as anyone I'd ever seen.

When he started having serious knee problems, he lost a bit of speed, which certainly affected his game. Being an offensive-minded defenceman, it was very difficult for him to see an opening and not go for it. But even when he started to slow down, he was head-and-shoulders above the competition – which explains his eight Norris Trophy selections in a row as the NHL's top defenceman.

Speaking as the Canadiens' captain, I was also impressed by the fact that Orr seemed to be well-liked by his teammates and regarded as a team man by everyone who played with him.

Of course, it wasn't long before other defencemen sought to emulate him – players such as my younger teammates, Serge Savard and Guy Lapointe, and Brad Park. Within a few years, a stream of talents who'd been profoundly affected by his example flowed into the NHL: Denis Potvin, Larry Robinson, Ray Bourque, Doug Wilson, Paul Coffey, Randy Carlyle, and Borje Salming.

All the defenders who've come along since then have Bobby Orr's stamp all over them – Chris Chelios, Phil Housley, Al MacInnis, Brian Leetch, Scott Stevens, Jeff Brown, Gary Suter, Steve Duchesne, Larry Murphy, Al Iafrate, Kevin Hatcher, Zarley Zalapski, Rob Blake, Rob Niedermayer, and Bryan Fogarty.

A few, like Housley, Brown, Fogarty, and Leetch, remind me of Bobby in terms of acceleration and offensive skills, but none possesses what I call the complete package.

The only defender I've seen who can match Orr for speed is Coffey, even though their styles are radically different. Coffey skates with his knees bent, almost in a sitting position. Orr's style was more esthetic or classic; his posture was more upright, even at full speed. Players like Denis Potvin and Larry Robinson were great defencemen, with a predominantly physical style. They could control the game, but they lacked Orr's speed.

I compare Potvin more to Ray Bourque than to Orr, especially in terms of strength, endurance, and the way each shoots. Bourque, in particular, releases the puck very quickly. Both he and Potvin are in the top rank, one step down from Orr and of course Doug Harvey.

One final point, to highlight Bobby's contribution – a quick glance at the scoring statistics.

In 1,113 games over nineteen seasons, Doug Harvey scored eighty-eight goals and had a total of 540 points. I had to look it up. If you'd asked me a month ago whether he had scored more or fewer than 100 career goals, I'd have said more, by far. In fact, the most he could manage in a single season was nine, and he never accumulated more than fifty points in a year. But he wasn't alone in this. Tom Johnson, another excellent Hall-of-Fame defence-man, totalled only fifty-one goals in sixteen seasons.

Enter Bobby Orr. In only 657 regular-season games, he turned in 915 points, a phenomenal 1.39 points-per-game average. He had season totals of 139, 135, 122, 120, 117, and 101 points. He racked up 102, 90, 89, 87, and 80 assists per season – breaking all the pre-vious records for defencemen in the process. He did something no other defenceman has ever done, before or since: he won the scoring championship, and he won it twice. In 1970, he won the Norris (top defenceman), Art Ross (scoring championship), Hart (Most Valuable Player), and Conn Smythe (Playoff MVP) trophies, and was selected as Sportsman of the Year. He was all of twenty-one years old.

How much has Bobby Orr changed the game? During the 1993-94 season, Paul Coffey became the first defenceman to surpass my 1,219 total career points. I was fifteenth overall when that season began, and everybody else was a forward like me. In 1985-86, Paul scored forty-eight goals; two seasons before that, he'd bagged forty. In other words, his output in those two seasons alone equalled Doug Harvey's entire career scoring.

In fact, three other players passed me in career scoring during 1993-94: Dale Hawerchuk, Denis Savard, and Jari Kurri. Ray Bourque will be the next defenceman to leave me in his wake, sometime during 1994-95, as will Mario Lemieux and Mike Gartner in the not-too-distant future.

Conversely, the change in the 1990s game is reflected in netminders' lifetime goals-against averages. Ken Dryden's was 2.24, Jacques Plante's 2.38, Glenn Hall's 2.51, Terry Sawchuk's and Johnny Bower's were 2.52, and Bernie Parent finished at 2.55.

Going into 1993-94, Ed Belfour's was 2.70, Patrick Roy's 2.79, Curtis Joseph's 3.06, Mike Richter's 3.27, Ron Hextall's 3.30, Andy Moog's 3.32, Kirk McLean's 3.35, Bill Ranford's 3.43, John Vanbiesbrouck's 3.45, Kelly Hrudey's 3.48, and Grant Fuhr's was 3.64. Roughly speaking, the average difference is somewhere between a goal and a goal-and-a-half. I think that says a lot about what's happening in today's NHL – and it's all because a defenceman from Parry Sound liked to skate fast and carry the puck.

Another of Bobby's legacies came long after he, and the players who were in the league when he arrived, had retired. As I've mentioned, Orr's hiring of Alan Eagleson was a watershed, and paved the way for the representation of players' interests by professional agents throughout the NHL. That, in turn, led to more money for all of us.

In December 1966, the Bruins were in Montreal. Bobby was having dinner with Eagleson at the Queen Elizabeth Hotel, when two of his teammates appeared at the table and asked both of them to come upstairs.

Eagleson was surprised to find that the entire Boston team had gathered in Bobby's room – and overwhelmed when they asked him to form a players' association. Within a year, nearly everyone on every club had joined. But Eagleson proceeded cautiously, and left the Canadiens until last, because he was "afraid" of the team, and of me as captain and my position in the Canadiens' organization. Montreal's management had always taken very good care of us. We went first-class all the way, and were considered to be a pretty conservative bunch, content with our situation. Eagleson assumed that he'd have a hard selling job in front of him.

I remember that meeting very clearly. My teammates listened as Eagleson talked and talked, perhaps selling a little bit too hard, because he'd misinterpreted success as complacency. As captain I'd always felt that I had to be as objective as possible, to say and do what was right for the team, whether or not I necessarily agreed as an individual.

After Eagleson had spoken for about an hour, I finally got up and said that I was in favour of the Canadiens joining the NHLPA. "It will be good for you young guys," I said.

Alan Eagleson didn't know that one of the reasons the Canadiens were successful was because everyone was free to speak his mind. All in all, I still believe that the NHLPA helped the players, especially in its early years – just as, at one point, Alan Eagleson was good for hockey.

A great deal has been written about John Ziegler, the Detroit lawyer who was league president from 1977 to 1992, and Alan Eagleson, about the roles they played in the development of the NHL and professional hockey in general throughout the 1970s and 1980s. I don't intend to rehash all that, or to discuss the recent allegations in the United States. Eagleson's troubles are before several different courts, and I am prevented from commenting on them in detail, even if I wished to do so.

I will say that I got a first-hand view of how despised Alan Eagleson had become, and how far his once close relationship with Orr had deteriorated, when I was sitting beside Bobby one night at a league function. Eagleson entered the room, and the normally mild-mannered Orr reacted with profound disgust.

It's also a fact that the American grand jury investigation into Eagleson's activities was launched only after a Boston-area journalist alleged that he had discovered a large number of "irregularities" in Eagleson's doings within the NHLPA and Hockey Canada, and as a player representative. Many people suspect that Orr was the journalist's original source for this story, although that has never been verified. If so, Orr's final legacy was helping to topple both John Ziegler and Alan Eagleson.

If I have any quarrel with John and Alan, it relates to the NHL players' pension fund. I had been concerned about this situation since 1991, when Stan Mikita and I served as honorary captains at the All-Star Game in Chicago. On Friday morning, I joined the Oldtimers for a skate, although I wasn't scheduled to play in the Legends game that night. I spoke with Carl Brewer and Mark Zigler, a lawyer with expertise in pensions, as we rode a bus to the Stadium, and they began to explain their position on the fund in general, particularly the elusive "surplus."

For years, players like Bobby Baun had wondered why a sixteen-season NHL career was worth only $7,600 a year in pension. Gordie Howe's twenty-six years in the NHL paid only $13,000 per annum. I heard that Baun had spent a lot of his own money trying to get to the bottom of this, but without success. Ironically, some of Eagleson's very first clients on the Toronto Maple Leafs would be responsible for launching the first serious investigation of the pension fund.

This group included Carl Brewer, Eddie Shack, Andy Bathgate, Gordie Howe, and Bobby Hull. They would eventually launch the suit against Eagleson and the NHL owners. The Players' Association itself was sympathetic, but kept its distance.

When the Toronto group got started, Norma Shack (Eddie's wife) became heavily involved, and called to solicit my support. I told her that I wanted the group's lawyers to ask several questions.

"First of all, were there any surpluses? Every time we've asked that question in the past, we never received a direct answer. If there aren't any surpluses, then that's the end of it. But if there is a surplus, how much is it? That's question two. Thirdly, where is it; what's become of it? And fourthly, what has been done with the money; how has it been used? I would like answers to those four questions."

I have always prepared a financial statement at the end of each year, and the only thing I could never establish to my own satisfaction was the value of my pension. In the early 1980s, when interest rates went up to eighteen or twenty per cent, you were allowed to roll your pension into an RRSP, which I did. I'd always felt that the interest paid on the pension fund's investments was too low – although, as I say, I had no firm numbers to justify that opinion.

The trouble was that all the other players were in the dark as well. No one was minding the store, even though it was our money. The pension fund began in 1948, and both individual players and the league contributed. Everyone paid throughout his playing years. For example, in 1953, I was putting in $900 a year. Later, this rose to something like $1,500. While the fund was run by the league, the players' association had two representatives on the pension fund committee.

In 1969, Eagleson negotiated an agreement by which the league would fund the plan entirely by itself. The owners then said that, if they did this, there was no longer any need for players to be represented on the committee. Eagleson accepted this position.

I believe that Eagleson was wrong. A review process of some sort was necessary. He made a mistake – but I'm not convinced, as many former players are, that he led us intentionally down the proverbial garden path.

In 1990, the Toronto-based group of former players hired Mark Zigler to study the plan. He determined that there was a surplus of $25 million sitting in the fund, as well as indications that the league owners had used some portion of this – I think the figure was $13 million – as an excuse to take a "contribution holiday." Their point was that, if there was indeed a surplus, they didn't have to keep on adding money.

The situation was quite complex, which is one reason why it's before the courts. But I felt strongly that the matter had to be cleared up, one way or another, and sent a cheque to help the players' group defray its legal costs.

Time passed, and on the morning before the 1993 All-Star Game in Montreal, I joined several members of the Canadiens Alumni for breakfast with Zigler, Eddie Shack, and Billy Harris. They briefed us on what had been happening in the interim. When they'd finished, Réjean Houle proposed that the Canadiens Alumni donate $10,000 toward their legal costs. But I interceded.

"The Canadiens Alumni are seen as leaders in this area, and the other groups are going to watch what we do before they act," I said. "If we donate $10,000, they'll feel okay giving $3,000 or $4,000. I propose that we donate $25,000; that way they'll have to come in with $10,000 or so. Lawyers are expensive."

After a short discussion, it was agreed that the Canadiens Alumni would donate $25,000, and now the hard part began: I had to discuss the matter with team president Ronald Corey. This was a delicate situation for all concerned. I was by that time part of the management team. The Canadiens had treated the Alumni very well throughout the years. For example, we had been given the Forum, rent-free, to stage money-raising exhibition games and skate-a-thons. Now I was about to tell Ronald that we wanted to take some of these proceeds and use them to support a suit against the team and its NHL partners.

"I proposed to the Alumni that we should be leaders in this," I told him. "I wanted you to know immediately, because it's going to upset a lot of people."

Ronald grimaced, and acknowledged that he was going to take "some flak."

"I realize that, Ronald," I replied, "but you always told me that the Alumni's money should be used for the good of the players. Frankly, no other project touches the former players more. There's no better way to use it."

Ronald agreed. "It makes for a funny situation, but I respect your right to do this." And so we used a small part of the Alumni's bank account in this way.

As has been reported in the media, the group of veterans who initiated the suit against the NHL won their case at the first two levels of the courts, but the league and the individual teams insisted on taking the matter on appeal to the Supreme Court of Canada.

That decision prolonged the agony for Ronald Corey and myself. Ronald agreed with me that the players had a case, but he was supposed to demonstrate his solidarity with the rest of the league management. As I was preparing this book, the Canadiens had joined with the other teams in voting for the Supreme Court test. It was an unpopular decision among the Montreal media, and left me very uncomfortable, but it was taken for a specific reason. The league's lawyers told the board of governors that the chances are good that the Supreme Court will rule with the lower courts. If this transpires (which, in fact, it did on July 28, 1994), the league would have to turn its attention to an American legal firm, which had advised the owners to reject the players' claims at the outset.

"If the appeal is rejected by the Supreme Court, which it probably will be, we'll sue the American firm," Ronald told me. "I don't like this whole thing; it's a no-win situation for us. But, if we don't exhaust every level of appeal, and then try to sue the law firm, they could easily defend themselves by saying we didn't take the case to the highest court. So we have to go through with this."

Meanwhile, the Canadiens have been putting money aside in a special account, to meet their obligations if the Supreme Court rules against the league. By these obligations, I mean the monies that would then be owing to the former players. The "original-six" teams will carry a much greater burden in this regard. Those are the players whose careers were the longest, but whose pensions are the smallest. They have the most to gain by a settlement in their favour – a settlement that will come out of the pockets of the teams they played for.

The thing that bothers me about this case is the old saying: "Justice delayed is justice denied." The end result of a similar pension fight was covered recently on the television news. This one concerned the shutdown of a St. Jean manufacturing plant. Its 220 workers were left in the lurch when the facility closed in the early 1970s. They sued for $4 million in pension benefits owing. When the suit had dragged through the various courts, the surviving workers numbered fewer than one-third of the original group. All of the others had passed away in the interim.

In 1991 and 1992, I told anyone who'd listen that the league faced a no-win situation, and a public relations disaster.

"Today we're talking millions and millions in salaries, but you have former players, referees, and linesmen – and their widows – with pensions of $100 a month. It's bad public relations to go to court. When this comes out, the league will have a big black eye, and I believe you should try to find a way to settle the situation."

But my words fell on deaf ears, because yet another hockey business story had captured the headlines – the league's first strike. Despite several warnings from the NHLPA, John Ziegler had convinced the board of governors in September of 1991 that there was no real danger of a strike at that time, or at any other time during the season. Events proved him wrong: a month before the 1992 playoffs, he had a full-scale walkout on his hands.

Ziegler genuinely thought that there would be no strike; therefore his strategy was totally off base. If he'd wanted to force a showdown, he should have acted in September, when the players had just reported for duty, and hadn't received any money for the upcoming season. In April, the players had already been paid for the year. The pressure was off them, and they were prepared to gamble.

Prior to the walkout, Ziegler demanded that the players put the issue to a vote by secret ballot. He still felt he had a chance, and told the owners so. When the vote was 500–4 in favour of a strike, Ziegler's credibility was shot forever.

John Ziegler received a $2 million buy-out and a pension of $250,000 a year when he left the NHL in 1992, having served as president for fifteen years.

Gordie Howe, Maurice Richard, Bobby Orr, and I also received pensions when we left the NHL, after playing for a combined total of seventy-six seasons. Our four pensions total roughly $45,000 a year.

10

✦

THE SECOND FLOOR

For those Canadiens who hang up their skates, then agree to wear a suit for the team, the relationship with the front office (also known as the Second Floor) usually begins with the retirement press conference.

In my case, however, this relationship had begun many years ago, back in the days when I was twenty-one and playing with the Quebec Aces. In late 1951 or early 1952, Zotique Lespérance came to see me after a game. At that time he wore three hats: as newspaper columnist with *La Patrie*, broadcaster with CKAC radio in Montreal, and vice-president, public affairs, of Molson Brewery. What might sound to us in the 1990s like a walking package of conflicts of interest was, in fact, relatively commonplace back then. Journalists were poorly paid, and many moonlighted to all points of the compass, sometimes supplementing their incomes as part-time public relations consultants with sports teams or commercial sponsors.

"I'm not here tonight as a sportswriter or sportscaster," he said with a chuckle. "I'm here as a delegate of Molson Brewery. Well, Jean, we've been watching you. If you ever decide to come to Montreal, we'll have a job for you."

I was a trifle nonplussed by his offer, because I didn't know a thing about the beer business. But it stuck in my mind. I used to go back to Victoriaville regularly in the off-season, and the next summer I looked up a good friend of the family named Mr. Garon, a hotel owner who later became president of the Hotel Owners Association of Quebec.

I told him about Zotique's invitation.

"Jean, in my position, I should not favour anybody," he said. "I sell every product and I've dealt with all of the breweries. If you're asking me as a friend, I can say it might be a good idea if you go with Molson. It's a family-run company, and they have a reputation for being very fair with their people."

What I didn't comprehend entirely, of course, was that Molson was interested in me for several good reasons. I was the right athlete (a prominent French-Canadian hockey star) in the right place (Quebec City, but Montreal-bound, which was better still) at the right time (when television had begun to arrive in the world of sports and in the province of Quebec).

In 1952, Molson's marketing and sales forces had pretty much decided to concentrate on television to promote their product line. Molson and Imperial Oil co-sponsored Canadiens games on radio, but Imperial Oil took the lion's share. If Imperial was unwilling to take a chance on TV, Molson was prepared to jump in. If Imperial maintained its position here as well, Molson would remain as secondary sponsor but would seek primary sponsorship of the Quebec Senior Hockey League's Sunday afternoon telecasts.

Frank Selke was the man with his finger on the switch. If Molson could help him, he would obviously be disposed to help them.

Zotique Lespérance met with him in the summer of 1953 and proposed a mutually beneficial arrangement.

"I'm off to Quebec City, where I'm going to offer Jean Béliveau a full-time position with the brewery," Zotique said. "After a trainee period, he will become a full-timer in our sales promotion department. If he does well with the *bleu-blanc-rouge*, or even if he fails, he'll still be our employee, and we have a reputation of keeping our employees." This was no exaggeration. At this time, Molson was one of the few major corporations in Montreal with a "cradle-to-grave" employment policy. Others included the two railways, Bell Telephone, Northern Electric, and Canadian Marconi.

Frank Selke's ears perked up when Zotique added what proved to be the clincher. "Of course, he will work for us in Montreal during his trainee period. Now, in exchange for bringing him here from Quebec City, we want you to sell us the television rights for the senior league games at the Forum on Sunday afternoons."

"My friend," Selke replied, "that's a bargain, and I'm going to hold you to it."

Returning to the provincial capital, Zotique and I met on August 9 to discuss these developments. "Jean," he said, "this is job security for you. You start at $10,000 a year, including all benefits, pension plan, and health and dental coverage, which is certainly far above scale for a trainee." And he was right: in 1953, a $10,000 salary was almost triple the amount needed to raise a family of four in middle-class comfort.

Four days later, I was in Montreal, in the offices of Hartland de Montarville Molson. We sealed the deal with a handshake, and began a relationship that is still alive and well.

Later that afternoon, Zotique Lespérance hustled off to the Forum. "Frank, it's a deal! Jean will begin work in Montreal for Molson in the fall."

"Zotique, you have your senior league TV advertising rights."

Six weeks later, I signed with the Canadiens – a five-year

contract that would pay me a total of $105,000 in salary and bonuses. That same October, I started work at Molson, and for the next eighteen years I was in double harness. It wasn't piece-work, or part-time employment with the brewery. I was a full-time Molson employee who happened to have special dispensation to play hockey for the Montreal Canadiens. (I suppose that the distinction blurred in 1957, when the Molson family cemented ties with the club by purchasing it from Senator Donat Raymond.)

Although I was one of the NHL's best-paid players throughout my career, my hockey salary alone in no way guaranteed that I was "fixed for life." No player of my era was in that position. Molson, thankfully, presented an opportunity for me to develop a parallel career without waiting until my retirement party. Needless to say, I jumped at the chance.

When the Canadiens were at home, we would practise at ten o'clock and wrap up by noon. I would shower, don my suit, and go to my office. My first several years were spent at what I call Molson Business School. Each year I would "major" in something new: marketing, production, distribution, public relations. As time went by, my responsibilities increased, and by 1962, I was sports promotions director for Molson Lévis Limitée. This meant that I spent my summers in Quebec City. Eventually, we purchased a second home in Ste-Foy, just west of Quebec, and lived there from mid-April to mid-September, when I would report to the Canadiens' training camp.

I met a great many influential people at Molson, among them the senator himself, Campbell Smart, and Edgar Genest. Later, when I went off to Molson (Québec) Limitée, I worked with a variety of top people in the business, including Paul Falardeau, Jean-Jacques Côté, and Jean-Luc Doyon.

In mid-May 1964, several nominations were made public at Molson (Québec) Limitée: Charles L. Dumais became chairman of the board, Paul Falardeau was named executive vice-president and general manager, and I became vice-president.

Recently, I came upon a picture of the three of us taken during the press conference in Montreal, seated at a table with David Molson, the cousin of the senator and president of Canadian Arena Company. We were young, serious, and capable, prepared to do great things for the company. Then I turned the page of the scrap-book and memories of a tragedy came flooding back. Barely three weeks after his promotion, Charles Dumais was sleeping on his boat which was moored in the St. Lawrence River at Sorel, when he was overcome by fumes from the gas heater. It was a great loss to the company and to Quebec City. Charles was well respected, and would indeed have done great things, had he lived.

Thus, when I hung up my skates in 1971, I was able to look back on the experiences and memories of not one but two careers. Upon retiring, my plan had been to continue with Molson, but David Molson persuaded me otherwise.

"Jean," he said, "hockey is changing. There will be a lot of marketing surrounding every professional sport, not just hockey. You're going to be our spokesman."

I could appreciate David's logic, and thought I'd be willing to give the marketing side of hockey a try. In reality, as team captain, I'd been the Canadiens' spokesman for a decade already. Arrangements were made for the transfer of my Molson pension plan and benefits package, and I moved into the office across the hall from Sam Pollock in June 1971.

It was easy to accept the new position in the Montreal front office. I had great respect for David, and great admiration for general manager Sam Pollock, perhaps the finest hockey man who ever existed (and I say this knowing that Frank Selke preceded him). When people ask how the Canadiens could be so good over such a long period of time, two answers come immediately to mind:

Frank Selke and Sam Pollock. Together they consecutively over-saw the club's fortunes for thirty-three seasons, from 1946 to 1978.

I first met and played against Sam Pollock in junior. His 1950 Junior Canadiens won the Memorial Cup, after which he moved up to the Eastern Professional Hockey League in the early 1960s with the Hull-Ottawa Canadiens. I admired not only his supreme hockey knowledge, but also his tremendous ability to shoulder a killing workload. Whenever a deal beckoned, Sam would go day and night until it was resolved, refusing to leave the slightest ele-ment to chance, or to last-minute cold feet on the part of the other participants.

He selected hockey players in his own image, those who could combine their talent with hard work — which, when you think about it, is a short but effective definition of a winner. Sam was a motivator long before the word became overused. When you saw him running as hard as he always did, it always got you moving.

Throughout his long career, Sam earned everything he got, which was quite a lot. He started at the bottom of the Canadiens' organization as a scout, and coached his way up through the junior, senior, and minor professional ranks, before becoming assistant general manager and director of player personnel, and then finally replaced Frank Selke in 1964.

Just as I'd welcomed the prospect of starting with Molson Brew-ery as a sales and promotion trainee, I looked forward to working with David Molson and Sam Pollock. I knew they offered the best course in sports administration available at the time. The list of future NHL coaches and general managers who have passed through Pollock University is long, and includes Cliff Fletcher (St. Louis, Atlanta, Calgary, Toronto), John Ferguson (New York, Winnipeg, Ottawa), "Professor" Ron Caron (St. Louis), Scotty Bowman (St. Louis, Buffalo, Pittsburgh, Detroit), Bob Gainey (Minnesota, Dallas), and Jacques Lemaire (New Jersey).

Sam not only built the Canadiens, he helped to build the

National Hockey League. When the league was seriously contemplating expansion in 1964-65, it asked a general managers' committee headed by Sam to study the viability of such a move. Sam's committee reported back that the league should double in size to include franchises in major American markets in California (Los Angeles and Oakland), the midwest (Minnesota and St. Louis), and the industrial east (Pittsburgh and Philadelphia), if it was to entertain any hopes of securing a network television contract. As well, those teams should be stocked with quality players, and begin play in their own division, to ensure they would not be relegated to second-division status in the first decade of post-expansion play. That's how the league's West Division came into being and why Scotty Bowman's veteran-laden St. Louis Blues ended up playing against the Canadiens in the 1967-68 Cup final.

Sam also designed the draft system that would be used. Each of the "original-six" teams was allowed to protect eleven skaters and one goaltender, then allowed to "fill" a player from its list for each player drafted. NHL president Clarence Campbell had argued for protecting only nine players, but the six teams were not in that generous a mood.

Nine or eleven would have hurt most other teams, but not Montreal. We had more farm teams and more players in reserve than anyone else, as well as a far more elaborate scouting system than the competition. As I mentioned earlier, Sam succeeded in turning expansion to the Canadiens' advantage, while offering the richest collection of players available for the new teams. Part of his strategy included preparing a complete classification of all our talent, which is why our 1966 training camp featured more than 110 players. Our scouts worked overtime that year, but when the 1967 expansion draft took place, we kept more of our nucleus intact, while furnishing more players to the new franchises, than any other of the "original-six" teams.

Since the late 1940s, Frank Selke had built up the Canadiens' farm system and nurtured it carefully, before turning over management to Sam Pollock as director of player personnel. Those players we "grew" but couldn't keep were sold at the annual "market garden," and the proceeds funnelled right back into the system. Other teams scrambled to copy our way of doing this, but Sam was always two or three jumps ahead. When his committee was studying the communications potential inherent in league expansion, he quickly perceived that many minor leagues would atrophy with the arrival of television, and was the first general manager to start divesting himself of multiple farm teams.

Expansion presented an opportunity for the team to make a profit after many years of patient cultivation, and to use that profit to set us up for the medium and long term. Two years later, when the NHL adopted the universal draft, Sam traded off large numbers of players to guarantee a one-time shot at drafting the top two francophone juniors in the country at the time, Réjean Houle and Marc Tardif.

The Montreal Canadiens benefited at every turn. As a player and team captain, I can say that Trader Sam was regarded with awe in the dressing room. Moving upstairs to work even closer with this man was a privilege.

That fall, I joined Sam and his public relations staff – Camil Des Roches and, two years later, Claude Mouton, whom I hired – and we began moving the team further into the community through a variety of programs – blood donor clinics, cultural exchanges, charity appearances of every kind. All these things have since become standard fare, for the Canadiens and every other team. At the time, however, we were innovators. My associates believed that a new age was about to dawn, and that previously "throwaway" functions such as marketing and communications would assume far greater importance in coming years. Sam wanted to position me as the person who could oversee their development.

Several months into my new duties, the Molson connection was severed when, to take advantage of various tax provisions, the family sold the team to a consortium headed by Edward and Peter Bronfman and John Bassett of Toronto (who dropped out after a year, leaving the Bronfmans to go it alone). Seven years later, the team was sold again, and found itself back in familiar hands – this time, Molson Breweries of Canada Limited, which paid $20 million, after a bidding war with Labatt's Brewery of Canada Ltd.

While I was happy to welcome all my friends and former fellow employees at Molson back to the fold, it was time to say goodbye to Sam Pollock. During the seven years of Bronfman ownership, Sam had built up a good deal of equity in the Bronfmans' enterprises, including Edper Investments and the Canadian Arena Company (which retained control of the Forum after the sale of the franchise itself to Molson Breweries). Now, in his early fifties, he found himself at a crossroads. The Canadiens were solid at every level, and under his stewardship had just won three straight Stanley Cups (and would win another in the coming season).

"Jean," he said, "I've been in hockey since high school and it's time for me to move on. I have a rare opportunity to continue with the Bronfmans and I'm going to take advantage of it." Needless to say, the corporate world viewed Sam's managerial and administrative skills with the same admiration as had the hockey world. He has continued to prosper. As I write these words, he is the chairman of the board of John Labatt and Company in Toronto.

The only hitch in Sam Pollock's happiness concerned the selection of his replacement as general manager. It wasn't in his nature to leave loose strings untied, and he agonized over the responsibility of the succession.

Morgan McCammon of Molson, who was appointed president of the team, met with Sam and me to discuss this thorny issue. Actually, two meetings were held, one at the Forum, another at Molson Brewery. The most obvious candidate – by which I mean the one whom the media thought of right away, and the one who'd campaigned most actively and overtly for the job – was coach Scotty Bowman.

Scotty had been trained by Frank Selke and Sam Pollock, and had worked within the Canadiens' organization as a coach and scout after a high stick from Jean-Guy Talbot had fractured his skull and ended his playing days with the Junior Canadiens (then coached by Sam) in the early 1950s. When expansion arrived in 1967, he left his position as Sam's assistant to become coach of the St. Louis Blues, where he did a tremendous job, then returned to Montreal after our 1971 Stanley Cup win. In the eight seasons between 1971-72 and 1978-79, he won five Stanley Cups and was considered, along with Al Arbour of the New York Islanders and Fred Shero of Philadelphia, the foremost coach in the league. Whatever his personal quirks, Scotty had proved himself behind the bench.

The trouble was, he'd "proved" himself behind the scenes as well. This had resulted in negative entries on his balance sheet. Whenever Scotty took issue with a player for any reason at all, he'd run upstairs to Sam's office and demand an instant trade. Bringing all his experience and knowledge to bear, Sam would calm him down. Sam knew that no one was about to turn in eighty perfect games.

Sometimes Scotty would barge in while I was meeting with Sam, whereupon I'd personally witness these unfortunate harangues. I made my mind up that if this guy was ever in the running for general manager, or for any position within the organization in which he'd have the final say on personnel matters, the Canadiens were going to be in trouble. Scotty had fractious relations with some of his more colourful players, especially Peter Mahovlich, but virtually any player who had a bad game would be enough to send him scampering to the Second Floor. He wouldn't be general manager if I had a vote. With Scotty at the helm, it seemed likely that our team would change dramatically from year to year, if not from hour to hour.

There was a problem, of course, in taking this negative

position. Scotty had run an effective media campaign, and appeared to be a shoo-in because the short list of candidates was very short indeed – down to one, as far as several observers were concerned. Like any good general manager, Sam Pollock had refrained from tipping his hand, but I'm pretty sure that he'd made up his own mind on Scotty's aspirations long before.

When the Bronfmans purchased the Canadiens in 1971, they brought along a financial adviser named Irving Grundman. In his seven years under Sam Pollock, Irving learned a great deal about hockey and hockey management. He was a quiet, reflective man, who carefully considered all the possibilities and weighed every option before rendering an opinion. Sam and I both agreed that he should get the job, and Morgan McCammon, as president, made it unanimous.

When you vote against a guy whom everybody expects will be the next general manager, you have to have a few good reasons handy. The new president will want to know what's going on, as will the other members of the board. My views and those of Sam became known, but they were limited to a very small circle because Scotty had a year remaining on his coaching contract. He would, in fact, stay in Montreal for another, admittedly difficult, season, before moving on to Buffalo as coach and general manager.

I was asked once if what I saw of Scotty's performance as Buffalo's general manager vindicated Sam and me. It's a difficult question to answer. On the one hand, he wasn't an unqualified success, winning 216 of 404 games and "batting" .500 in playoff action. I thought him to be a great coach, but an impatient general manager. On the other hand, Irving Grundman wasn't entirely successful, either. There's no doubt that Irving was well respected as a gentleman and a good businessman. He never claimed to have Sam Pollock's store of hockey knowledge, but he'd tried very hard during his stint as the Canadiens' managing director to learn how the game was run.

On balance, I don't think that Sam and I made a mistake by selecting Irving Grundman over Scotty Bowman, if only because I don't think that things would have been any better under somebody else.

Our decision undoubtedly disappointed Scotty, and he didn't bother to hide his feelings during the 1978-79 season. Unhappy as he may have been, he still saw to it that the team won the Stanley Cup.

The team of the 1970s, which won five Stanley Cups of its own, was clearly Sam Pollock's creation – a testament to his abilities and strategies. With Frank Selke's departure in 1964, it was his alone to mould and manoeuvre.

I mentioned earlier how the January 1971 trade for Frank Mahovlich delivered a Stanley Cup to the Canadiens the year that I retired. It also delivered one in 1973, after John Ferguson and I were gone. Frank's presence took his brother Peter's performance up a couple of notches, but his most important contribution was as another senior veteran in the room alongside Henri Richard, my replacement as captain, J.C. Tremblay, Terry Harper, and Jacques Laperrière. They settled down a young team which had a corps of middle-level veterans in Serge Savard, Guy Lapointe, Yvan Cournoyer, Jacques Lemaire, and Claude Larose, and a large group of rising young players in the persons of Yvon Lambert, Steve Shutt, Guy Lafleur, Marc Tardif, Réjean Houle, Murray Wilson, Larry Robinson, and Ken Dryden.

When the World Hockey Association claimed the likes of Big Frank, Tremblay, Houle, and Tardif, and Henri Richard and Jacques Laperrière retired after the 1973 Cup, Lemaire, Cournoyer, Savard, Jim Roberts, and Lapointe stepped forward to provide veteran leadership, while Sam's system continued to produce new stars such as Bob Gainey, Doug Jarvis, Doug Risebrough, Mario

Tremblay, Bill Nyrop, John Van Boxmeer, Michel Plasse, and Michel (Bunny) Larocque. At the same time, the Bruins, Hawks, and Leafs were being devastated by defections to the WHA.

If Sam experienced one minor setback in the 1970s, it came at the hands of Ken Dryden, the goalie who, in taking a break from his law studies at McGill, had backstopped the team to two Stanley Cups in 1971 and 1973. After accomplishing this, Dryden felt obliged to make what Sam felt were exorbitant salary demands. Complicating matters was the knowledge that the WHA was offering journeymen goaltenders up to $100,000 a year. Ken's older brother, Dave, himself a goaltender, had already made the move to the new league.

Dryden felt he was worth a lot more in this accelerated marketplace. Sam, however, adamantly refused to alter his system of steadily increasing a player's salary over a lengthy proving period. When the two reached an impasse, Dryden quit the team to article for a Toronto law firm at $135 a week.

Sam was a fiscal conservative, who believed in the traditional values of money for services rendered and championships earned. I never had difficulty negotiating my salary with him, and we always were on the same wavelength in our contract discussions. Then again, I retired before the WHA threw the scale out of whack, so I didn't experience the new salary explosion as a player. Sam never really discussed the Dryden situation with anyone, especially during the 1973-74 season that Ken sat out, but I could see he was concerned by it. Not only had a player turned his back on a good sum of money to prove his point (an unheard-of occurrence), but that player was Ken Dryden, an athlete whom Sam greatly admired.

Like the players, though, Sam couldn't seem to draw a bead on Kenny. We knew he was a scholar when he originally joined us at the tail end of the 1971 season. As such, he was a first for our dressing room. I've always told my teammates to respect the temperaments of each person in the room, because it takes all kinds to make a successful team. Ken proved his worth spectacularly, and continued to do so the following season when he won the Calder Trophy as the league's top rookie.

Still, as his captain for two months, and then as a Second Floor observer, I noted that Ken always placed a little extra distance between himself and his teammates. You couldn't construe it as being anti-team or egotistical. Far from it. Ken just seemed to be both a participant and an observer, all at once. It must have been disconcerting for Sam to negotiate with him at the beginning. His return after his self-exile set the Canadiens back on the road to the Stanley Cup, and Sam was the first person to recognize that fact.

To be sure, I had my own opportunity to join the new league and make fabulous money. The Quebec Nordiques were one of the WHA's founding teams, and it seemed natural that the new franchise should go after the two players whose names loomed largest in the public's imagination – Guy Lafleur and Jean Béliveau. Guy was out of the question. He had signed a three-year deal upon joining the Canadiens and still had two years and an option year remaining.

As for me, well, in 1971, Jacques Plante was the Nordiques' general manager, and one of the club's principal backers was Paul Racine, a shopping-centre magnate who had known me for many years. In other words, the two guys offering me millions of dollars weren't fast-money boys or strangers from another hockey planet. One was a former teammate, the other a guy at whose home I would stop off for a post-game beer in my junior days. When we met, it was almost like a family reunion.

Paul was a go-getter who had spearheaded construction of the massive Laurier shopping centre in Ste-Foy and others in the United States. He had other backers, but he drove the deals and, as a result, was a very wealthy man when he became the first president of the Nordiques. When I met with him and Jacques at the Dorval Hilton in Montreal, they offered me a four-year deal – but with all

After I retired as a player in 1971, the Montreal Expos hosted an appreciation night at Jarry Park. On hand was the great outfielder and hitter of the San Francisco Giants, Willie Mays.

Above: In 1969 I was proud to be inducted as an Officer of the Order of Canada by Governor General Roland Michener (centre). Fellow inductee Gordie Howe is on the right. (*John Evans Photography / Ottawa*)
Below: In September 1972 I travelled with Team Canada to Moscow for the final games of the epic Summit Series against the Soviet Union. Here I am shaking hands with the great Russian forward Valeri Kharlamov.

Above: One of the greatest moments of my life occurred in August 1971 when our family had a private audience with Pope Paul VI at his summer residence in Castel Gandolfo, Italy. (UPI/*Bettmann*) *Below:* In 1972 I was most pleased to receive an honorary doctorate from the Université de Moncton. (*Arnold's Studio/Moncton*)

I've had many opportunities to travel in my life, both in Canada and abroad. *Above*: Here I am travelling to Canadian Forces Base Gagetown in New Brunswick with the pilot of General Jean Allard, Canadian chief of defence staff. *Left*: During a visit to Nova Scotia I was able to land this huge blue-fin tuna. For several years I was a member of the Canadian team in the International Tuna Tournament. My biggest catch weighed eight hundred pounds. (*Nova Scotia Communications and Information Centre*)

Above: Guy Lafleur (centre) joined the Canadiens the season after I retired. Here he is with me and another great right-winger, Rocket Richard, at the Forum. The Canadiens, it seems, always find a way to "pass the torch." (*Denis Brodeur*) *Below:* In January 1985 fans voted for an all-time Canadiens "dream team." Here I am with (from left): Jacques Plante, Larry Robinson, Toe Blake, Dickie Moore, Aurel Joliat, Doug Harvey, Maurice Richard, Bob Gainey. (*Denis Brodeur*)

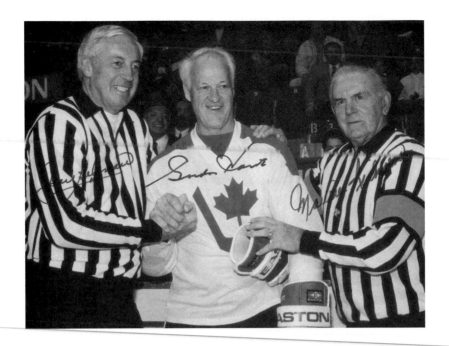

In the late 1980s Maurice Richard and I refereed at an Old-Timers game in the Forum. Gordie Howe (centre) was a player. (*Andre Viau / Journal de Montreal*)

In 1988 I received, at centre ice of the Forum, the Olympic Torch that was en route to the winter games in Calgary. (*Denis Brodeur*)

Giving a television interview in my office on the second floor of the Montreal Forum.

In 1985 the Canadiens marked their 75th season and yours truly was asked to give a speech. (*Denis Brodeur*)

Leaving the Forum's administration offices at 1414 Rue Lambert-Closse.

Here is a recent photograph of me and my family (clockwise from centre) – my wife Élise, my daughter Hélène, granddaughters Mylène and Magalie. (*Bob Fisher*)

monies paid even if it turned out I could only play for one season.

"Whatever you put on the table, I won't go back," I told them. "Ten million, twenty million, it doesn't matter. I'm forty, going on forty-one. I can't play the quality of hockey I liked to play any more. If I could, and if I wanted to play again, I'd play with the Canadiens. It wouldn't be fair to you, the fans, or me . . . I just can't do it any more, and I'm the first guy to recognize it."

Of course, the very fact that we were talking millions certainly gave one pause. I wasn't under the illusion that they wanted me for my playing skills. They wanted the name Béliveau on the marquee, and on the front page of the season-ticket subscription forms. Both Jacques and Paul were certain that they'd make money on the deal. Yet it was Jacques, as a former player (who would return to play yet again), who immediately understood what I was saying.

I know that some people have returned to professional hockey after a few years away from the game, but, by and large, I view this as a mistake. Jacques Plante would prove to be an exception to the rule – but he was a goalie, not a skater, and his powers did not decline. You shouldn't trade on the past. You have to ask yourself tough questions. Are you helping your teammates? Are you producing on the ice? Or are you merely helping the owners, because your name is on the marquee? If you're satisfied to play that kind of hockey – scoring fifteen goals and deceiving yourself into thinking that you've had a good comeback season – it's your choice, and you'll have to live with yourself. All I can say is that, after the story surfaced, I got a great deal of mail from Quebec City. Most of it came from people who congratulated me for not being cynical, and for turning down the Nordiques' offer.

The Canadiens of the 1970s were an all-star group, with Hall of Fame talents such as Yvan Cournoyer, Ken Dryden, Guy Lafleur, Larry Robinson, Serge Savard, Guy Lapointe, Steve Shutt, and

Bob Gainey lining up for four straight Stanley Cup parades down St. Catherine Street. In many ways, however, Jacques Lemaire may have been the most important of all. His nickname was Coco, but someone with a sense of his presence on that team might have labelled him the Quiet Man. Jacques was a low-key but highly effective leader who did all his talking on the ice.

If Ken Dryden was an intellectual, then Jacques Lemaire was a hockey intellectual – but few people realized this until after his playing career was over. He scored Cup-winning goals in the 1978 and 1979 playoffs, and constantly brought out the best in Guy Lafleur. Still, I think his post-playing contributions have proved even more important.

After Jacques retired as a player, he coached in Europe, the U.S. college ranks, and the Quebec Major Junior Hockey League, before returning to the Canadiens as assistant to coach Bob Berry. He replaced Berry late in the 1984-85 season, at a time when the team was playing below .500 hockey for the first time in twenty-five years, and very nearly took them to the Stanley Cup final. After resigning this position, he became Serge Savard's right-hand man. Both Savard, as general manager, and Ronald Corey were impressed by his efforts, which paid off handsomely. He studied every player in the league, much as Sam Pollock had done before him. When the time came for trades and acquisitions, Jacques had a master file on hand, and could offer an instant and accurate evaluation.

Jacques was a major contributor to our 1986 and 1993 Stanley Cup wins. He did this by helping Savard identify and acquire important talents such as Bobby Smith, Gaston Gingras, Brian Skrudland, Mike Lalor, Kirk Muller, Vincent Damphousse, and Brian Bellows. There's no doubt that he's one of the foremost students of the game – and, although his departure was a loss to the team, I think that going to New Jersey was perfect for him. Jacques itched to get behind the bench, but knew that he couldn't do it under the media microscope in Montreal. Along with Larry

Robinson as his defensive coach, he's proved his mettle in his first season with the Devils.

I know that Scott Stevens, the Devils' captain and a twelve-year veteran of the league, paid the Lemaire–Robinson duo (and the Montreal Canadiens) a compliment during the 1994 playoffs. In an interview with Réjean Tremblay of *La Presse*, he remarked: "I couldn't imagine how much I had to learn. Larry especially taught me how to play my position, but he also taught me patience. I had the tendency to commit myself too quickly, to get caught out of position. He also showed me a bunch of little tricks that were taught to him during his years with the Canadiens: how to hold your stick when a player is skating down on you; how not to fall for a move. Teaching is what distinguishes Larry and Jacques Lemaire. They themselves learned from the best. The Canadiens teach young players what to do. That is why, good year or bad, the Canadiens always have a top team."

By the time of my second retirement from the Canadiens, Frank Selke and Sam Pollock had been long gone from the Second Floor, as were Toe Blake and Scotty Bowman from the bench. But their lessons, I think, live on, passed down from generation to generation, on and off the ice, and throughout the sport of hockey.

11

THE MONEY GAME

During the hot debate that preceded the entry of Disney's Mighty Ducks of Anaheim into the National Hockey League, I was reminded of a scene that took place in Pittsburgh in October 1967.

Many hockey conservatives, you'll recall, complained about the "shameless marketing ploy" and "Disney hype" when it was announced in 1993 that the Disney entertainment conglomerate had obtained a franchise. The clamour intensified when NHL president Gary Bettman joined Disney chairman Michael Eisner and Los Angeles Kings owner Bruce McNall in quacking duck calls at the team launch. A team named after a kids' movie seemed to strike a nerve. So intense was the reaction that it took at least some of the heat off the Florida Panthers, owned by none other than Blockbuster Video.

But none of this was new. That night in Pittsburgh, twenty-six years before the duck calls, Penguins captain Andy Bathgate and

I were front and centre for the ceremonial face-off, prior to the expansion team's first-ever NHL game. Midway through an eternity of introductions, a special visitor was escorted onto the ice. It was a live penguin, who, I remember, was clearly unnerved by 14,000 cheering fans in the stands. I'd never seen anything like it at the time. Both Andy and I found ourselves looking down at a penguin instead of the puck.

Maybe that night marked the beginning of the NHL's move into big-league marketing. At the time, I don't remember thinking, "Well, this isn't so bad, because in twenty-five years, Mickey Mouse and Goofy will join us." Mind you, on Penguin Night in Pittsburgh, I wouldn't have been surprised at anything the future could or would bring. That summer, the league had doubled in size, and for the first time since the 1941-42 season there were more than six teams involved in the quest for the Stanley Cup. The league expanded again in 1970 (Vancouver and Buffalo), 1972 (Atlanta and the New York Islanders) and 1974 (Washington and Kansas City). Just to keep things interesting, we also saw the arrival and departure of the World Hockey Association, and the subsequent addition of four of its teams to the NHL in 1979.

In the meantime, baseball, football, and basketball were expanding into newer markets with clockwork regularity, securing bigger and better network contracts, which, in turn, were bringing in more and more varied marketing opportunities, thereby swelling the coffers even more. That led to the establishment of other layers in the hierarchy of professional sports: agents and management corporations; marketing conglomerates; sports networks, cable television, and pay-per-view; million-dollar salaries and multi-million-dollar endorsement and personal services contracts.

Generally speaking, I have always been in favour of growth of every kind. After all, if you don't or can't expand, it means your business is in trouble. When the twelve-team WHA showed up in 1972, the NHL was composed of fourteen teams. Can you imagine what would have happened to the league, if the WHA had been created back in the days of the six-team league? Eighteen organizations would have had to fight for the best talent of a half-dozen clubs. As it was, the WHA made inroads right from the beginning, especially among the NHL's top players, because they'd been underpaid for several years.

Nonetheless, I've heard fans express reservations about the three most recent expansions, wondering aloud whether the NHL was moving too fast with regard to the talent available. I don't think so, because the league has opted to stock the expansion draft pool with better quality players. The results were there for everyone to see during the 1993–94 season: San José, a third-year team, made the playoffs, while Anaheim was not far behind in the Western Conference. In the East, the Panthers went down to the final week of regular-season play before they were edged out by Washington and the New York Islanders. These performances proved that the talent was there, and offered eloquent testimony to the NHL's intention to move swiftly and effectively into new markets.

Many players of my generation are baffled, even troubled, by what has taken place with respect to money in recent years. I have a somewhat different perspective, because I had a front-row seat as the money game took hold, and, I think, developed a fuller understanding of how it came to pass. My thoughts, therefore, are dedicated to two groups of people: the hockey fan of the 1990s, who has known nothing but the current hyper-marketed world of staggering salaries, "athlete-spokespersons," and corporate endorsements; and the hockey player of the six-team NHL, who has difficulty comprehending how his "grandchildren" can demand, and receive, such staggering compensation.

Am I surprised, or even envious, when I see how the money game has changed the rules of professional sport? I'm not surprised, because I have been in hockey management for more than twenty years and have participated in the process. Nor am I envious, because one cannot be consumed by envy or dwell in the past. An athlete must do all he can to make all he can in the short time allotted to him. He only charges what the market will bear, and the market shifts with time.

How different has the money game become for the professional athlete today? Some in-house (Montreal Canadiens) comparisons are in order:

• On October 3, 1953, Frank Selke "opened the Forum vault" (as he put it) and signed me to my first five-year contract, for a total of $105,000 in salary and bonuses.

• In 1970-71, my final season as a player with the Montreal Canadiens, our entire team was paid a total of $1,110,687.73 to win the Stanley Cup. That figure includes every player's regular-season salary and signing bonuses, as well as all playoff monies.

• In his eighteen-year NHL career, Maurice Richard made less than $500,000.

In 1994, Montreal Canadiens' managing director Serge Savard signed Patrick Roy to a new deal that paid the golden goaltender $4 million a season. (I firmly believe that Patrick is worth every penny.) In other words:

• Patrick will be paid more to play *two games* than I was paid throughout my first *five seasons*, not including playoffs.

• Patrick's deal pays him three-and-a-half times more than the entire Canadiens team earned in 1970-71.

• Patrick will earn more in two months than did Rocket Richard *in his entire career*.

We can quibble about what constitutes real dollars in 1953, 1971, and 1994, but even when that is factored in, today's superstars come out miles ahead. Properly managed, the money they earn in their professional sports careers will last a lifetime. No superstar of my generation – Gordie Howe, Maurice Richard, Stan Mikita, Bobby Hull, or Frank Mahovlich – could say the same.

Perhaps I can further illustrate my point by returning to the so-called Lindros Affair, which caused such a furor several years ago. It was a reminder to the NHL, the NHL Players' Association, sports television executives, and fans in markets both large and small that the money game is here to stay.

Eric's refusal to report to the Quebec Nordiques was, in fact, the logical follow-up to Wayne Gretzky's move to Los Angeles, which had prompted heightened efforts to sell the game of hockey in major U.S. markets.

Eric Lindros didn't refuse to play in Quebec City because of a "language issue" or some such nationalistic argument. If we think of him and his advisers as a hockey "corporation" – the superstar CEO and his board of directors – it was more a case of their looking around and coldly assessing the impact of new baseball stadiums being built or planned in Cleveland, Baltimore, Chicago, and Texas; new hockey rinks that are soon to appear in Montreal, Boston, Ottawa, San José, Vancouver, and Tampa Bay; and brand new franchises being awarded in these sports (and in basketball and football) to cities all over North America, but especially in the southern U.S. Hockey does not exist in a vacuum. All sports are interconnected. Nor does the money game acknowledge national boundaries. Many young Canadian players, in fact, are hoping and praying that they'll be drafted by American teams.

Unfortunately, Eric's situation became fraught with emotional and political baggage which pitted the Lindros camp and the Toronto media against the Nordiques and the Quebec media. Harsh words were spoken and written. People on both sides said things they probably regretted afterwards. As a Quebecer, I would have liked to have seen this talented player leading the Nordiques, but I don't think they could or would have paid him what Philadelphia wound up offering.

Once the dust had settled, Lindros – who'd never played a single NHL game – had signed an agreement that gave him $3.5 million a year for four or five years. It was also a terrific deal for the Flyers. They're putting up a new building and they have their own cable television network. If they're lucky, Eric will be their headliner for twelve to fifteen years. That's why they fought so hard to get him: they needed Lindros (or a Lindros) to make their investments pay off.

Nordiques president Marcel Aubut had the same thing in mind. He was busy mounting a campaign for a new Colisée, to ensure that Quebec could compete on a "level playing field." He, too, was looking for a young player with star quality (another Jean Béliveau, some said) whose presence would attract investors in the building and help fill the seats during those important early years of the new operation. But even if Marcel could have paid Lindros as much as the Flyers did, nobody could argue that Eric had a far better chance for non-hockey income in Philadelphia.

Still, many people criticized the NHL for not taking charge as *l'affaire Lindros* heated up and boiled over. According to this point of view, Lindros should have been "forced to play" – and, if he wouldn't, fined or banned. But in my view, the situation was cut and dried: Lindros was within his rights. His right not to play was protected by American anti-trust legislation and by the Sherman Act – no employer or potential employer can prevent someone from making a living in his or her chosen field. If the NHL had chosen to intervene, it might well have been taken to court for restraint of trade. The universal draft would not survive a court challenge, as baseball and football leagues discovered to their sorrow in previous judicial proceedings.

"Why are you blaming the NHL?" I would ask. "The rules have been there for several years, and everybody is simply following them." Any attempt on the NHL's part to sanction Lindros would have led to his being declared a free agent by the courts, and Quebec would have been left without recourse or compensation of any kind.

Another point: I'm pretty sure that the Lindros family was actually hoping that Eric would go to New York, not Philadelphia. If I'd been in his shoes, that would have been my choice. Philadelphia isn't a bad place, but it's not the media capital. (Although that seems not to be as important as it once was. Shaquille O'Neal is doing very well in Orlando, as did Larry Bird in Boston.) If Eric hoped to do a great deal of commercial work or promote himself in other ways, New York was a more obvious destination.

In any case, Eric went with the Flyers – and was, on the day he signed, the highest-paid player in the league, until Gretzky and Lemieux played catch-up. This sounds familiar; I was the highest-paid player the day I first signed, until Gordie Howe and Maurice Richard put matters right. The only difference between Eric and myself was about $3,479,000 a year.

How did the National Hockey League and the Montreal Canadiens get from my day to his? By 1977, the WHA was experiencing difficulties. That year and the next, approaches were made to the NHL board of governors, with a view to merger. This would have made life easier for everyone. The bidding war between the leagues had driven players' salaries out of sight (and several hockey entrepreneurs into bankruptcy) in four short years. When I retired, a year before the arrival of the WHA, highly rated NHL players were being paid in the range of $150,000 U.S. When players including Bobby Hull, Derek Sanderson, and Bernie Parent received offers of one million dollars each from WHA teams, those salaries doubled and tripled, as NHL teams strove to keep their top talent more or less satisfied.

Before Sam Pollock left the Second Floor, he very accurately predicted what was on the hockey horizon. Professional sports were going to become even more of a business than before, he said. Front offices would require the services of capable administrators, tax-law and investment specialists, and marketing and communications gurus, because competition was going to get fiercer by the day. Until that time, most of a hockey organization's decision-making and planning power had rested in the hands of the managing director or the general manager. Both these positions had traditionally been filled by people who knew the game inside out. The presidency was to a degree ceremonial in many franchises, even though, in the case of the Canadiens, individuals like David Molson and Jacques Courtois certainly contributed a great deal to the team's business affairs.

When Courtois left the presidency after the team was sold to Molson, I was asked to replace him. At the time, I was involved in all sorts of things, including my foundation and the community outreach side of my job. I also felt that I knew my capacities, and that it would take someone with extensive experience at the top of a corporation to handle the task. I preferred to stay where I was and to become the new president's right-hand man, if called upon to do so. Eventually, Morgan McCammon took the helm.

We got our first glimpse of the new reality Pollock predicted almost right away, right in our own back yard. In May 1977 when the Canadiens won the Stanley Cup, and the Quebec Nordiques defeated the Winnipeg Jets to win the WHA's Avco Cup, talk began to circulate of a "super series" between the two champions. It didn't get much beyond a couple of days of media speculation and a mini-tempest on talk shows, but it gave everybody on the Second Floor a clear indication of the passions a renewed Quebec City–Montreal rivalry would arouse.

When the first merger feelers were put forth in 1977 by a group representing the strongest WHA franchises, Sam Pollock had grave qualms about any agreement that would involve the Nordiques.

The province of Quebec was exclusive Montreal Canadiens territory within the NHL, and Sam wanted it to stay that way. By the time of his departure a year later, there was yet another reason for the Canadiens to oppose the Nordiques' entry: both teams now belonged to rival breweries. Carling O'Keefe had become the Nordiques' majority shareholder in 1976.

Given this situation, Molson's ownership of the Canadiens meant that the organization was susceptible to pressure of various kinds. When it became apparent that Montreal intended to impede Quebec's admittance to the NHL, anti-Canadiens sentiment grew in and around the provincial capital. Molson sales representatives and distributors there reported back to head office that there was a serious threat of a boycott of all Molson products. For a time, it seemed that such a boycott (which never really got underway) might spread as far west as Edmonton and Winnipeg.

On June 22, 1979, the threat of a boycott was nullified when the Nordiques and three other WHA teams – the Whalers, Oilers, and Jets – joined the NHL. The Canadiens were no longer Quebec's uncontested team. Molson was no longer the only brewery with an NHL squad in Quebec. Indeed, we were under attack by an aggressive new NHL franchise determined to get out from under the giant shadow cast by the building at Atwater and St. Catherine. The Nordiques were very much an expansion team that season, but there were well-recognized names in the lineup, many of them French, and many more French names among the Nordiques' management.

A key player in the Nordiques' organization was the president of O'Keefe Breweries, a tireless marketing specialist from Montreal named Ronald Corey. Another was Marcel Aubut, the team's thirty-year-old general counsel, who assumed the presidency and became the impetus behind the merger talks. These two men showed vision and daring, and the Nordiques became competitive on the ice within three short years. Unfortunately, one of their very first marketing ploys was to position themselves as French Quebec's team, and to subtly paint Montreal as the team of the "English establishment."

Fifteen years later, long after the Nordiques abandoned this dubious strategy, there remain Quebecers who've never forgotten or forgiven it. It certainly upset the Canadiens' players, their fans, and everyone in the Montreal organization. To my mind, it went too far. This kind of rivalry was not healthy. Nobody plays it tougher on the ice than the Bruins and the Canadiens, but each team has always viewed the other with respect, and this has led to a healthy competition over the decades. Not so for the Canadiens and the Nordiques. There are many Montreal fans who would tell you that they glory in the fact that Quebec has missed the playoffs six of the last seven years.

The Nordiques continued to make inroads in the Quebec marketplace between 1979 and 1982. After Dale Hunter's overtime goal eliminated us in the fifth game of the 1982 conference semifinal, the pressure for change on the Second Floor grew overwhelming. The message was that the Canadiens had to be smarter, more savvy, more attuned to the marketplace. It wasn't enough any more to distribute fold-out schedules at gas stations, and expect that people would automatically come.

I was an advocate of change, because, as you've seen, I've always thought that competition makes you better, on the ice and in the front office. Montrealers, we realized, had only so much disposable income, and we found ourselves in a battle for their entertainment dollars with the Expos, musical concerts of every kind, cable television, dance and theatre, and many other sources of diversion. To stand out, we had to be creative in our promotions and performance.

Molson needed a marketing expert with a strong background in sports, a man recognized as a motivator and a leader. That man was Ronald Corey, who joined the team as president in November 1982.

I'd known Ronald as a TV sports producer with Radio-Canada in the 1960s, before he went to Carling O'Keefe. When he settled in on the second floor of the Forum, he would often talk about his days as a teenage hockey fan.

"Jean, I used to buy standing-room tickets to watch you and the Aces play the Royals on Sunday afternoons at the Forum. Later, I did the same for the Saturday night games when you joined the Canadiens. I'm going to depend on your inside hockey knowledge to help me. The impression out there is that this team has distanced itself from its fans, and from its history. The saddest thing about that is that the history of the NHL's greatest franchise and its greatest building is our greatest marketing device. We can sell success, and use it to build even more success. The first job I have to do is to give this team back to its players and its fans."

Ronald's first move was to welcome back the Canadiens Alumni to the Forum, and make the old-timers comfortable. He asked me, as vice-president of corporate affairs, to help, and Louise Richer and I jumped in enthusiastically. A special ticket allotment was created for the former players, and one of my most enjoyable tasks was to escort Ronald all over the Forum as we tried to find space for the Alumni's permanent quarters. Players who'd felt forgotten had a home again, and a family feeling spread throughout the building. Our new president was quickly proving to be far more "hands-on" than his predecessors. Indeed, he may prove in time to be the most innovative and successful leader of them all.

Within a year, Ronald hired François-Xavier Seigneur, a fellow marketing whiz. A chain of Canadiens boutiques was launched. The old-fashioned game program was transformed into a glossy, well-produced magazine. Now fans went looking for it, rather than looking upon the program sellers as irritants. Then came the Mise au Jeu lounges, full-service dining rooms that were soon overbooked by businessmen eager to entertain clients before and after the games. The traditional hot dog and beer stands were augmented by food-court-style concession areas which introduced pizza, smoked meat, and other choices for the fans. A refurbished Canadiens Hall of Fame exhibit followed. With these changes, the Forum started to belong to the paying customers once again

Ronald Corey's enthusiasm made my tasks a great deal easier, too. Working with Claude Mouton, Camil Des Roches, and F.-X. Seigneur, our projects grew in stature: food drives, Alumni exhibition games on behalf of various charities, and Jean Béliveau Foundation work. I worked long hours, but under ideal conditions. Ronald made sure that I was free to pursue the causes I was championing at the time. If I needed to hold a press conference, the Mise au Jeu or Molson's reception room was always available.

As I mentioned earlier, the original expansion of the six-team NHL was spurred by the hope of securing a U.S. network television contract. CBS did, in fact, broadcast games for a brief period, but this arrangement had ended even before I finished playing, and the league has been unable to sign another contract since. Faced with this, the NHL went to the cable and private networks, which led to inequities within the league, since clubs in larger television markets were able to benefit from higher revenues – just as Montreal and Toronto were the major beneficiaries of *Hockey Night in Canada*.

Meanwhile, players' associations proliferated and gained in strength, with baseball and football leading the way. These activities put pressure on the NHL to pay our players more and more – but hockey franchises were not receiving (and still do not receive) the fabulous sums in TV revenue that basketball, baseball, and football teams enjoyed. The worst thing to happen to professional sports in North America was the ridiculous contract that CBS gave to Major League Baseball, to broadcast even fewer games than had been shown in the days of NBC's *Game of the Week*. That contract almost broke the network, and threw salary structures in every sport out of whack.

Meanwhile, the number of agents and athlete-management groups proliferated as well. The hockey business manager first appeared in the mid-1960s, with individuals such as Bob Woolf in Boston, Gerry Patterson in Montreal, and Alan Eagleson in Toronto vigorously promoting the game's major stars. Bobby Orr, for example, became a spokesman for General Motors, Coca-Cola, and Standard Brands, while endorsing other products. By the 1990s, big stars were making more money this way than they earned playing their particular sport. In 1994, the Sports Marketing Letter reported that Michael Jordan topped the list, with $31 million U.S. in off-court earnings annually, followed by Shaquille O'Neal, at $13.5 million. Wayne Gretzky was in ninth place, but first among hockey players, with $8.75 million in endorsement income, which eclipsed his $8 million annual salary.

With salaries rising across the board, hockey managements scrambled to identify and control new sources of money. Front offices began to talk about "revenue streams" – from logo marketing, food concessions, and parking lots, to luxury boxes, building rentals, and television rights. This spelled trouble for medium-sized cities on both sides of the border, where stadiums and arenas tended to be public buildings, owned by their communities. These facilities had been built in the first place because the communities looked forward to capturing the very sorts of revenues team owners were now talking about. As a result, prolonged tugs-of-war with local governments started to become commonplace.

Poor "revenue stream" franchises in more than one sport – think of the Baltimore Colts, St. Louis Cardinals, Atlanta Flames, Minnesota North Stars, and New Orleans Jazz – all folded, after acrimonious local debate, but were reborn in richer pastures where better deals could be made.

In 1992 and 1993 I was often asked how hockey hotbeds like

Minnesota or Edmonton could possibly be threatened with the loss of their teams. Each city had a knowledgeable fan base and a history of involvement with the sport. Would it not be a good idea for the NHL to step in, to protect its own long-term territorial interests against the short-term vision of certain franchise owners?

My answer never varied: how long can we expect team owners to lose upwards of five million dollars a year? If a professional sports franchise is faced with the deadly combination of increasing fixed costs, and rising player demands, many teams will reach the point where they'll be able to re-sign only two or three of their better players. The rest will be cut loose – just as the Pittsburgh Pirates were unable to retain stars such as Barry Bonds, Barry Bonilla, and Doug Drabek.

This leads to fears of a two-tiered league or sport – with franchises owned by giant corporations the best-placed to succeed because they have the most dollars. Why bother to build a team, if you can go out and buy one? This is an issue that must be addressed before it's too late – and I believe that every professional sports league will need a commissioner who is empowered to rule for the betterment of the sport.

Everyone is in this together. Sports organizations and fans are not on opposite wavelengths when it comes to a city losing its franchise. Nobody at the Forum was happy to see the North Stars leave Minnesota after the 1992-93 season, but we understood the business reasons behind the move. Canadians should be and are sensitive to this. As hockey gains in popularity in the United States, and the balance of NHL power shifts in that direction, several of our franchises may find themselves in the "have-not" category, when the inevitable shake-out occurs.

What happens in the short to medium term depends largely on the strength of an individual franchise's ownership. Building up that strength is what the race to discover more revenue streams is all about.

The league itself is also obsessed with finding "new money." Retail sales of NHL-licensed products grew from about $30 million in 1988 to more than $600 million in 1993. A thousand items bearing team logos are distributed by some 250 licencees – everything from caps, T-shirts, sweaters, jackets, and pyjama sets to bed linens, mugs, and posters. By late 1994, those sales should have nudged the $1 billion mark – a relatively small share of the $12 billion (per year) North American sports-licensing market.

NHL Enterprises, the league's marketing arm, also seeks out corporate sponsors such as Coca-Cola and McDonald's. We see this on every hockey telecast. When the Montreal Canadiens won the Stanley Cup in 1986, the series was played in rinks that featured pristine, white circumference boards. When the club repeated its victory in 1993, those same boards, and parts of the ice surface, were valuable money-makers for the teams. A 1992 survey by Ernst & Young of stadium and arena advertising found that the average NHL arena led the way with seventy-two signs and billboards, far ahead of basketball's fifty-four, football's twenty-five and baseball's eighteen. Canadian rinks contained an average of eighty-two signs, twenty-two per cent more than their U.S. counterparts. The Quebec Nordiques led the pack, with 100 signs promoting forty-six advertisers.

How much money is involved here? In Montreal, we bring in several million dollars a year on the boards alone, and the Molson Companies' Sports & Entertainment Group reported sales of more than $50 million in 1992 alone.

When the issue of advertising on the boards first arose, I mentioned that baseball teams had got rid of their outfield signs, while we in hockey were going the other way. Now, looking at the monthly numbers, I realize that we needed this particular revenue stream. It was good revenue and the fans accepted it fairly quickly. Amusingly, when I look at a tape of a game played ten years ago, the all-white boards seem strange and empty. On-ice corporate logos have been another matter. When I first saw advertisements on the ice surface itself, I confess it did something to me, even though I didn't fight against it.

It's human nature, I suppose. People adapt to new situations more quickly than we want to believe. No one thinks twice about the fact that players wear helmets with the brand names prominently displayed. These days, a manufacturer's name covers almost the entire shaft of a stick. When the Forum installed a new lighting system for colour television, it made an enormous difference. We asked ourselves how we could ever have played under the old lights, it seemed so dark by comparison. For a while, we kept the old lighting system functioning, for non-televised games – but then the fans complained, and we had the outmoded lights removed.

So far, so good. Business savvy, aggressive marketing, and full acceptance of the facts of life by understanding fans have led to impressive revenue figures. As the 1980s drew to a close, the Canadiens were in solid shape – but Ron Corey and his team could read a balance sheet with the best of them, and they could see trouble ahead.

When the Canadiens were sold by the Bronfmans to Molson, Edward and Peter Bronfman maintained control of the Canadian Arena Company (later Carena), which in turn owned the Forum. The Canadiens occupied the Forum under the terms of a thirty-year "net-net" lease, which permitted us to amortize improvements we made to the building.

However, one can only do so much with a building one doesn't own. Moreover, the Forum was not suited to the needs of a 1990s hockey franchise. Although it was one of the league's older structures, it had been renovated in 1949 and again in 1968. Luxury boxes, however, could not be added without taking away large numbers of seats and creating an uproar among average fans. The hard reality was that the Forum was outdated. Its hallways were narrow, which meant that traffic jams formed as people lined up at the food concessions during intermissions. The very ice – once among the league's finest – had become one of the worst surfaces around, because the ice plant dated from the building's original construction in 1924. Even the kids who skated there on Saturday afternoons were among its critics. As well, the Forum is hemmed in, located in a heavily built-up part of the city, on the western edge of downtown. There are exactly ten indoor parking spaces, and parking revenues – a major income source – are scooped by nearby private lots.

During one of our morning "coffee talks," Ronald Corey ran down this familiar litany of complaints. "Everywhere we turn, Jean, we're up against a wall that prevents us from finding the revenues that will keep the Canadiens at the top of the league and allow us to maintain our standards as a class organization," he said.

Then came the bombshell. "What would you think if we were to put up a new, state-of-the-art building on our own land?"

I can't say that images of the present Forum flashed before my eyes, like the lifetime of the proverbial drowning man. I loved the building, but I also recognized its many shortcomings. I knew we needed a new building if we wanted to maintain a solid revenue picture over the next decade and beyond. If we failed to do our duty now, another generation of managers in 2010 or so would probably look back and say, "Those guys were asleep at the switch in 1990. They didn't make the right decisions and now we're paying for them."

I also knew, however, that many hockey fans around the world saw the Forum as Leaf supporters see Maple Leaf Gardens. It is hockey's shrine, the Holy of Holies. Any replacement structure would have to be meticulously planned, carefully marketed, and backed by reams of persuasive documentation.

"What do you propose to do, Ronald?"

"I'd like to have a feasibility study done," he said, "to see if we can upgrade the present building, and then we'll take it from there."

"I think that's best," I agreed. "It will be the first step in mounting our case."

Days later, Ronald met with representatives of Lavalin, the prestigious engineering firm, which would undertake the study. A little over six months later their answer came back: it would take a $40-million investment to bring the Forum up to speed – after which, it would still be a seventy-odd-year-old building with a lot of improvements tacked on and built in. Some of its shortcomings – notably its size and location – could never be addressed, for any amount of money.

Lavalin concluded that the Forum needed to double in size from its existing 300,000 square feet, if it hoped to serve as a multi-functional, all-purpose entertainment venue for the 1990s. Plainly, another renovation would not suffice. To remain profitable and competitive, the Canadiens needed a brand new building.

Given this conclusion, a second phase began. Engineers, designers, and Canadiens executives began visiting the newest facilities all over North America. They had a two-edged mandate: to provide the team with a state-of-the-art building that would meet all of the needs identified by Lavalin's study, and to ensure that the new Forum would retain the warmth and ambience of the sport's most exciting building.

The fact-finding team had many projects to inspect. Stadiums and arenas are under construction or in the planning stages in San José, Chicago, Boston, St. Louis, San Antonio, St. Petersburg, and Vancouver. A wealth of information and technology was available – and the team came back most impressed by The Palace of Auburn Hills, home to the Detroit Pistons of the NBA.

These information-gathering visits were undertaken in utmost secrecy. We wanted to assemble all the facts, and present the world with a well-conceived *fait accompli* when we judged that the time was right.

After Canadiens management unanimously endorsed Lavalin's conclusions, research began into downtown real estate. This led to contacts with Marathon Realty, the commercial real estate arm of Canadian Pacific Limited – and to a spectacular project that, if realized, will position the new Forum as the centrepiece of a vast office and entertainment complex. Indeed, the development as a whole is the city's largest project since Place Ville-Marie, which helped propel Montreal into the second half of the twentieth century.

The new arena, planned for construction just south of historic Windsor Station, will be surrounded by the twenty-storey Terminal Building, at St. Antoine and Mountain streets; the forty-four-storey Forum building at Mountain and Lagauchetière; and the fifty-one-storey Windsor building to the east, on St. Antoine. The nineteenth and twentieth centuries will stand side-by-side, with a huge courtyard between the arena and the refurbished Windsor Station minimizing shadows cast by the new buildings on neighbouring Dominion Square, Saint George's Anglican Church, and the courtyard itself.

The existing Forum at Atwater and St. Catherine has averaged 1.2 million spectators a year for fifty hockey games and another 100 entertainment events. The new building should substantially raise those numbers, with seating for 21,260 (up from 16,900), and 134 luxury boxes that should generate about $12 million in revenue a year. Needless to say, the food courts will be state-of-the-art, as will be the scoreboard and its replay screen. There will be 700 indoor parking spaces available, and another 5,000 within easy walking distance. Should it come to pass, the whole project will cost in the neighbourhood of $450 million.

Because this is Montreal, and only the Canadiens can market their history as the sport's most successful franchise, great care will be taken throughout the new facility to maintain the team's long-standing character.

"It is one of the most interesting challenges I've ever faced," said

F.-X. Seigneur, who is charged with moving the "ghosts" across town. "We aren't sure whether or not to have a single area designated as the Canadiens Museum, or to make each floor a museum in itself. But rest assured that the historical links will not be lost."

After our plans were made public, all the parties involved were subjected to an arduous round of zoning and heritage hearings – but our preparations had been so complete that we met with little opposition to the news that the team would leave the old Forum in 1995-96. With a waiting list of 2,000-plus for season tickets, and a city anxious to renew its downtown core, Montrealers responded positively and with great excitement.

A final question is: what will the new building be called? A name can be a revenue stream all by itself, worth untold millions over the long haul. Up until the 1993 season, both the NHL's Washington Capitals and the NBA's Bullets played their home games at the Capital Center in Landover, Maryland. In 1994, they began playing at something called the U.S. Air Arena. They hadn't moved. The airline had simply negotiated a ten-year, $10 million agreement to rename the Capital Center. Its logo appears at both centre ice and centre court, and on every program and ticket stub. For ten years, every time the Capitals and Bullets are mentioned in a sports report, U.S. Air will get a mention, too.

This sort of practice is becoming more and more widespread. Few people objected in the mid-1980s when the Los Angeles Forum became the Great Western Forum, and few complaints will arise in 1995 when the Bruins, Black Hawks, and Canucks move, respectively, to the Shawmut Center (a bank), the United Center (the airline), and General Motors Place.

Will our new arena be the Molson Forum, Centre, or Place? Will other Montreal-based conglomerates such as Air Canada, Bombardier, the Bank of Montreal, or Canadian Pacific wish to advertise on and in the building? What will that sort of exposure be worth to them?

I don't know what the official name will be. I do know that it may meet with a degree of public resistance. When the Impact Research survey firm and *La Presse* carried out a survey among 300 French-speaking Montrealers in February 1994, seventy-eight per cent of the respondents indicated they were against a "corporately affiliated" Forum. *La Presse* also interviewed Ronald Corey – who needless to say espoused an opposite view.

But we'll cross that bridge when we come to it. It took a great deal of courage for Ronald Corey to recognize what had to be done in 1990, and then move forward with the force and enthusiasm that this sort of project requires. When it's completed, it will be the crowning glory of his leadership. But knowing him as I do, once the new Forum opens in 1996, he'll immediately turn to the ongoing challenge of keeping the franchise at the top of the heap.

"You can't rest on your laurels in this business," he is fond of saying. "The day after you've won the Stanley Cup, you have to get up and start selling the next one."

This is his nature, which everyone has come to respect. When Ronald Corey first arrived, he seemed too brash, too confident, too much of a fan to be presidential material. Of course, he proved the *mauvaises langues* wrong. His style was a perfect match for the challenges at hand. He did the job that had to be done at the time.

And so did Serge Savard, our managing director, who replaced Irving Grundman in 1983. In the past, when the stakes were somewhat less, the team's managing director operated with a greater degree of autonomy, because hockey decisions did not necessarily have a profound impact on the entire corporation. Now, however, when we sign Patrick Roy to a $4 million contract, Ronald Corey and Molson have to be involved. Matters must be clarified at the very top.

Ever since Serge came in, the Canadiens have always won the first round of the playoffs, with the sole exception of 1994. While this might seem a rather minor achievement, I mention it to show

how it's become part and parcel of the money game. When you prepare your budget for the year, and you factor in five or six at-home playoff games, it's very important for the team's financial health that those games, in fact, take place. Each one represents a take of somewhere between $500,000 and $750,000 – which could very well work out to be the team's profit margin for the entire season.

Success breeds success, and the long-term success that has been our good fortune for so many years has allowed the team to remain rock-solid throughout the past decade. Winners build up a long-term bank account that dwindles only a little when the pendulum swings.

This holds true throughout the world of sports. Maybe the Boston Celtics haven't been winning like they used to – but are we going to lose sight of them? You hear a lot more about the Chicago Bulls these days, but they'll have to perform for ten or fifteen years, before they achieve a similar mystique. Although we have won "only" two Cups in the last eight seasons, it will be many a long year before the Montreal Canadiens' reputation decreases.

Of course, shrewd marketing is only partially responsible for maintaining a franchise's mystique, even through the lean times. But marketing, finally, can do only so much. I used to say that the best marketing device is performance. You can conceive all the best ideas in the world, but your task will be easier if the team is bringing home the bacon. Fame endures, and a team's supporters stay on board. So what if the Yankees haven't won anything since the late 1970s? Don't worry, they'll be back. The diehard fan is unequivocally tied to the team, and marketing keeps him there.

The Quebec Nordiques are an excellent case in point: they missed the playoffs for five consecutive seasons and suffered through the Lindros episode, but good marketing filled the rink and moved the merchandise. Then, in 1992-93, the young and exciting post-Lindros Nordiques enjoyed a terrific regular-season surge, only to falter in the playoffs, a performance they repeated the next season.

A lot of people, as I've said, were annoyed by the deference shown the Mighty Ducks and the Panthers on their arrival in the NHL. Oddly enough, fans in the teams' home cities did not share these misgivings and filled the rinks at once.

Other people are worried about the growing influence of the NHL's New York headquarters, far away from the traditional hockey strongholds of Toronto and Montreal. They fear that both the league and the game will lose their Canadian roots. This may occur, but the league will always have a Canadian flavour. As for the American expansion teams, their success as they age will depend on their performance. That holds true everywhere: the Nordiques will have to start winning consistently pretty soon if they hope to build themselves a name. History is a grand thing, but the Canadiens wouldn't be recognized throughout the world if they'd been losers. Performance is the key to longevity.

We have to face facts, and not get sidetracked by hockey nationalism or sentimentality. The survival of today's franchises in Canadian cities will hinge both on performance and on solid, responsible ownership. Quebec, Edmonton, Winnipeg, and Ottawa must come to grips with their particular situations. Toronto and Montreal, because of the size of their markets and their wealth of history, are in a different league, so to speak.

Will one or more of these small-market franchises disappear? Small-market teams have to make do with small-market resources, and some have had well-documented problems at the top. But even the most trouble-plagued franchise is aware of what it has to do. Both Vancouver and Ottawa, for instance, have new arenas in their future. So does Quebec, thanks to Marcel Aubut, who has spent what seems like every waking hour of the past three years trying to convince three levels of government that the Nordiques need a new building if they are to survive and prosper.

Tied in with these concerns is the fear that the Canadian or long-established teams will lose their influence in the NHL's board-room. The rapid rise of Bruce McNall of the Los Angeles Kings struck some as disquieting. One year he was a new owner; a few years later, he'd replaced Chicago's venerable Bill Wirtz as chairman of the league's board of governors. But I saw no evidence of an anti-Canadian bias in anything he did. Besides which, his influence, not to mention ownership clout, has waned of late.

It all comes down to the money game. You can begin to grasp how the sports world has changed over the past decade, simply by tracking the media coverage. In my day, the business media had no interest in the Montreal Canadiens or the Maple Leafs. Today, they focus on sports franchises in the same way as they would any other corporation or industrial sector.

Each spring, one of the most anticipated sports-cum-business stories is *Financial World*'s annual rating of North American franchises. In 1993, the Dallas Cowboys (repeat winners of the Super Bowl) were deemed Number One, with an estimated value of $190 million. How was this figure arrived at? It factored in all the usual profit-and-loss yardsticks – revenues, players' salaries, operating costs, and so on – as well as something the publication called a franchise's "software value" (referring to how much money was derived from broadcasts of the team's games), and its value as a vehicle for the sale of consumer products.

The highest ranked baseball team was the New York Yankees, in sixth place overall, at $166 million, followed by the Toronto Blue Jays ($150 million). The Montreal Expos were dead last in the baseball category, at a mere $75 million.

Nor was hockey doing all that well. The Detroit Red Wings were first among NHL teams at $104 million, followed by the Boston Bruins ($88 million), the Los Angeles Kings ($85 million), and the Montreal Canadiens ($82 million). The other Canadian NHL franchises checked in at $77 million (Toronto), $69 million

(Vancouver), $50 million (Calgary and Ottawa), $46 million (Edmonton), $43 million (Quebec), and $35 million (Winnipeg). The Jets, interestingly, held the unenviable distinction of being the franchise with the lowest value in all four sports surveyed.

These figures reveal extraordinary disparities, and show clearly which franchises are at risk. When $69 million separates the Red Wings and the Jets, something's got to give. I would suggest that any professional sports franchise of the 1990s that's not supported by large corporate assets, or by major media agreements, will find itself in trouble sooner or later. A salary cap may be the answer for hockey. If the players are going to ask for more money each time revenues increase (or each time salaries in some other sport take a wild jump), the weaker franchises will remain forever in a bind.

A spirit of common sense and compromise is plainly necessary. But that's easy to say and harder to achieve. Perhaps there are too many hands on the NHL wheel now. In the era of the six-team league, the board meetings, chaired by Clarence Campbell, often were over and done with in a morning or an afternoon. Sometimes we settled matters with a conference call. Now, with twenty-six teams – which means twenty-six owners, twenty-six lawyers, and who knows how many experts and advisers – league meetings often have more than fifty individuals on hand. Fortunately, by 1996, the brand new Forum likely will be ready for occupancy. By that time, they may need that sort of space, if all of hockey's constituencies hope to sit down together and thrash things out.

Perhaps the sports world is getting so big, and is moving so fast toward major corporation status, that the end-user is being lost in the shuffle. I hope not. The fans are, and must remain, paramount. But the crystal ball is clouded, and, truthfully, I can't foresee the eventual winners and losers of the money game. I can only say that I've enjoyed my front-row seat, as professional sports went through this quite remarkable metamorphosis. It was, and continues to be, an education for us all.

12

✦

THE PEOPLE
AND PLACES

To echo the great Lou Gehrig's farewell at Yankee Stadium in 1939, "I consider myself the luckiest guy in the world." I am a religious person, and I thank God daily for the natural abilities that enabled me to become a professional hockey player, and for the countless opportunities that were presented to me over my career with the Montreal Canadiens.

The eighteen-year-old boy who left Victoriaville in December 1949 could not possibly have guessed that he was embarking on a voyage through life that would never cease to enrich him. Hockey enabled me to educate myself, to meet my wife, to pursue a career off-ice both during and after my playing days. Hockey introduced me to wonderful friends: my teammates, the Côtés and the Byrnes, Roland Mercier, Zotique Lespérance, Jack Latter and Charlie Smith, the Molson and Bronfman families, Raymond Lemay, the Selkes, Sam Pollock . . . the list goes on. I have been truly blessed, and I am truly grateful.

But hockey is a business – and none of these things would have happened without the people who paid money to sit in the stands. A player makes a basic decision early in a sports career – how to balance his own need for privacy with the demands that will be placed upon him by virtue of his profession. An athlete should be involved in his community. He must treat the public with respect, if he wishes to gain respect in turn. It's not always easy. But anyone who thinks that he's there only for the paycheque and the good times will be bitterly disappointed in the end.

As a hockey player – and later as a member of various corporate boards – I was fortunate enough to travel all around the world. First, however, I came to experience the wonderful country in which I live. I have crossed it many times over the past forty-five years, and have come to know it well.

Today, I am asked a number of inevitable questions, given the current climate of political doubt. I think my actions over the years have made my position clear. People know where I stand. I like to reply that I am first and foremost a Canadian – and a Canadien.

One of the proudest days in my life was in 1969, when Gordie Howe and I were received as Officers of the Order of Canada by Governor General Roland Michener. It was and is a great honour, and I wear my pin every day.

I've always said that we are so fortunate to be Canadian. Even if you travel as extensively as I have done, you are always glad to come home. I've seen great things all over the world, but Canada is to my mind the best place to live, bar none.

The Club de Hockey Canadien has always been a metaphor for Canada, a fine example of different ethnic groups working together to achieve something. Language and cultural differences were never problems among the team. I learned English from my teammates in the room. When I went to Quebec City, I couldn't speak a word. I picked it up from them, and I very quickly realized that there are good people everywhere. I believe that part of

our present difficulties lies in the fact that the majority of Quebecers have never had the chance to visit the rest of the country,
to see its beauty, to meet its people.

I am very disturbed, not only by what is happening here in
Quebec, but also by events all around the world. So many countries are going through miserable difficulties. Can we not learn
from these things? Every day it seems there's a new trouble spot
or an old trouble spot renewing ancient hatreds ... Yugoslavia,
Haiti, Rwanda, Yemen. Closer to home, the guiding principles
of my youth have virtually disappeared. Respect and discipline
seem to be in large part absent from the education of our young
people. If you don't have discipline, you don't have limits. If you
don't have limits, it leads to situations like the one we're facing in
our society.

I think the situation we have here in Quebec had its wellsprings
in 1960, with Jean Lesage's Quiet Revolution, or perhaps in 1955,
with the Maurice Richard incident. One thing is certain: the
negative fall-out, the climate of uncertainty, has lasted too long.
For almost thirty-five years, people in Quebec haven't known
where the future will take them. It makes a lot of people very
uncomfortable.

What I find difficult to understand is why, at a time when large
corporations and countries worldwide are getting together to
confront the global marketplace, some Quebecers want to go the
other way. I've always thought that if you're not getting any bigger,
then through the years you'll regress and become smaller. Once,
Quebecers made up thirty per cent of the Canadian population.
Now, I believe, they're down to roughly twenty-one per cent.
Before the turn of the century, that will have fallen even more, to
about eighteen per cent. Immigrants may make a difference, but
who knows what will happen if they don't arrive, and the birth
rate remains as low as it's been in the past several years.

The situation in Quebec today is very sad, and has produced

only hard feelings among families here. I know many families where some members aren't talking to each other, caught up, as they are, in disputes over Quebec and Canadian politics.

I myself have never been tempted to enter politics. I suppose that, throughout the years, my name has been on everybody's "wish list" of ideal candidates, and, yes, I was approached in round-about ways from time to time. But when I showed no interest, these overtures no longer came my way. It's true that I was twice offered a Senate seat by Prime Minister Mulroney, whom I knew quite well. The first call came in 1992, when there were several vacancies in the Upper House which he wanted to fill with Conservatives.

"First of all," I told him, "I've always stayed away from politics. Secondly, I certainly wouldn't have anything to do with politics unless I were elected, not appointed. Thirdly, I certainly wouldn't go to the Senate merely because the Conservatives need more votes."

The prime minister understood this, and the matter rested. A year later, however, he tried again, just before he resigned as prime minster, about the time that I was counting down to my corporate retirement. When word got out about this offer, I was in Toronto on business. I knew I couldn't hide from the press on this so I had Louise Richer reroute all the calls. I sat in my room at the Royal York for two hours answering reporters' questions.

Again, I had to refuse Mr. Mulroney and told him I had to be consistent: "The Canadiens want me to stay, but I want more freedom. I want control of my agenda. If I accept your offer, I simply transfer my time at the Forum to Ottawa. And you know me. I wouldn't be a figurehead. I'd want to work at it, just as I've worked for the team. I'm a well-known person. I'd be asked to go everywhere. When I left Ottawa on the weekend, I wouldn't go home. They'd have me off in Halifax or Vancouver. I'm sixty-two years old, and I want to give more time to my family." And that was that.

Besides, I think I did my small part in showing how close Canadians of every background and heritage could become when we undertook twenty years of sports cultural exchanges at the Forum. I worked with Bob Beale and Marcel Bonin all throughout the project, which started in 1972. At that time, Peter and Edward Bronfman were directors of a student exchange program. One day, Peter Bronfman came to me and said: "Jean, our program works fine in the summer, but there's nothing in the winter."

The idea came. "If you give me a budget, we'll use the same principle, and set up an exchange among French- and English-speaking minor hockey organizations. The kids can play on Forum ice and attend the Saturday night game together." Over the years, this was a tremendous success, but it ended in 1993. I always thought that the person responsible for the program should be there, actively working on it. When I retired, we had to close it down.

I have received hundreds of letters from parents expressing their happiness and satisfaction with the exchanges, telling me how pleased they were with the values and lessons that their children learned. What a great experience it was for a kid from the Beauce, who couldn't speak a word of English, to come to Beaconsfield in the West Island of Montreal on Friday night, and stay with a family there throughout the weekend. When he left on Sunday, he and the kid from Beaconsfield were friends and fellow players. Then, the Beaconsfield kid would return the visit by going to the Beauce. It showed those kids at an early age that there were other people, other places, other lifestyles, other viewpoints in the world.

One of my most memorable trips across Canada took place in the mid-1970s. One Sunday afternoon, I flew to St. John's, Newfoundland, where I met the current Miss Canada and Bruno Gerussi, the long-time star of the CBC television program *The Beachcombers*. The Rock was our jumping-off point for a unique marathon on behalf of the Big Brothers organization: the next day we would embark on a twenty-four-hour, coast-to-coast media tour.

Accompanied by a couple of directors of the Big Brothers of Canada national office, we attended a local press conference very early that Monday morning, and then flew to Halifax, then Montreal, Toronto, Winnipeg, Regina, Edmonton, and Vancouver, all on the same day. At each airport in each city, the local Big Brothers set up a press conference. After we had wrapped up at Vancouver airport at nine o'clock Pacific time, we went to a television studio. Needless to say, we were absolutely exhausted after seven take-offs and landings, and collapsed in our beds like zombies.

The greatest contrast to that trip was the one I took with Élise in 1960. This was the year, you may recall, that Molson acquired several western breweries, and sent me to tour them. I could pick any mode of transportation I wanted – plane, train, whatever – but I said to Élise, "We're still young, so let's drive. We'll have a second honeymoon all the way across the country."

Élise didn't hesitate. She's always been an enthusiastic traveller. Her sister Rita agreed to take care of Hélène, who had just turned three, while we took our car and toured Canada.

The first stop was in Winnipeg, and we went on from there. We'd spend two or three days in each city, and I'd visit hospitals, radio stations, and service clubs. Then we'd hit the road for our next stop. One month later we found ourselves in Vancouver.

Before we'd left, Molson's told me: "When you finish up in Vancouver, take all the time you need for yourselves." You can imagine that after a month of long, full days, we were pretty pooped. We caught our breaths, got back in the car, and drove all the way down the coasts of Washington, Oregon, and California, to San Diego. Then we took another month to come back home.

By the time we arrived in Quebec, after two months of missing our daughter, we were all travelled out for a while. In retrospect, though, this was the trip that gave us the "travel bug" for life. Later on, whenever I got the opportunity, off I'd go to experience more and more of our country – especially what many people would consider its more "remote" areas. That all depends on your point of view: Canadians who live in these far-off corners don't consider themselves remote at all, but neither do they have the same chance to meet and greet sports personalities as do their fellow citizens in major centres, so every time I was invited, I tried to go. I was invited often – because, for the longest time, the Canadiens were the only team who had someone to do this sort of thing.

One day early in 1976 I got a call at the Forum from the mayor of Dawson City, Yukon. "Jean, we're about to open a new sports complex, and the major part of it is the arena. We'd be honoured if you would come." This was a marathon trek by anybody's standards, and I hesitated at first. "Surely there's someone in Vancouver who could go," I said. "I'd have to fly there, sleep overnight, and take the plane the next morning to Whitehorse. And after that, another hour-and-a-half in a small plane . . . I don't say no very often, but this time it has to be no."

I hung up the phone, and immediately felt bad. These people felt that the opening was a very special occasion in their lives. If I could help, I should, even if it meant travelling all that way.

I called him back an hour later. "Have you found somebody else?"

"No, we still want you."

"Okay, I'll go."

The sights and sounds of many different places tend to meld together with time, but I have a great memory aid when it comes to the Dawson trip. That night in my Vancouver hotel room, I saw Darryl Sittler of Toronto set a league record with six goals and four assists for ten points in a single game.

I arrived in Whitehorse the next morning, on February 8, and flew to Dawson after a change of plane. It was a crisp winter day.

You could see the mountains, lakes, and forests, deep beneath a blanket of snow.

About 800 people winter in Dawson City, mostly Inuit and Indians, but the town's population swells to 3,000 or 4,000 in the summer. The whole town (and half the surrounding countryside) came to the opening ceremonies.

The mayor began by giving a little speech. "Down east, you cut a ceremonial ribbon when you open a new building," he said, "Here, we do things differently." Two Inuit came toward us. One carried a sawhorse and saw, the other a white birch log.

The mayor and I each took an end of the saw, and cut the birch in two (taking me back to Victoriaville and the cedar poles). When we were done, he gave me a key to the front door and invited the crowd inside. We promptly did what every Canadian does at an arena opening – we went for a skate.

Before the Montreal casino opened on Ile Notre-Dame, Dawson was the only place in Canada where you could gamble legally. Its casino usually operated only in the summertime, but they made an exception that night, and we packed the place. It was like an old saloon in western movies, complete with cancan showgirls and plenty of local colour.

Before the opening ceremonies, I was taken by helicopter over the Klondike River. We landed, and I was shown how to pan for gold with a sluice. That night, an old prospector came by our table at dinner, and showed me a nugget the size of my fist. That thing was so heavy, it must have been worth thousands of dollars. And he was carrying it around in his pocket! Just before the evening ended, they called me up on stage and told me to take off my jacket and roll up my sleeves. A big bucket full of sandy water appeared, and I panned for gold. After a while, I came up with about an ounce, all in tiny flakes. I still have them in a plastic vial. It was one of the most original gifts I'd ever received on my travels. After all, it's not very often that you can make money during dessert.

I was up at seven the next morning, despite a late night. I was staying at the mayor's house, and had only three or four hours before my plane went back to Whitehorse, so I wanted to look around a bit. I dressed warmly and walked through the town in 40-below weather – just me and the crunching of my boots in the half-light of a Northern sunrise. Suddenly I looked up, and saw I had company. I thought at first they were crows, but later was told they were huge ravens. They and a few dogs were my only companions, plus a lonely fireman on duty at the firehall.

Northern travels define this country for me. Several years later I was asked by the federal government to visit the community of Frobisher Bay (now called Iqaluit) for a weekend. I was to watch the *Hockey Night in Canada* game that Saturday with local residents, and, after each period, answer their questions about the contest, and about hockey in general.

Frobisher Bay is on Baffin Island, which is 1,100 miles long, and dotted with tiny settlements. The bush plane is the lifeline of the North, especially when you have to pick up someone who's fallen ill 500 miles away from the nearest hospital. In this case, the only hospital is located in Iqaluit (which means "place where the fish are"), along with the only high school. You might have a teacher or a nurse in some of the bigger settlements, but for the most part, those things are centralized.

During my visit, I was taken by plane to Pangnirtung, on the Cumberland Peninsula. Quite a few tourists go there now because it's an important centre for Inuit art, especially woven tapestries and soapstone carvings. Pangnirtung is at the base of a mountain. As you fly in, the plane clears the peak, banks sharply and then drops like a stone to land on a frozen clearing right in the middle of the village. When I disembarked, a group of kids were playing hockey in thirty-five-below weather. I joined them for a few minutes and then continued my tour, which included a visit to the local museum.

Pangnirtung is famous for reasons other than art. It's said that the first Europeans landed there in 1585, four hundred years before me. By 1840, it was established as the northernmost port for whalers plying their trade in the Arctic waters.

To fly out, we had to follow the course of a river canyon for several miles, with mountains flanking us on either side. All of a sudden, we reached a pass, the pilot pointed the nose straight up, and we were out of there.

Pangnirtung, a local guide told me, is Inuit for "place of the bull caribou." I soon found out why. One of the sights below us was a caribou herd, hundreds if not thousands of them, moving across the landscape. Later, as we neared Iqaluit and darkness fell, I could see the lights of Inuit hunters, returning to their villages from all directions on their snowmobiles.

At dinner in Iqaluit that night, the mayor introduced me to a dentist who had retired from his practice in Jonquière, and had decided to experience the Far North for a year. Three years later, he was still there (just like my uncles, who went to the western harvest and stayed forever).

During our meal, I asked the mayor if I could see a dog sled.

"Sure, Jean, but I have to tell you that there's only one in town."

This surprised me – but what surprised me even more was that the only dog sled and team in Iqaluit was owned by the dentist from Jonquière. Everybody else relied on snowmobiles!

I experienced memorable trips outside the country, as well. My first came in 1966, when I went to visit the Canadian forces who were part of a six-country United Nations peacekeeping contingent in the Sinai Desert. Each night, the CBC provided footage of the latest Stanley Cup playoff game, and I'd show it to the soldiers. Our troupe numbered about twenty persons, including the entertainer Danièle Dorice and Miss Canada, Diane Landry, of St.

Boniface, Manitoba. But we also toured the camps of the other countries' troops. There wasn't much ice in sight, so I played softball and golf. They'd set up a small course in the nearby desert, and we'd tee off from carpets. For greens, they'd empty a barrel of oil, and roll the surface smooth. Of course, there wasn't any need for them to construct sand traps.

We stayed in Rafah, on the coast, and visited places that would become household names eighteen months later during the 1967 Arab–Israeli War, including El Arish, only six miles distant, where the Israeli army would launch a major tank offensive in the first days of the conflict.

I returned to the Middle East nineteen years later, when Gary Ulrich, Eddie Wilzer, and Gordie Schwartz invited me to visit Israel as honourary captain of the Canadian team competing in that year's Maccabiah Games, a sort of Jewish Olympics. It was a great trip for both Élise and me, because we had lots of free time to visit the cities and the nearby countryside. Tel Aviv gets extremely hot in July. As a result, the competitions were confined to early mornings, late afternoons, and evenings. Most events took place in Tel Aviv's Ramat Gan Stadium, with golf near Netanya and swimming in Jerusalem.

Israel is quite small, and very easy to get around. Most days, we'd go to Jerusalem for the early competitions, then ask our driver to take us to the Dead Sea, the mountains, or to the ancient city of Jericho.

One afternoon in Jericho, I decided that I wanted a Bedouin teapot, and asked our chauffeur to find a reputable antique shop.

"Antique shops are more numerous than people in Jericho," he smiled.

"Then take us to the best one," I said.

As it happened, we got there just as units of the Israeli Army did. Troop transports disgorged helmeted and flak-jacketed soldiers who fanned out in all directions. The canvas top of one two-ton truck was rolled back to reveal the biggest, ugliest machine gun I'd ever seen. The troops quickly secured the area immediately in front of us, roped it off, and took up their positions.

Of course, our destination was on the other side of the rope.

Our chauffeur, who obviously had some kind of governmental (if not military) connection, hailed an officer. "What's happening?"

The officer pointed to a stone bridge not two hundred yards from where we stood.

"We just received a call that the bridge over there is mined with several hundred pounds of explosive."

There was nothing to do but wait, as the sappers went to work. Meanwhile, our antique shop beckoned to us, a scant thirty yards away.

"Listen," our chauffeur said to the officer, "these people are from Montreal. Mr. Béliveau is honorary captain of the Canadian team at the Maccabiah Games. We want to go to that store. They'll be safer inside it than standing here, should this whole thing blow, God forbid."

The officer thought about it, and I could see him visualizing how much trouble would come down on his head if we were blown to bits because he refused us shelter.

"Go ahead, but be careful," he said, and waved us through.

As a Canadian who lives in a country of a million lakes and hundreds of rivers, surrounded by three oceans, I was struck by the self-sufficiency of an Israeli kibbutz and the country's irrigation system. I'd wondered out loud how they could have turned the desert so green, and they showed me the giant desalination plants.

We saw the modern Israel, and the country of Biblical times ... the Roman amphitheatre at Caesarea ... Masada ... Galilee and the Jordan River ... Bethlehem and Nazareth. I spent a few moments in contemplation and prayer at Manger Square and the Church of the Nativity in Bethlehem. I was shocked when we reached the ninth or tenth Station of the Cross and discovered a Coca-Cola sign on the wall.

But the most unforgettable moment of the Israel trip for me had to do with the reason why we were there, the Maccabiah Games. I can't remember anything in my professional career that matched marching into Ramat Gan Stadium at the head of the Canadian contingent, with 60,000 spectators cheering us on. Canada got an extra-special salute, and everyone felt this as we walked proudly behind our flag.

One day in 1976, I received a call from Montreal Mayor Jean Drapeau, who the year before had hosted the Montreal Games, a full-dress rehearsal for the Olympics. He was asking for a bit of eleventh-hour help – because, as he put it, everyone involved was working forty-eight-hour days. "The Games are only a few weeks away," he said. "The organizing committee needs somebody to receive the flame on behalf of Canada. Could you do this for us?" Actually, I'd already lent a hand at the Montreal Games themselves, standing in for Roger Rousseau, the president of COJO, the organizing committee, when we performed the opening, closing, and medal ceremonies, so I was pleased to oblige.

That's how, in July 1976, I played a small part in Olympic history. One of my duties was to speak at a general meeting of the Academy of Amateur Sport, located in Olympia itself, right across from the ruins of the first, ancient stadium. Representatives of perhaps 130 countries were in attendance there in Greece, and I began my speech by admitting that, as a former professional athlete, it felt rather odd to be addressing them there, in the birthplace of amateurism.

The Olympic torch is lit in Olympia at eleven o'clock in the morning. The high priestess and her attendants, a dozen or so maidens in long robes, preside over the ceremonies, which take place amid the columns of the stadium. Then the torch is carried by runners to Athens, about 240 miles away. The flame arrived in Athens two nights later. The last torch-bearer entered the modern Olympic stadium, to the cheers of the audience. A satellite link had been established with Canada, and we could follow the results on a monitor in our box when, as the signal was relayed, a torch burst into flame on Parliament Hill in Ottawa. Another of my duties as flame recipient was to escort the high priestess to the ceremony at the stadium in Athens. That night, she gave Élise and me a tour around Plaka, near the Parthenon, and took us to an authentic Greek psarotaverna, where they break plates and sing and dance into the early morning hours.

In December 1984, I was invited by the Canadian Association of Hong Kong to attend the Colony's Canada Week and serve as honorary president of the festivities, which included a golf tournament, a press conference, and several receptions and parties. Just before Christmas, right across from our hotel on the Kowloon side, the governor's wife threw a switch to turn on the myriad holiday lights that decorated all the buildings. Thousands upon thousands of Chinese armed with tripod cameras set to special exposures added to the atmosphere, and a tremendous cheer went up when the lights came on.

As I was preparing to leave for Hong Kong, an External Affairs representative presented another intriguing proposition. "Would you be interested in going to Beijing?" he asked. "We've received an invitation from the Canadian embassy there. Our ambassador has just been installed, and not too many Canadian sports figures ever get down his way. He told us that if you could come, it would give him an opportunity to meet the Chinese sports authorities, by hosting a reception or a dinner with you as guest."

Away we went, and visited Tienanmen Square, the Great Wall of China, and the Forbidden City. The country seemed endless. Beijing was spectacular, with wide avenues, huge squares, and millions of bicycles everywhere you looked.

I told Élise that I wanted to see all those bicycles in motion all at once, so I got up at five-thirty one morning, dressed rapidly, and went downstairs to find the streets a sea of bicycles, piled high with everything imaginable.

After the official functions were over, the embassy offered us a couple of more days of travel time, and we took advantage of this to visit Shanghai. It's the most European of Chinese cities. Half a century after communism arrived, it still retains a vaguely familiar air. Indeed, its narrow streets reminded me a little bit of Quebec City, except for one fact: I had never in my life experienced that kind of population density. Although China has become richer (at least in capitalistic terms) in recent years, Shanghai hasn't yet reaped the benefits of the free economic zone farther south in Guangzhou (Canton). There are fewer automobiles and other signs of affluence, which adds to the impact of the teeming throngs. Most are on foot, or pedalling bicycles of their own.

Our first impression of the city involved teeming of another kind: our hotel room was infested with cockroaches. Thankfully, matters improved when we shifted accommodation. I've always been a voracious reader, and the China visit brought to new and exciting life the many, many pages I had read about the country.

The saddest trip I undertook had a sports connection. It occurred in February 1986. On the last day of that month, I was attending a Chamber of Commerce luncheon in South Shore St. Jean. When it wrapped up in the mid-afternoon, I decided to go straight home, instead of returning to the Forum, and telephone my office to see if anything else demanded my attention. As I pulled into the driveway, I was greeted by the Longueuil police.

Élise was in Barbados, so there had been no one home all day.

"A break-in?" I asked the officer. Once, several years earlier, thieves had ransacked our house during a hockey game, assured of my absence because they were following my progress on television — my television, which they then stole. Domestic security had been a concern ever since.

"No, no, Mr. Béliveau," said the officer. "The Forum has been trying to get hold of you all afternoon. Please call them."

I thanked them, and phoned Louise Richer, who immediately passed me on to François Seigneur.

"Jean, we've just learned that Jacques Plante will be buried in Switzerland on Saturday," he said. We had heard that Jacques had died the previous day, and assumed that his remains would be returned to Canada for burial. It was 4 p.m. on Thursday in Montreal, 10 p.m. in Sierre, Switzerland, and Jacques Plante would be going to his final rest there in about thirty-six hours.

"We've found a ticket on Air Canada to Zurich via Paris," François continued, "and the plane leaves at seven-fifty tonight from Mirabel. You're the only one who can go, and the league is asking, too. They'd like to be represented there, if possible. It's your choice, but you're the last person in the current organization who knew him and his family well. Can you make it?"

I threw a few things into an overnight bag, and plunged into rush-hour traffic, heading for Mirabel International Airport, twenty-five miles on the other side of the city, and almost forty miles from my house. By 11 a.m. Friday, local time, I was in Zurich.

It took another three hours by car to reach Sierre, the same small centre where Jacques Lemaire went to coach after he retired from the Canadiens in 1979. The Valais region is very beautiful, and I was amazed to see that spring had already arrived down in the valleys, while up on the heights, winter maintained its hold. I'd assumed that the Swiss climate was similar to ours.

I arrived at my hotel at two o'clock that afternoon, and tried to lie down for a bit, because I'd only managed to doze lightly on the plane. When sleep wouldn't come, I went for a short walk in the fresh air, returned to my hotel, and telephoned Raymonde Plante, Jacques's second wife. His ex-wife, Jacqueline, lived in the Montreal suburb of Laval.

Raymonde was very happy to hear my voice.

"At what time will you be receiving people at the funeral parlour?" I enquired.

"Six o'clock, Jean. Thank you very much for coming."

I stayed at the funeral home until nine o'clock and heard the story of Jacques's final year from Raymonde. I'd last seen Jacques in January 1985, when the Canadiens held a promotion to celebrate a double anniversary: the team's seventy-fifth, and the Forum's sixtieth. As part of the promotion, the fans had been asked to vote for an all-time Canadiens Dream Team. Jacques was the people's choice for goalie, edging out Ken Dryden, with Doug Harvey and Larry Robinson on defence, me at centre, Maurice on right wing, and Dickie Moore on left. Aurèl Joliat represented the players of the 1920s and 1930s.

Look at that list, and count the missing names. Can you imagine a "Dream Team" without Henri, Boom, Guy Lafleur, Howie Morenz, Newsy Lalonde, Tom Johnson, Guy Lapointe, Serge Savard, Butch Bouchard, Toe Blake, and Elmer Lach? There, if any were required, is proof of the enduring strength of hockey's greatest franchise.

That selection and the special gala at the Queen Elizabeth brought Jacques back to Canada. He spent several days here and we had occasion to talk a couple of times. It was clear that he had been supremely happy in Switzerland with Raymonde, and that his life there was what he had always sought.

Later that fall, Jacques returned to North America to work with the goaltenders of the St. Louis Blues. On his way to St.

Louis, he experienced stomach pains and could hardly eat. When he reached Missouri, he visited the team doctor, who, in turn, consulted a specialist. The diagnosis? Stomach cancer.

"Jacques," the doctors told him, "we can operate on you here, or you can have it done in Switzerland, but it has to be done soon." Jacques returned to Switzerland, and was admitted to a hospital in Geneva, one of the world's foremost medical centres. They operated immediately and he underwent therapy, but to no avail.

On the night Jacques Plante would die, Raymonde stayed with her husband until ten o'clock. After they watched the late news on TV in his hospital room, she returned home. A few hours later, Jacques's aorta burst, and he died of the resulting haemorrhage.

His funeral took place Saturday morning in a small church packed to overflowing. Raymonde had invited me for dinner the previous night, and had told me that she and Jacques had many friends in the area. The number of mourners indicated that, clearly, this was true. I could only assume that Jacques had become more outgoing among his new friends here than he had been back in Canada.

At the church, Raymonde led me by the hand into the first row of family mourners and I sat beside her during the service. Outside the church, I learned once again how small our modern world can sometimes be. Two teams of peewee hockey players, wearing their sweaters over shirts and ties, had formed an honour guard at the door. One of their coaches looked very familiar to me – and I was staggered to learn that the peewees came from Victoriaville. They were scheduled to play an exhibition game in Sierre later that day, having just crossed the Alps from Chamonix, France. When the coach heard of Jacques's death, and learned that his funeral would take place on Saturday morning, he booked his team on an earlier train, to ensure they could attend and pay their respects to a fellow Canadian and Quebecer. It was a beautiful gesture appreciated by everyone.

After the service, the funeral party moved in a procession to the cemetery gates, where, according to Swiss custom, the priest said a few more words, then accompanied the casket to the gravesite for private burial.

After a memorial reception in town, I returned to the graveside with Raymonde and her family, and a few more prayers were said. A huge mound of flowers identified the spot where Jacques had been laid to rest. We stood alone with our memories for several moments, before returning to his home.

Raymonde had a special way to remember her late husband.

"Jean, there's a Swiss National League hockey game between Sierre and Kolten (a Zurich suburb) at quarter to six. Would you like to go?" Jacques, it seemed, often went to the Saturday afternoon games, so we attended this one, which began with a moving moment of silence in his memory.

The next morning, Raymonde presented me with a bottle of wine from a small vineyard nearby, where Jacques had made his own wine, meticulously recording and numbering by hand all the bottles produced. I received Bottle Number 187 – the last personal memento from my former teammate.

Then it was back to Geneva for an early flight home. From the moment I'd first received news of the funeral until my plane took off from Switzerland at eleven on Sunday morning, I'd had less than ten hours' sleep. We landed at four o'clock at Mirabel, seventy-two hours after the original phone call, and right in the middle of the usual Sunday evening traffic jam as thousands of skiers returned to the city from the Laurentians.

But my duties to the legacy of Jacques Plante weren't over quite yet. When I got to the Forum on Monday morning, I met with Ronald Corey right away.

"There are other families to be considered, who've lost a husband and father, as well as a brother," I said, referring first to Jacqueline Plante and Jacques's surviving son. Another son had been killed in a motorcycle crash many years before. Jacques had been the eldest of eleven children, and several surviving brothers and sisters in his hometown of Shawinigan wanted a memorial of some kind.

"You're right, Jean," said Ronald. "See what you can do."

I called Marcel de la Sablonnière at Immaculate Conception Church. Père Sablon, as he is known to thousands, is Montreal's unofficial athletes' priest, and several times he has served as chaplain to Canadian Olympic teams. The following day at eleven, a second memorial was held for Jacques Plante. The sundry Plante families were very happy to have an occasion to say good-bye to Jacques in this way, and they gathered around me with questions about Sierre. In life, Jacques had been a bit of a loner. In death, he was surrounded by hundreds of friends.

The last trip I'll mention here was one done on my own for purely selfish, family reasons. It turned out to be a highlight of my life.

In August 1971, two months after I'd retired as a player, a doctor told me my father had a touch of atherosclerosis and had apparently suffered a very minor stroke a couple of years earlier. Arthur Béliveau was nearing his seventieth year at that time, but, amazingly, he had never been on a plane. We decided on a five-week holiday in Europe for the five of us – Élise, Hélène, myself, and my father and stepmother. The pleasure of seeing Dad's reaction to his first plane trip was worth the price of the tickets. Moreover, since I'd done a bit of advertising work with Citröen in Canada, I was able to pick up a complimentary station wagon and set off through Germany, Switzerland, Italy, and France. We slowed down to enjoy five lovely days in Nice on the Côte d'Azur in August, with a final stop in Paris.

Before we left, seasoned travellers warned me that I was foolhardy to visit Europe in high season with no reservations. Still, this was our plan. I wanted five weeks of freedom, gallivanting around with no set itinerary. We made reservations for our first morning in Frankfurt, but thereafter I dealt with the concierge of whatever hotel we happened to stop at. Before dinner on the eve of departure I'd tell him our next destination, and describe our requirements: a quality hotel, close to downtown, with two available suites.

European concierges have a sophisticated network and they never failed us. Even in Nice in August we stayed at a four-star hotel a few blocks away from the Promenade des Anglais.

Before we left, I met with former Montrealer Louis Laurendeau, a Jesuit priest stationed in Rome, to ask if he could arrange a visit to the Vatican. The headquarters of the director-general of the Order of Jesus is right next to the Vatican. At that time, Father Laurendeau was the director-general's first secretary.

"Could you get us a pass into the gardens so we can see Pope Paul VI at Castel Gandolfo?" I asked. During the summer, I knew the pontiff held regular audiences on Wednesday mornings at his summer retreat just outside Rome.

When we got to Rome, we went out to dinner with Father Laurendeau, who happened to be there at the same time as us.

"Jean, I have good news for you." When he told me we were not just going to see the Pope but have a private audience with His Holiness, I was speechless.

Needless to say, we were all quite nervous when we left our hotel at eight-thirty the following morning. As we drove off, our driver informed us that we had plenty of time. "It starts in the garden at ten," he said, "but the private audiences are at eleven." So he took us to the catacombs first, and we toured them before driving down to the little town of Castel Gandolfo.

A total of twenty-three people, fifteen of them missionaries, had private audiences that day. We sat in the marble reception chamber while the Pope went out for his audience in the garden. We could hear the cheering as he spoke to the various delegations in their own language. Then, shortly after eleven o'clock, there was movement at the end of the room, some cardinals walked by, and the Pope's assistants began calling us up by groups.

When our turn came, it was clear the Pope had been well-briefed as to who we were. He knew what my career was about, and that the Canadiens had had a retirement night for me on March 24.

"I know that you didn't accept gifts, that you created a foundation to help others." Then he told me, "I was in Montreal when I was a young priest. I am very pleased that you brought your parents with you." He then gave us beads and medals.

The audience lasted only two or three minutes, although it's stayed with each of us in the years since. What really remains with me was our walking into the room, then seeing the Pontiff all dressed in white, and how that set off his blue eyes. While there is a no-camera policy during private audiences, the papal staff nevertheless take discreet pictures to commemorate the occasion. Ours were delivered to us later that evening. When the hotel staff saw the envelope, our service got even better.

The next day, we visited Vatican City again. And, once again, everything had been laid on by Father Laurendeau.

We reached the Gate at ten o'clock, and were greeted by a huge member of the Swiss Guard. He looked at me and said, "You have the shape of an athlete. Where are you from?"

"Montreal. What made you say that I look like an athlete?"

"I'm sure you are one."

I finally admitted that he was right and that I'd played for the Montreal Canadiens.

"The hockey club? You're Jean Béliveau of the Canadiens?" He almost put down his halberd to shake my hand. As it turned out, he knew everything about hockey. We exchanged addresses, he sent me a book on Switzerland, and later on, I returned the favour.

It was like that all throughout our trip, an idyllic five weeks made even better for me by the pleasure of seeing my father's delight in visiting the Leaning Tower of Pisa, the Blue Grotto of Capri, the Pont d'Avignon, the Eiffel Tower – places and things he had only read about, and had never hoped to see.

I was so happy that I could share these things with him. He had been there for me in 1949, when his eighteen-year-old son set out from Victoriaville on the trip that started it all.

Our European trip together was, of course, scant repayment for all that he had done. But it was my way of saying, "Thank you, Papa. I hope that my best was enough."

Appendix

Jean Béliveau's Semi-Pro and Professional Statistical Record

QUEBEC ACES

Regular Schedule

Season	League	GP	G	A	TP	PIM
1951–52	QSHL	59	45	38	83	88
1952–53	QSHL	57	50	39	89	59
	QSHL Totals	116	95	77	172	147

MONTREAL CANADIENS

Regular Schedule

Season	League	GP	G	A	TP	PIM
1950–51	NHL	2	1	1	2	0
1952–53	NHL	3	5	0	5	0
1953–54	NHL	44	13	21	34	22
1954–55	NHL	70	37	36	73	58
1955–56[ab]	NHL	70	★47	41	★88	143
1956–57	NHL	69	33	51	84	105
1957–58	NHL	55	27	32	59	93
1958–59	NHL	64	★45	46	91	67
1959–60	NHL	60	34	40	74	57
1960–61	NHL	69	32	★58	90	57
1961–62	NHL	43	18	23	41	36
1962–63	NHL	69	18	49	67	68
1963–64[b]	NHL	68	28	50	78	42
1964–65	NHL	58	20	23	43	76
1965–66	NHL	67	29	★48	77	50

(continued)

Regular Schedule

Season	League	GP	G	A	TP	PIM
1966–67	NHL	53	12	26	38	22
1967–68	NHL	59	31	37	68	28
1968–69	NHL	69	33	49	82	55
1969–70	NHL	63	19	30	49	10
1970–71	NHL	70	25	51	76	40
	NHL Totals	1125	507	712	1219	1029

Playoffs

Season	League	GP	G	A	TP	PIM
1953–54	NHL	10	2	★8	10	4
1954–55	NHL	12	6	7	13	18
1955–56	NHL	10	★12	7	★19	22
1956–57	NHL	10	6	6	12	15
1957–58	NHL	10	4	8	12	10
1958–59	NHL	3	1	4	5	4
1959–60	NHL	8	5	2	7	6
1960–61	NHL	6	0	5	5	0
1961–62	NHL	6	2	1	3	4
1962–63	NHL	5	2	1	3	2
1963–64	NHL	5	2	0	2	18
1964–65[c]	NHL	13	8	8	16	34
1965–66	NHL	10	5	5	10	6
1966–67	NHL	10	6	5	11	★26
1967–68	NHL	10	7	4	11	6
1968–69	NHL	14	5	★10	15	8
1969–70	NHL	–	–	–	–	–
1970–71[d]	NHL	20	6	★16	22	28
	NHL Totals	162	79	97	176	211

[a] Won Art Ross Trophy.
[b] Won Hart Trophy.
[c] Won Conn Smythe Trophy.
[d] NHL record for assists in Stanley Cup Playoffs.
★ Highest individual total in NHL for season.

Acknowledgements

The greatest fear of a team captain is to overlook the contribution of a teammate or, for that matter, of a worthy opponent. Therefore, I would like to acknowledge all of my teammates, stars and otherwise, who helped me throughout my career. My success is their success. In addition, I would be remiss if I didn't thank the media, led by the late Jacques Beauchamp and Danny Gallivan, as well as René Lecavalier, Red Fisher, Marcel Desjardins, and Dick Irvin, who are still with us. I also cannot forget the fans who were very good to me throughout more than forty years of hockey.

On a more personal level, I would like to acknowledge the friendship and contributions of the following persons in my careers, both within and without hockey: Roland Mercier, Raymond Lemay, the Byrne family, Roland Hébert, Jack Latter, Rita and Jean Proulx, Punch Imlach, Jacques Côté and the entire Côté family, Father Leonard Murphy, René Corbeil, Camil DesRoches, Pierre Roux, the Sacred-Heart Brothers of L'Académie Saint-Louis de Gonzague and Collège de Victoriaville, Raynald Deslandes, Thérèse and Yves Robitaille, Irène and Paul Brouillard, Paul Aquin, George Lengvari, Doug Kinnear, M.D., David Mulder, M.D., Senator Hartland de Montarville Molson and the Molson families, Peter and Edward Bronfman, Zotique Lespérance, Frank Selke, Sr., Dick Irvin, Sr., Toe Blake, and Ronald Corey.

And, in a very special category of one, there is Louise Richer. This book, and many of the memories it contains, are as much hers as mine.

Index

308 ✦ MY LIFE IN HOCKEY